city-pick

ISTANBUL

Oxygen Books

This book has been published with the support of the Ministry of Culture and Tourism of Turkey in the Framework of TEDA Program

Published by Oxygen Books Ltd. 2013

This selection and commentary copyright © Heather Reyes 2013

Illustrations © Eduardo Reyes 2013

Copyright Acknowledgements at the end of this volume constitute an
extension of this copyright page.

A CIP catalogue record for this book is available from the British Library.

ISBN 978-0-9559700-9-2

Typeset in Sabon by Bookcraft Limited, Stroud, Gloucestershire

Printed and bound in Great Britain by Henry Ling Ltd,
Dorset Press, Dorchester

Praise for the series

'Brilliant ... the best way to get under the skin of a city. The perfect read for travellers and book lovers of all ages'

Kate Mosse, author of *Labyrinth*

'An inviting new series of travel guides which collects some of the best writing on European cities to give a real flavour of the place ... Such an *idée formidable*, it seems amazing it hasn't been done before'

Editor's Pick, *The Bookseller*

'An attractive-looking list of destination-based literature anthologies ... a great range of writers' *The Independent*

'... something for everyone – an ideal gift' *Travel Bookseller*

'*city-pick*'s method of including blogs, novels, letters and memoirs of famous artists, filmmakers and writers is endlessly inspiring' *Scotland on Sunday*

'All of a sudden the traditional travel guide seems a little dull. The *Rough Guide* and *Lonely Planet* series have conditioned us to expect certain things: accommodation listings from budget to luxury, the lowdown on the best bars, restaurants and cafés, information on all the obvious sights, and the kind of prose which even makes civil war, poverty and dictatorial government seem as if they were established just to make our trip more interesting.

city-pick offers a more soulful guide to the metropolises of the world in the company of journalists, musicians, playwrights, bloggers and novelists past and present. They are beautifully produced books and can be read from cover to cover or just dipped into. They not only fill you with an intense desire to pack bags and head away, but also to seek out the complete texts from which the extracts are taken.

Oxygen Books is restoring intellectual discovery to travelling, inviting would-be adventurers to view cities as irrepressible compositions of wisdom, wit, conflict and culture, rather than excuses to get the digital camera out and tick off another sight from the list. A very hearty bravo indeed!'

Garan Holcombe, *The Good Web Guide*

'It's not hard to see why Oxygen Books' *city-pick* series continues to go from strength to strength: these snappy literary collages of the world's most written-about cities combine erudition with inspiration, bookishness with approachability, and a near-encyclopaedic range of reference with a canny appreciation for whatever it is that would make you want to visit a city in the first place. It's like having a playlist of all the bits of books that you'd want to read before you visited a place, but would never have the time or energy to find on your own. ... if you weren't already planning to, it makes you desperately want to visit the city it celebrates.' **Booktrust**

Editor's Note

In a radio interview in January 2013,[1] Orhan Pamuk – the Nobel-Prize winning Turkish writer – observed that allowing differences to confront each other, placing contradictory voices or elements in juxtaposition, was a key factor in creativity. Istanbul itself is, and always has been, a place where contrasts and differences co-exist and compete. Societies that are multi-voiced thrive, while those that supress variety deprive themselves of creative dynamism. (Significantly, the first three chapters of Pamuk's 1998 novel, *My Name is Red* – the novel which secured his international reputation – are told by a corpse, a man, and a dog.) It isn't surprising that Istanbul itself, with its fabled meeting of East and West, is a positive cauldron of creativity and that many of its best creative spirits are its writers.

The method of this anthology is, likewise, to place contrasting voices and perspectives next to each other to create a dynamic portrait of one of the world's greatest and most fascinating cities. And the city's many different literary voices deserve to be made more available to Anglophone readers.

It would have been easy to fill an anthology with lengthy extracts from the work of Orhan Pamuk, Elif Shafak and the few other Turkish writers widely available in English translation. However, we decided to allow those too rarely heard voices of some of Turkey's other writers on the city to take precedence, to give readers a chance to taste them in a kind of literary *mezze* and to expand their awareness of just how rich a feast Turkish publishing has to offer. We can only regret that space prevented us from including more of them, while defending the inclusion of multiple extracts from those writers whose work most fulfilled the needs of this themed anthology.

---

1 Interviewed by Michael Barclay, on 'Private Passions', BBC Radio 3, Sunday 13 January 2013.

Istanbul has always attracted visitors and immigrants, so, side-by-side with the Turkish perspectives on the city are those of travellers, past and present, from a dozen different nations. While exploring the many beauties and wonders of the city, this collage portrait does not ignore its darker and more difficult sides: like any huge city, there are great contrasts in wealth and levels of happiness, and these discrepancies are certainly represented – mainly by Turkish writers themselves. But all invite the reader to engage with Istanbul – its glorious past, its difficulties, its present vibrant ascendancy, its culture, its food, and its people.

We would like to record our extreme gratitude for the help received in preparing this volume: to the committee of TEDA (the Ministry of Culture and Tourism of Turkey) for awarding a grant towards the printing costs; to Nermin Mollaoğlu, director of the Kalem Agency, for her enthusiasm, support and help in suggesting writers and works, and for checking the rendering of Turkish names and vocabulary; to Amy Spangler and İdil Aydoğan (the Anatolialit Agency) also for their suggestions and enthusiastic co-operation; to Jonathan Lee and Rebecca Hart (British Council) for their help and enthusiasm; to Barbara Nadel for her excellent introduction; to Eduardo Reyes for his atmospheric illustrations; and not least to the many translators – especially Feyza Howell – who have made such a wonderful range of writing available to English readers.

We hope you enjoy your visit.

Heather Reyes, 2013

Contents

Introducing Istanbul, by Barbara Nadel 1

What is it about Istanbul?

David Byrne, *Bicycle Diaries* 7
Michael Booth, *Just As Well I'm Leaving* 8
Edmondo de Amicis, *Constantinople* 8
Eveline Zoutendijk, 'Interview' 8
Anya von Bremzen, 'Eating in Istanbul' 8
Edmondo de Amicis, *Constantinople* 9
Gérard de Nerval, *Journey to the Orient* 9
Edmondo de Amicis, *Constantinople* 10
İnci Aral, *The Colour Saffron* 11
Willam Dalrymple, *From the Holy Mountain* 12
Hilary Sumner-Boyd and John Freely, *Strolling
    Through Istanbul* 12
Virginia Woolf, *Orlando* 13
Mehmet Zaman Saçlıoğlu, 'Winter' 14

'A garland of waters'

Hilary Sumner-Boyd and John Freely, *Strolling
    Through Istanbul* 16
Rory Maclean, *Magic Bus* 17
Mehmet Zaman Saçlıoğlu, 'Winter' 17
Kai Strittmatter, *User's Guide to Istanbul* 18
Maureen Freely, *Enlightenment* 19
Daniel Rondeau, *Istanbul* 20
A. W. Kinglake, *Eöthen* 21
Willam Dalrymple, *From the Holy Mountain* 22
Ahmet Hamdi Tanpınar, *A Mind at Peace* 23
Geert Mak, *In Europe: Travels Through the
    Twentieth Century* 25

Contents

Geert Mak, *The Bridge: A Journey Between
Orient and Occident* 26
Jan Neruda, *Pictures from Abroad* 27
Edmondo de Amicis, *Constantinople* 29
Geert Mak, *The Bridge: A Journey Between
Orient and Occident* 31
Tuna Kiremitçi, *The Way of Loneliness* 32

Travellers' tales

Edmondo de Amicis, *Constantinople* 33
Edmondo de Amicis, *Constantinople* 34
Lady Mary Wortley Montagu, *The Turkish
Embassy Letters* 35
Hans Christian Andersen, *The Poet's Bazaar* 39
Jan Neruda, *Pictures from Abroad* 41
Gustave Flaubert, *The Letters of Gustave Flaubert
1830–1857* 43
Jeremy Seal, *A Fez of the Heart* 44
Simone de Beauvoir, *Force of Circumstance* 45
Rory Maclean, *Magic Bus* 47
Michael Booth, *Just As Well I'm Leaving* 48
Geert Mak, *In Europe: Travels Through the
Twentieth Century* 48
Michael Booth, *Just As Well I'm Leaving* 49
Tuna Kiremitçi, *Leave Before I Fall In Love With You* 51
Marian Edmunds, 'Don't forget your toothbrush' 53
Yiannis Xanthoulis, *The Istanbul of My
Disrespectful Fears* 55
Daniel Rondeau, *Istanbul* 57
David Byrne, *Bicycle Diaries* 57

The glorious past

Gül İrepoğlu, *Unto the Tulip Gardens: My Shadow* 61
Philip Mansel, *Constantinople: City of the World's Desire,
1453–1924* 63
Reha Çamuroğlu, *A Momentary Delay* 65

Contents

Philip Mansel, *Constantinople: City of the World's Desire,*
1453–1924 67
Philip Mansel, *Constantinople: City of the World's Desire,*
1453–1924 70
Gül İrepoğlu, *Unto the Tulip Gardens: My Shadow* 72
Lady Mary Wortley Montagu, *The Turkish*
Embassy Letters 74
Gül İrepoğlu, *Unto the Tulip Gardens: My Shadow* 75
William Dalrymple, *From the Holy Mountain* 75
Yashar Kemal, *The Birds Have Also Gone* 76

A city for all seasons

Lady Mary Wortley Montagu, *The Turkish*
Embassy Letters 78
Oya Baydar, *The Gate of the Judas Tree* 79
Esmahan Aykol, *Hotel Bosphorous* 79
Sema Kaygusuz, 'A Couple of People' 80
Füruzan, 'In the Park by the Pier' 81
Maureen Freely, *Enlightenment* 83
Geert Mak, *The Bridge: A Journey Between*
Orient and Occident 84
Kai Strittmatter, *User's Guide to Istanbul* 85
Feryal Tilmaç, 'Hitching in the *Lodos*' 86
Gaye Boralıoğlu, *Syncopated Rhythm* 90
Ahmet Hamdi Tanpınar, *A Mind at Peace* 91
Elif Shafak, *The Bastard of Istanbul* 91
Tuna Kiremitçi, *The Way of Loneliness* 92
Murat Gülsoy, 'Marked in Writing' 93
Daniel Rondeau, *Istanbul* 93
Mehmet Zaman Saçlıoğlu, 'Winter' 93

'The imam fainted'

Anya von Bremzen, 'The Soul of a City' 98
Berrin Torolsan, 'The Milky Way' 101

Rory Maclean, *Magic Bus* 103
Kai Strittmatter, *User's Guide to Istanbul* 105
Maureen Freely, *Enlightenment* 107
Jan Neruda, *Pictures from Abroad* 107
Mehmet Zaman Saçlıoğlu, 'Winter' 108
Michael Booth, *Just As Well I'm Leaving* 109
Elif Shafak, *The Bastard of Istanbul* 111
Mehmet Zaman Saçlıoğlu, 'Winter' 111
Çiler İlhan, 'Groundnut Sky Cake' 113
Daniel Rondeau, *Istanbul* 115

Stamboullus

Elif Shafak, *The Bastard of Istanbul* 117
Hikmet Hükümenoğlu, 'The Smell of Fish' 119
Esmahan Aykol, *Hotel Bosphorus* 120
Yashar Kemal, *The Birds Have Also Gone* 121
Emine Sevgi Özdamar, *My Istanbul* 123
Ahmet Hamdi Tanpınar, *A Mind at Peace* 125
İnci Aral, *The Colour Saffron* 127
Mehmet Zaman Saçlıoğlu, 'Winter' 130
Barış Müstecaplıoğlu, 'An Extra Body' 131
Gönül Kıvılcım, *Razor Boy* 132
Gaye Boralıoğlu, *Syncopated Rhythm* 134
Hatice Meryem, *It Takes All Kinds* 139
Geert Mak, *The Bridge: A Journey Between*
    Occident and Orient 142
Moris Farhi, *Young Turk* 143
Yiannis Xanthoulis, *The Istanbul of my*
    Disrespectful Fears 145
Mario Levi, *Istanbul was a Fairy Tale* 146
Elif Shafak, *The Bastard of Istanbul* 149
Mehmet Zaman Saçlıoğlu, 'The Intersection' 150
Oya Baydar, *Its Warm Ashes Remain* 153
Barbara Nadel, *Death by Design* 155
Kai Strittmatter, *User's Guide to Istanbul* 157
Esmahan Aykol, *Hotel Bosphorus* 159

Orhan Pamuk interviewed by Shaun Walker,
    The Independent 159
Cem Mumcu, *Sarcophagus* 163

Exiles

Orhan Kemal, *The Idle Years* 165
Mehmet Bilâl, 'The Stepson' 167
Tuna Kiremitçi, *Leave Before I Fall In Love With You* ... 168
Jeremy Seal, *A Fez of the Heart* 171
Ece Vahapoğlu, *The Other* 173
İnci Aral, *The Colour Saffron* 174
Maureen Freely, *Enlightenment* 176
Aslı Perker, *Soufflé* 178
Wendy Buonaventura, *I Put A Spell On You* 180
Oya Baydar, *The Gate of the Judas Tree* 181
Maureen Freely, *Enlightenment* 182
Daniel Rondeau, *Istanbul* 182

Built to last

Edmondo de Amicis, *Constantinople* 184
Eduardo Reyes, 'Big Architecture' 186
William Dalrymple, *From the Holy Mountain* 187
Lady Mary Wortley Montagu, *The Turkish
    Embassy Letters* 188
John K. McDonald, 'Istanbul's Caravan Stops' 189
Lady Mary Wortley Montagu, *The Turkish
    Embassy Letters* 190
Gül İrepoğlu, *Unto the Tulip Gardens: My Shadow* 191
Edmondo de Amicis, *Constantinople* 193
Philip Mansel, *Constantinople: City of the World's Desire,
    1453–1924* 194
William Dalrymple, *From the Holy Mountain* 197
Kai Strittmatter, *User's Guide to Istanbul* 198
Chris Hellier, 'Mansions on the Water' 199
Gül İrepoğlu, *Unto the Tulip Gardens: My Shadow* 203

Contents

Edmondo de Amicis, *Constantinople* 204
Pat Yale, 'Istanbul's Forgotten Art Nouveau Heritage' ...206
Pat Yale, 'Nationalism in Stone: Istanbul's Forgotten
    Treasures' 208

From *hüzün* to *huzur*: the city in all its moods

Ayfer Tunç, *The Night of Green Fairy* 211
Behçet Çelik, *The Drone of the World* 212
César Antonio Molina 'Impregnable in his Sorrows' 213
Suzan Samancı 'In the melancholy of wisteria' 215
Oya Baydar, *Returning Nowhere* 217
Maureen Freely, *Enlightenment* 219
Rory Maclean, *Magic Bus* 220
Emine Sevgi Özdamar, *My Istanbul* 221
Daniel Rondeau, *Istanbul* 222

Here and now

Rory Maclean, *Magic Bus* 223
Maureen Freely, *Enlightenment* 224
Anya von Bremzen, 'Soul of a City' 225
Michael Booth, *Just As Well I'm Leaving* 226
Elif Shafak, *The Bastard of Istanbul* 228
Geert Mak, *The Bridge: A Journey Between
    Orient and Occident* 228
Esmahan Aykol, *Hotel Bosphorus* 230
Kai Strittmatter, *User's Guide to Istanbul* 230
İnci Aral, *The Colour Saffron* 231
Cem Selcen, *Blame the Apple* 232
Çiler İlhan, 'Big city hunter' 234
Barış Müstecaplıoğlu, *The Brother's Blood* 236
Jeremy Seal, *A Fez of the Heart* 237
Daniel Rondeau, *Istanbul* 238
Sally Pomme Clayton, 'With music in Istanbul' 240
Rory Maclean, *Magic Bus* 243

Selective Index 245

Introducing Istanbul

by Barbara Nadel

The late, great raconteur and eccentric Quentin Crisp once said that the first time he saw Manhattan he 'wanted it.' When I first went to Istanbul back in the 1970s, Mr Crisp had yet to discover New York. But when I heard his words some years later, I knew what he meant. As soon as I saw the domes of the Imperial Mosques of Sultanahmet rising up out of an early morning springtime mist for that magical first time, I knew I was in the presence of something beyond extraordinary. I was in Byzantium, the New Rome, Constantinople, Istanbul – the City of the World's Desire. And I wanted it.

Ever since it was founded by the Greek King Byzas in 667BC the city now known as Istanbul has been coveted, fought over, occupied and dreamed about by civilisations as diverse as the Romans, the Greeks, the Venetians, Imperial Russia, the Seljuk Turks and the Ottoman Turks. Strategically pivotal, it was also, and remains, a city of religious significance for both Christianity and Islam. Even today, Muslim Turkish Istanbul continues to be the centre of the Eastern Orthodox world because it is still where the Patriarch of Constantinople resides. It is also home to one of the world's greatest religious buildings, Hagia Sophia (or Aya Sofya) – once the foremost church in Christendom, then an Imperial Ottoman mosque, now a museum.

As one would expect of a city that spans two continents, Istanbul was the capital of both the Byzantine and the Ottoman empires. However on the 13th October 1923 it was downgraded to the second city of the newly formed Turkish Republic which was officially inaugurated by its founder Mustafa Kemal Atatürk on 19th October 1923. In order to mark the infant

Republic's break with its imperial past, a new Anatolian capital devoid of the trappings of empire and state religion was required and Istanbul, for many years, became something of a backwater. When I first remember the city back in the nineteen seventies it was not only a lot smaller than it is now, but also much scruffier and a lot darker. I can still remember pressing my nose up against the window of an all male coffee house in the centre of the historical Sultanahmet district which was lit by one single hurricane lamp. Night life was minimal and the only tourists in town were either wealthy people passing through on cruises or hippy kids on their way to Kathmandu.

However things changed a lot during the course of the nineteen eighties when Turkey began to open its doors to the world both as a tourist destination and as a place to do business. The world responded with interest and Istanbul, slowly at first, began to blossom into the fascinating, funky and intellectually lively place it is today. It also grew from the two million inhabitants recorded in the late nineteen seventies to the twelve million plus people it has today. Mainly migrants from Anatolia, these new residents started to come when Istanbul began to rise again and to this day they keep on arriving, together with other foreign nationals from the Balkans, central Asia and the Middle East. Istanbul is and always has been a multiethnic city with new immigrants joining the much older communities of Istanbul Sephardic Jews, ethnic Greeks and Armenians who still live and work in the city.

Culturally this makes for a very diverse and vibrant artistic scene that has been greatly enhanced in recent years by the high profile career of the writer Orhan Pamuk and the creation of one of the world's foremost art galleries, Istanbul Modern. But people, both local and foreign have written about this city for millennia. Somewhere between 550 and 562AD the Byzantine lawyer and historian Procopius wrote a book called *The Secret History* which was a somewhat salacious account of what went on in the Great Palace of the Byzantines when Istanbul was ruled by the Emperor Justinian and his wife the Empress Theodora. Half of it, or more, was probably made up by a man who was very disillusioned with his rulers and the system under which Byzantium was governed. But it is still a fascinating read providing as it does, evidence of the richness of culture, life and experience in the long gone world of the great Christian Empire in the East.

A lot of writers will lead you through Istanbul in the pages of this book. Some, like Orhan Pamuk and Elif Shafak – already well-known to Anglophone readers – are modern Turkish novelists with much to say about contemporary issues. They appear alongside a raft of other Turkish writers, such as Esmahan Aykol, Yashar Kemal, Orhan Kemal, Hatice Meryem and Ahmet Hamdi Tanpınar, as well as a number appearing in English for the first time. From Istanbul's past come the British aristocrat Lady Mary Wortley Montagu, the Italian writer Edmondo de Amicis and the Frenchman Gustave Flaubert. Literary superstars like Simone de Beauvoir feature also alongside travellers like William Dalrymple, Geert Mak and expatriate writers such as Moris Farhi.

Much of what will be found in this book chimes with my own experience. I can well remember, like Maureen Freely, the Russian ships passing through the Bosphorus strait in the 1970s and how people used to talk of defectors swimming away from vessels at night. David Byrne's description of his experiences with the gypsy dancers of Sulukule makes me sad because that district has now been cleared for redevelopment. That small world, like Rory Maclean's 'hippy' Istanbul, can only now be seen in glimpses. As recently as just four years ago I came across a shabby character who told me he'd got stuck in the city on his way back to England from India. He was sitting in the famous Pudding Shop where all the hippies and freaks used to hang out and he'd been in Istanbul, he thought, since well before the

1970s. Maybe he was just spinning me a line – Istanbul is after all a city of myth and legend – but maybe it was true. After all, if I was once lowered, by a policeman and a tea garden waiter, into an ancient Byzantine cistern underneath the Grand Bazaar by my wrists (and I have been!) then anything is possible.

Istanbul has often been described as a 'sensual' city and it is something that I agree with wholeheartedly. It is a city of great beauty, of spicy smells in ancient bazaars, of abundant, colourful food that is complex on the palate, and of the almost sexual kick one derives from being amongst so much diverse humanity. However Istanbul's sensuality, I believe, also derives from its stories, not all of which are exotic, but whose details arouse the soul. Sometimes people will tell you their tales, like the old imam who once, in perfect almost unaccented English, told me about his service in the Ottoman army. Then there was the soldier on a bus who treated me to the hundred and one (or so!) ways in which he was absolutely wonderful. Over the years I have spent time with jewellers, sellers of cheap cigarettes, simit (a bread roll a bit like a bagel) sellers, purveyors of leeches and amongst shops selling only buttons, or lighters, or corsets so antiquated even my grandmother would not have worn them. They all either tell or illustrate a story that cannot be found anywhere else. These are stories that can make your day. Or your year. People sometimes ask me if I ever have any problems getting hold of new material for my Istanbul based crime fiction series and my answer is always the same, 'Never.' The city always gives me everything I need – but always on its own terms and with a few surprises thrown in for good measure.

Whenever I visit the city in the winter, people who don't know Istanbul always assume I will come home to the UK with a tan. But as well as the stifling summers that Orhan Pamuk describes with such feeling, Istanbul can also be battered by rainstorms so bad that the narrow streets of the old city run with torrents of water and rubbish. I have also been in town when the snow was so deep it came up to my thighs and the skyline of the old city, with its Imperial Mosques, its domed tombs and fountains looked like a dreamscape of a Tsarist Russia that never was. Even now one still sees groups of people standing around braziers, toasting chestnuts, as well as their own fingers, in the winter. For a British person this is all very cosy and oddly familiar even if I do like to warm myself with the quintessential Turkish winter drink of *sahlep* (orchid root with milk and cinnamon).

But to sum up what I, as well as many other lovers of the city feel about it, I will turn to one of the contributors to this book for some last words on the matter. Eveline Zoutendijk is a Dutch chef and writer resident in the city. She says, 'Istanbul easily becomes an obsession.'

You have been warned ...

Barbara Nadel

What is it about Istanbul?

Be prepared to fall in love with Istanbul – as many have done before you ... and for many different reasons.

I love this city. I love its physical location – bounded by water, dispersed across three landmasses, one of which is where Asia begins. Its way of life, which seems Mediterranean, cosmopolitan, and yet tinged by the deep history of the Middle East, is intoxicating.

David Byrne, *Bicycle Diaries* (2009)

* * *

You come to believe anything is possible in Istanbul. It is a city of relentless surprises, most of them amusing, some surreal, a few alarming [...] – a place to go shopping for extraordinary sights and experiences.

Michael Booth, *Just As Well I'm Leaving* (2005)

❊ ❊ ❊

One leads a lighter, easier, more youthful kind of existence there than in any other city in Europe.

Edmondo de Amicis, *Constantinople* (1877)
translated by Stephen Parkin

❊ ❊ ❊

It was sort of love at first sight. After living in New York and Paris, Istanbul seemed to have just the perfect combination of energy, culture, history, and physical beauty. It was all so new, so different and exciting. I became quite obsessed by wanting to live there. Istanbul easily becomes an obsession, an addiction that gets into your blood and keeps you on a continuous high.

Eveline Zoutendijk, 'Interview' (2007)
in *Istanbul: The Collected Traveller: An Inspired Companion Guide*
(ed. Barrie Kerper)

❊ ❊ ❊

To me Istanbul is the most fascinating, most ravishing city on earth, a feeling that hasn't wavered since I first ate a peach on the Galata Bridge twenty years ago.

Everything one hears about Istanbul is pretty much true. Yes, the Hagia Sophia is big and Byzantine, the Grand Bazaar both a treasure trove and a tourist trap. Yes, the metropolis of twelve million people physically and metaphorically straddles Europe and Asia. It is by turns provincial and cosmopolitan, Muslim yet resolutely secular, exhilarating and exasperating. Even the rumours of Istanbul's transcendent new coolness aren't vastly exaggerated. Beyond the clichés, though, what keeps luring me back is the texture of everyday life. The ferry ride at dusk as the skies flare cinematically over the minarets. The tulip-shaped glasses at my corner tea garden. The courtly smile of my local pistachio vendor. And the food.

With the endless grills, the subtle spicing, the celebration of yogurt, legumes, and sun-ripened vegetables, Turkish cuisine is the last frontier of healthy Mediterranean cooking. The kebabs and savoury pastries called *börek* alone are reason enough to move here.

Anya von Bremzen 'Eating in Istanbul' (2007)
in *Departures* November/December 2007

❊ ❊ ❊

There is no doubt about Constantinople; even the wariest traveller can be certain they won't experience disappointment there. And it's not a case of nostalgic memories or conventional admiration. It is one of universal and sovereign beauty, before which poets and archaeologists, ambassadors and shopkeepers, princesses and sailors, sons of the north and of the south, are all alike overcome with wonder. All of the world thinks it is the most beautiful place on earth.

Edmondo de Amicis, *Constantinople* (1877)
translated by Stephen Parkin

❊ ❊ ❊

... that laughing and splendid city of Constantinople, whose fascinating and verdant outlines, painted houses and elegant mosques with their delicate minarets can inspire thoughts only of pleasure and sweet daydreams. Even death itself puts on a festive guise in this place.

Gérard de Nerval, *Journey to the Orient* (1851)
translated by Eloma Judd

❊ ❊ ❊

*Edmondo de Amicis' lengthy account of his visit in the
second half of the nineteenth century is sometimes a
little florid for modern tastes, but his enthusiasm and
deep appreciation of the Ottoman city are irresistible.*

The Golden Horn directly in front of us like a broad river; and
on either shore two lines of hills on which two parallel cities
stretch away into the distance, eight miles of hills, valleys, bays
and promontories; a hundred slopes covered with buildings and
gardens; a vast double terrace of houses, mosques, bazaars, sera-
glios, baths, kiosks, in an infinite variety of colours; among them
thousands of minarets with shining pinnacles rising into the sky
like tall ivory columns; groves of cypress trees descending in
long dark lines from the heights to the sea, encircling residen-
tial districts and harbours; and a lush vegetation springing up
everywhere, cresting the summits, weaving round the roofs and
hanging down into the water. To the right Galata, with a forest
of masts and pennants in front; above Galata, Pera, the great
outlines of her European palaces clear against the sky; in the
foreground, a bridge connecting the two shores, crossed in each
direction by two colourful streams of people; to the left Stamboul upon her broad hills, each of which is surmounted by a vast
mosque with lead dome and golden pinnacles; Hagia Sophia,
coloured white and rose; Sultan Ahmet, flanked by six minarets;
Süleyman the Great crowned with ten domes; Sultana Valide
mirrored in the waters; on the fourth hill the Mosque of Mehmet
II; and rising above them all the white tower of the Seraskerat
which overlooks the shores of both continents from the Dardanelles to the Black Sea. Beyond the sixth hill of Stamboul and
beyond Galata nothing but vague outlines can be seen, patches
of city or suburb, glimpses of harbours, fleets, groves – pale in
the azure air, unreal, like tricks of the light and atmosphere. How
will I ever grasp the details of this extraordinary picture? The
eye fixes a moment upon the nearer shore, upon a Turkish house
or gilded minaret; but immediately darts off into that luminous

depth, randomly roaming down and across the two shores and the two cities, with one's bewildered understanding painfully trying to keep up. All this loveliness has an air of serene majesty; there is something youthful and amorous about it which revives a thousand memories of childhood fairy tales and dreams; something ethereal, mysterious, sublime, carrying the imagination off beyond the real world. The sky, misted delicately with opal and with silver, forms a backdrop on which everything is drawn with marvellous clearness and precision; the sapphire-coloured sea, dotted with crimson buoys, mirrors the minarets in long, rippling reflections; the domes glitter; the trees sway and shimmer in the morning breeze; flocks of doves swoop over the mosques; a thousand gilded and painted caiques dart about the waters; the breeze from the Black Sea wafts the fragrance from ten thousand gardens; and when, drunk with the beauty of this paradise, and forgetful of all else, you turn away, you see behind you with renewed wonder the shores of Asia closing the panorama with the grandeur of Scutari and the snowy peaks of Mount Olympus, the Sea of Marmara sprinkled with islets and white with sails; and the Bosphorus covered with ships winding their way between the endless rows of kiosks, palaces and villas to vanish mysteriously among the fertile hills of the East. This is the most beautiful sight on earth and whoever denies it shows a lack of gratitude to both God and Nature! Our senses could not bear a greater beauty.

Edmondo de Amicis, *Constantinople* (1877)
translated by Stephen Parkin

✳ ✳ ✳

Back to the present with a young woman from another part of Turkey who comes to the capital.

She walked out intending to take a dolmuş and then she decided to walk. Since coming to Istanbul, she had not been bored outside the office. There were books and magazines to read, things to write, work to do. Istanbul was beautiful, very beautiful indeed. It would be fantastic if only she had a little money.

İnci Aral, *The Colour Saffron* (2007)
translated by Melahet Behlil

* * *

The sheer beauty of the city and its position is again emphasised by William Dalrymple.

At dawn the Sea of Marmara appears like a sheet of silver, with the stationary ships sitting as if welded to its surface. Now, at night, it becomes invisible but for the lights of passing ships and the distant lamps of Üsküdar and Kadıköy – Byzantine Chalcedon – shining across the Bosphorus.

From the old Byzantine Acropolis to the waters of the Golden Horn, the yellow glow of the sulphurous streetlights silhouettes the city's skyline, with its minarets and rippling domes and cupolas. The perfect reflections of the great Ottoman mosques and palaces that form in the water below are intermittently shattered by skiffs and caiques crossing and recrossing the Hellespont. No other city on earth has so magnificent a position. With its remarkable configuration of hills and water, sitting astride the land and sea routes connecting Europe with Asia, the Black Sea with the Mediterranean, and commanding one of the greatest anchorages in the world, there could be no more perfect position for a great imperial city.

William Dalrymple, *From the Holy Mountain* (1997)

* * *

And, of course, the Stamboullus themselves add to the pleasures of the city.

Istanbul is much more than just an inhabited museum, for the old town has a beauty and fascination that go quite beyond its history and its architecture. One is apt to feel this when seated at a *çayevi* or *meyhane* in a sun-dappled square, or while taking one's ease in a vine-shaded café beside the Bosphorus. Little has been said of the Stamboullus themselves, but the visitor will surely have experienced innumerable examples of their grave friendliness and unfailing hospitality. Much of the pleasure of visiting or living in this city derives from the warm and relaxed company of its residents. '*Hoş geldiniz!*' (Welcome), they say to the stranger who arrives in their city or their home; and when one leaves one is sent off with a '*Güle Güle!*' (Go With Smiles), as if to lessen the inevitable sadness of departure. But how can one not feel sad when leaving this beautiful city?

Hilary Sumner-Boyd and John Freely, *Strolling Through Istanbul*
(revised edition 2010)

Virginia Woolf's fleeting visit to the city found its way into her imaginative tour-de-force, the centuries-spanning, gender-shifting novel Orlando.

Orlando's day was passed, it would seem, somewhat in this fashion. About seven, he would rise, wrap himself in a long Turkish cloak, light a cheroot, and lean his elbows on the parapet. Thus he would stand, gazing at the city beneath him, apparently entranced. At this hour the mist would lie so thick that the domes of Santa Sofia and the rest would seem to be afloat; gradually the mist would uncover them; the bubbles would be seen to be firmly fixed; there would be the river; there the Galata Bridge; there the green-turbaned pilgrims without eyes or noses, begging alms; there the pariah dogs picking up offal; there the shawled women; there the innumerable donkeys; there men on horses carrying long poles. Soon, the whole town would be astir with the cracking of whips, the beating of gongs, cryings to prayer, lashing of mules, and rattle of brass-bound wheels, while sour odours, made from bread fermenting and incense, and spice, rose even to the heights of Pera itself and seemed the very breath of the strident multicoloured and barbaric population.

Nothing, he reflected, gazing at the view which was now sparkling in the sun, could well be less like the counties of Surrey and Kent or the towns of London and Tunbridge Wells. To the right and left rose in bald and stony prominence the inhospitable Asian mountains, to which the arid castle of a robber chief or two might hang; but parsonage there was none, nor manor house, nor cottage, nor oak, elm, violet, ivy, or wild eglantine. There were no hedges for ferns to grow on, and no fields for sheep to graze. The houses were white as egg-shells and as bald. That he, who was English root and fibre, should yet exult to the depths of his heart in this wild panorama, and gaze and gaze at those passes and far heights planning journeys alone there on foot where only the goat and shepherd had gone before, should feel a passion of affection for the bright, unseasonable flowers, love the unkempt, pariah dogs beyond even his elk hounds at home, and snuff the acrid, sharp smell of the streets eagerly into his nostrils, surprised him. He wondered if, in the season of the Crusades, one of his ancestors had taken up with a Circassian peasant woman; thought it possible; fancied a certain darkness in his complexion; and, going indoors again, withdrew to his bath.

Virginia Woolf, *Orlando* (1928)

❊ ❊ ❊

Finally, Istanbul writer Mehmet Zaman Saçlıoğlu (b.1955) on some of the things that make Istanbul what it is.

There are many things that make Istanbul, Istanbul. The winds, seagulls, turtledoves, cats come to mind at once. There are the islands, carriages, wooden houses, mimosa, and city walls. There are Judas trees, villas, architect Sinan's creations, mosques, narrow streets, children's parks with at least one broken swing. There are small primary schools, cobblestones, towers, prostitutes, rowdy people, bars, antique shops, second hand shops, drunks, mansions which overlook the Bosphorus. There are cemeteries, trains, boats, the snails which come out onto the pavements after the rain, the street dogs with their hopeful glances, the whistles of the night watchmen in our memories, the boza[1] sellers in winter, the tinsmiths who have left a shine in our eyes, the few remaining milkmen, all things that fill us with the joy of life.

Mehmet Zaman Saçlıoğlu, 'Winter' in
Four Seasons Istanbul from 1000 Feet (2010)
translated by Hatice Ahmet Salih and Joan Eroncel

---

1   a drink made from fermented millet

"Dancing ferries defy the noon-hot current, cutting between churning tankers"

Rory Maclean

'A garland of waters'

Part of the city's beauty, grandeur and interest is the result of its watery location.

A poet writing fourteen centuries ago described this city as being surrounded by a garland of waters. Much has changed since then, but modern Istanbul still owes much of its spirit and beauty to the waters which bind and divide it. There is perhaps nowhere else in town where one can appreciate this more than from the Galata Bridge, where all tours of the city should begin. There are other places in Istanbul with more panoramic views, but none where one can better sense the intimacy which

16

this city has with the sea, nor better understand how its maritime situation has influenced its character and its history. So the visitor is advised to stroll to the Galata Bridge for his first view of the city. But you should do your sight-seeing there as do the Stamboullus, seated at a teahouse or café on the lower level of the Bridge, enjoying your *keyif* over a cup of tea or glass of raki, looking out along the Golden Horn to where it meets the Bosphorus and the Sea of Marmara.

Hilary Sumner-Boyd and John Freely, *Strolling Through Istanbul*
(revised edition, 2010)

✻ ✻ ✻

The Bosphorus surges between the tail of Europe and toe of Asia, dipping, rising, rushing from the Black Sea to a silver-mirrored Marmara. Dancing ferries defy the noon-hot current, cutting between churning tankers, skeins of shearwater and two continents. Their almond-eyed passengers wash ashore, over decaying sea-walls caked with moss and mussels, around bobbing skiffs of fishermen flogging fried-fish sandwiches, into the great, jumbled capital of three empires.

Rory Maclean, *Magic Bus* (2007)

✻ ✻ ✻

It is not easy to be Istanbul. It is such a city that it is not quite clear whether it joins or separates two continents, whether it separates or joins two seas. The answer to these questions does not lie with nature but with humans. That is why Istanbul is different to every eye which looks upon it. Asia, in the poet's words, launches itself like a mare's head into Istanbul's sea. A little further down, on the opposite side, stands the daughter it bore so long ago that humans no longer remember. In her dreams, Europe knows she belongs to her mother Asia, but to someone else too; she is trying to analyse her dreams. Between the two, the waters are enchanted. The enchantment of the water stems from the tension between parting and bringing together. The almost touching of these two continents is like the fingers about to touch in Michelangelo's 'The Creation of Adam'. It is this touch, or anticipation of touch, that gives Istanbul life.

Mehmet Zaman Saçlıoğlu, 'Winter' in *Four Seasons Istanbul from 1000 Feet* (2010)
translated by Hatice Ahmet Salih and Joan Eroncel

✳ ✳ ✳

A recent German visitor, Kai Strittmatter, describes some very particular watery pleasures in this extract translated for the anthology.

I don't know why my heart starts beating faster whenever I stand at the *iskele*, the landing dock, as the siren announces the approach of the ferry long before it rounds the curve of the Bosphorus in front of Yeniköy. Is it because the Bosphorus ferries belong to another time or another world? They not only transport you, they run away with you. If someone came to Istanbul and only had a few hours of time in his luggage, I would put him on one of these old, iron boats. They don't just sail to the Black Sea, they don't merely go down to Istanbul – they drive straight toward Nirvana. You drift, look around, meditate, and feel like chuckling with joy. Worn-down boards, simple wooden benches, the only decorations here are the chains of white-painted iron rivets framing the stained windows. Swarms of gulls follow the boats like the clouds of steam in earlier times from which these vessels get their name: they are still called *vapur* today, from the French *vapeur*, steamer. Feeding gulls is the morning sport of the passengers, who toss bits of their sesame rings to them from the railing. Busy sailors serve copper-coloured tea for a few cents in small tulip glasses and (if they have brought supplies on board in Kalıca on the Asian side) the famous local yoghurt, sprinkling a white hood of powdered sugar on top with one hand. Sometimes sailors wave across from the tower of a submarine. And just when you feel you've reached the limits of pure bliss, the high-spirited gods send yet another school of somersaulting dolphins into the Bay of Tarabya.

Kai Strittmatter, *User's Guide to Istanbul* (2010)
translated by Susan Thorne

* * *

Maureen Freely is well known as the translator of Turkish Nobel Laureate Orhan Pamuk, but she is also a novelist in her own right. This extract, from her novel, Enlightenment, *captures the excitement of the international maritime traffic constantly present on the city's waterways.*

June 22nd 1970

'I wonder what it will be like when I leave this place and no longer wake up to ships. There's an endless procession passing beneath us, in darkness and in light. They're all shapes and sizes – from tankers, ocean liners and warships glistening with radar, to rowboats and ferries and wooden fishing boats that bounce along the water's surface like crescent moons. The little ones are as brightly painted as children's paintings, the ferries were built in Glasgow eighty years ago and look like artworks from a more innocent age. The Turkish Maritime Liners are white with orange anchors on their funnels, the cargo ships tend to be grey or black or rusting red, but there are no rules here and that's what's so exhilarating. You never know what's coming at you around the corner.

The ships look so stately from up here but Sinan says that the Russian pilots are often drunk and sometimes run aground. He's pointed out a few places – gruesome empty lots where once stood beautiful Ottoman waterside villas. No one can do anything about it, apparently. This is an international waterway and ships come and go as they please.

Some are high in the sea and others so low you can imagine them sinking under a single wave. They all have flags and I've taken to using Dad's binoculars to find out where they're registered. Most are Turkish, but it's the ominous Soviet vessels that linger in the mind. I have yet to master the Cyrillic alphabet so I can't decipher all their names, though obviously I have no trouble figuring out which are from the Bulgarian port of BAPNA.

Yesterday when Chloe and I were walking into Bebek, we saw nine people jumping off a ship from BAPNA. Defectors, we assume. Chloe says I should think of the Bosphorus as Berlin-on-the-Sea. She also claims she saw the missiles on their way to Cuba in 1962, and then on their way back again once the crisis was over. Dad says the Bosphorus is a lot more important than Berlin. It's our outermost outpost – not just where the free world ends, but where the free world has the best view of the other side. Where else can you watch the Soviet might pass before your eyes as you eat your breakfast?'

Maureen Freely, *Enlightenment* (2007)

❊ ❊ ❊

French writer and diplomat Daniel Rondeau observes the endless task of keeping the quaysides free of the large stones that accumulate there. (Translated for this anthology.)

A diver in a wetsuit is working the length of the quayside under water. He's gathering the large stones pushed towards the shore by the current and by boats' propellers and which get in the way of the ferries when they're docking. He works without let-up and with a great deal of visible effort, bringing up the stones one at a time, carrying them away from the waterside and finally depositing them as far away as possible. When the stones are too heavy, he prises them free from the mud with a crow-bar, resurfaces out of breath, gets a rope thrown by the sailor on the ferry – the *Sabri-K* – secures the stone with a system of complicated knots, dives to check whether the rope is firm, then sticks his thumb up out of the water. The *Sabri-K* moves towards the middle of the channel dragging its load, but two out of three times the stone breaks free and falls to the bottom again and the whole process has to recommence. His yellow diving mask, along with his exhaustion, makes the diver's eyes look big and bulging, ringed with black. The fishermen abandon their bamboo rods in order to watch this Sisyphian task, and sit themselves down comfortably next to me, their legs dangling above the water. Little shoe-shine boys settle themselves on their boxes behind us. Each time the rope unravels or the stone escapes, the *Sabri-K* gives a jolt, the captain sets the engine to slow down, then manoeuvres into a position that will allow the diver to go down once again and disappear beneath the boat's stem with his rope, close to the quayside. By the time an hour has passed, fishermen, shoe-shine boys and passers-by are forming quite a crowd, everyone uniting to direct the operation, until I too had to stop myself from adding my own voice to those yelling advice.

Daniel Rondeau, *Istanbul* (2002)
translated by Erica King

✳ ✳ ✳

A British visitor of the nineteenth century waxes lyrical about the city's waters ...

Even if we don't take part in the chant about 'Mosques and Minarets,' we can still yield praises to Stamboul. We can chant about the harbour; we can say and sing that nowhere else does the sea come so home to a city: there are no pebbly shores – no sand bars – no slimy river beds – no black canals – no locks or docks to divide the very heart of the place from the deep waters. If, being in the noisiest mart of Stamboul, you would stroll to the quiet side of the way amidst those cypresses opposite, you will cross the fathomless Bosphorus; if you would go from your hotel to the Bazaars, you must pass through the bright blue pathway of the Golden Horn, that can carry a thousand sail of the line. You are accustomed to the gondolas that glide among the palaces of St. Mark, but here at Stamboul it is a hundred-and-twenty-gun ship that meets you in the street. Venice strains out from the steadfast land, and in old times would send forth the Chief of the State to woo and wed the reluctant sea; but the stormy bride of the Doge is the bowing slave of the Sultan – she comes to his feet with the treasures of the world – she bears him from palace to palace – by some unfailing witchcraft she entices the breezes to follow her,[1] and fan the pale cheek of her lord – she lifts his armed navies to the very gates of his garden – she watches the walls of his Serail – she stifles the intrigues of his Ministers – she quiets the scandals of his Court – she extinguishes his rivals, and hushes his naughty wives all one by one. So vast are the wonders of the deep!

A. W. Kinglake, *Eöthen* (1844)

❖ ❖ ❖

William Dalrymple describes fellow-passengers on one of Istanbul's many ferries.

ISTANBUL, 28 JULY

By ferry to the island known to the Turks as Büyük Ada, and to the Greeks as Prinkipo. Hazy, all-enveloping heat. Boys bathing by the Bosphorus. The scent of sea-salt, hot wood, rotting fish. We pull away from the Golden Horn, pass around the wooded ridge of the Topkapı Saray, and head out across the narrow stretch of water that separates Europe from Asia.

The other passengers: beside me, a sad-eyed conscript, perhaps eighteen years old, in ill-fitting fatigues. Small moustache. Cropped hair. Gazes vacantly over the sea. Perhaps he is on his way to do his military service on the Kurdish front.

---

1   There is almost always a breeze either from the Marmora or from the Black Sea that passes along the course of the Bosphorus.

Opposite, a girl in a lilac headscarf and long Islamic rain-coat. She is earnestly studying an English-language pharma-cology textbook: 'Chapter Two – Drug Permeation'.

On the bench at the back, an old labourer with toothbrush moustache and no teeth. Unbuttoned flies. Cigarette hangs from the side of his mouth.

Shady-looking character in tight T-shirt. Stubble chin. He clacks worry beads from the palm to the back of his hand, and darts furtive looks around him. Fare dodger?

Shaven-headed sailor in war-movie sailor's suit. Thickset and swarthy. His cap is on his knee. Drags deeply on a cigarette, then loses interest and throws it overboard.

Moving from bench to bench: a blind violinist, led by his son who bangs a small wooden hand-drum. Both wear flat caps.

Various salesmen selling Coke, biros, potato peelers, Rolex watches (fake), Lacoste socks (fake), Ray-Ban sunglasses (fake) and Bic cigarette lighters (apparently genuine, but of the poorest quality). I buy a Coke and it turns out to be fake too: tastes of warm deodorant.

Halfway through the voyage another fearsome-looking head-scarf-and-raincoat lady appears at the top of the stair-well and begins to harangue us all. I assume she is telling us to vote *Refah*, or ticking off those few middle-aged women who are not wearing a veil. But I'm quite wrong. Her daughter is in hospital and she needs money for medicine. The passengers give generously, especially the old labourer with his flies open, who extinguishes his cigarette to dig deep in his pockets.

William Dalrymple, *From the Holy Mountain* (1997)

❊ ❊ ❊

One of Turkey's great writers of the twentieth century, Ahmet Hamdi Tanpınar (1901–1962), also contemplates the Bosphorus and some of the people who regularly travel on its waters in his beautiful novel A Mind at Peace.

On the Bosphorus, in contrast, everything summoned one inward, and plummeted one into one's own depths. Here everything belonged to us, those facets that governed the grand synthesis, including the panorama and the architecture, as temporal as it was ... those facets that we founded and subsequently came into being along with us. This was a realm of squat-minareted and small-mosqued villages whose lime-washed walls defined Istanbul neighbourhoods; a realm of sprawling cemeteries that at times dominated a panorama from edge to edge; a realm of fountains with broken ornamental fascia whose long-dry spouts nevertheless provided a cooling tonic; a realm of large Bosphorus residences, of wooden dervish houses in whose courtyards goats now grazed, of quayside coffeehouses, the shouts of whose apprentice waiters mingled into the otherworld of Istanbul ramadans like a salutation from the mortal world, of public squares filled with the memories of bygone wrestling matches with drums and shrill pipes and contenders bedecked in outfits like national holiday costumes, of enormous chinar trees, of overcast evenings, of eerie and emotive echoes and of daybreaks during which nymphs of dawn bore torches aloft, hovering in mother-of-pearl visions reflected in mirrors of the metaphysical.

Besides, everything on the Bosphorus was a reflection. Light was reflection, sound was reflection; sporadically, here, one might become the echo of an array of things unbeknownst to oneself.

Whenever Mümtaz lent an ear to his early childhood memories and listened to the echoes of the ferry horns that reached him after ricocheting from the surrounding hilltops, he might discern from which wellsprings the incurable *hüzün*[1] within him sometimes rose and flowed forth and made him so opulent amid everyday routine.

The ferry gathered civil servants returning from their city jobs,

1 See start of section 'From *hüzün* to *huzur*' for an attempt to define this emotion. (Ed.)

sightseers, beachgoers, young students, military officers, elderly women, and congregants on deck, the remorse of whose lives, and the day's fatigue, dripping from their faces, intentionally or not, seemed to surrender to this waning evening hour. Like the potter described by Omar Khayyám, the evening took up all those heads and worked them from the inside and outside, transfigured their lines, painted them, varnished and shellacked them, made their eyes dreamier, softened their lips, and filled their stares with renewed glimmers of yearning and hope. They came to the centre of this radiance as themselves, but, as if fallen into the midst of sorcery, they changed with the transformation of light. Intermittently, a guffaw verging on the obnoxious rose from the centre of a group; in the distance, all the way at the bow, well-to-do children raised along the Bosphorus played harmonicas and sang songs in callow voices; and passengers who'd grown accustomed to commuting together called out to one another. These were passing interruptions, however. Quiescence, rather resembling expectation, expanded again – its arboreal growth and boundless leaves beshrouding all.

Ahmet Hamdi Tanpınar, *A Mind at Peace* (1949)
translated by Erdağ Göknar (2008)

❊ ❊ ❊

*Renowned Dutch travel writer Geert Mak describes
sailing from the Black Sea into the Bosphorus.*

From the Black Sea, the first thing one sees are the green hills of Kilyos, behind them the elegant houses and gardens where Irfan Orga once spent the last, light summer of his childhood, and amid them the modern suburbs of Istanbul, lying in folds across the hillsides like cotton wool. We are sailing into the Bosphorus. The villas glide by left and right, one more extravagant than the other, with carved wooden balconies, stoops and terraces looking out on the water, brightly coloured gardens, trees, a village square, a minaret, a little wharf, a few cafés, a beach.

It is 7 a.m., but the sun is already hot. We pass a tiny fishing boat, the nets half spread in the water, three tanned and weathered men wave to the girls on the *Passat*. The great bridge between Europe and Asia lies in the distance, a flimsy thread being crossed by hundreds of bugs and beetles.

Geert Mak, *In Europe:*
Travels Through the Twentieth Century (2004)
translated by Sam Garrett

❊ ❊ · ❊

Where there is water, there are bridges. Geert Mak
again – this time an extract from his fascinating
book The Bridge: A Journey Between Occident and
Orient *– a study of the Galata Bridge and the people*
who 'populate' it. Plans to build a bridge across the
Golden Horn had existed for centuries before the
first one was actually built. Letters exist to the sultan
from both Leonardo da Vinci and Michelangelo with
their proposals for such a bridge. There have been five
Galata Bridges altogether (not counting the one put
together by Mehmet II during his conquest of the city
in 1453). Wooden ones were built in 1845 and 1863,
iron ones in 1875 and 1912, and in 1994 the current
concrete one.

The bridge is not hard to identify. You come flying in over the city, over these ten million souls, their villas and tower blocks rolling away across the hillsides, over the inland seas and bays that divide the city, over the suspension bridges where the freight convoys between Europe and Asia grind along bumper to bumper, over the dozens of ships rusting eternally in the harbours, over the fallen bastions and city walls of the long-vanished empire, over the Blue Mosque, above which, in sharp relief against the evening sky, white birds are always flying. And then unavoidably, your eye is drawn to the bridge.

Or else you discover it by accident. You walk down the

narrow streets past the bazaar, past the cheeses, the olives, the display cases filled with jars of honey and fruit conserves, past the ironmongers' shops, the saws, the stoves and tea pots, past the men standing solemnly beside their boxes full of ball-point pens and paper hankies, past the butchers with their sausage, tripe and goat heads, past the vendors of lottery tickets and luck. Or you follow the quay where the ferry boats dock; you fade into the vast morning masses rolling into the city, the young businessmen, the porters, the office girls, the farm-women, that whole parade of briefcases and threadbare suit jackets; you plough your way through the engines' throb, the fast tick of the girls' heels, the street merchants' shouts; the light reflects across the water, each day in a different way, always in motion; the gulls cry and, suddenly, there, round the corner, behind the kiosks and the stairways, begins the bridge.

The bridge, in fact, is not a pretty sight. Built of concrete, it is little more than half a kilometre long, four lanes and a set of tram tracks wide, a counterweight construction at its middle, its access ramps surrounded by tunnels and shopping arcades. The paved surface climbs gradually, so that smaller boats can easily pass beneath in mid-river. Under the bridge, on the waterfront, lies a long row of restaurants and teahouses – pedestrians can also cross beneath the bridge itself; that's cosier, but halfway across, close to the control towers, you have to negotiate an extra set of steps. And of course you miss all that space, the sea, the autumn mists, the dolphins that on occasion roll up across a distant wave.

Geert Mak, *The Bridge:*
A Journey Between Orient and Occident (2007)
translated by Sam Garrett

✻ ✻ ✻

Geert Mak is not the first visitor to be fascinated by the people of the bridge. Here's Jan Neruda in the late nineteenth century in an extract translated from Czech for this anthology.

Let's lean on the balcony. Beneath us strain the blue waters of the Golden Horn, schooners dart like arrows, and steamers veer; before us – a flowing potpourri of peoples. Yet another European caravan, but clearly one that has been here longer. Two ladies carried in an elegant, golden Sedan, behind them the men: all with fezzes on their heads, one of them with a large white felt hat similar to those worn by our firemen: the top of the hat, jutting forward, is open and serves as a ventilator. Beggars, sitting in a row along the pavement, hold out their tin bowls to him and bray. A poorly dressed, but gorgeously-built Bulgarian, with a shaggy fur cap on a bushy head of hair, leads an enormous bear on a chain; behind him his wife, also beautifully formed, with a monkey and a drum. A tall, thin Circassian fusilier, breast belted in ammunition, wants to cross to the other side; the bear stands in his way, and the fusilier jumps over as if it were but a coffee table. With calm, majestic step a sun-shrivelled Egyptian approaches; he has a silk scarf wrapped around his turban, with silk ribbons streaming from it by way of decoration. A crowd of Moroccan Jews, Sephardim, walking quickly as they argue among themselves, prattling in Spanish. Behind them, a crowd of half-naked workwomen; almost all of them with a child at their neck. [...]

Onwards and onwards in droves they come. Women from Damascus wrapped in colourful floral veils that make it impossible to see so much as an eye; Moorish women, almost all unlovely, but constantly smiling and coquetting to all sides; muscular boat pullers with their sleeves rolled up, bearing coils of rope; chatty Greeks all dressed up, waistcoats dripping in silver, skirts like snow, shoes adorned with roses; Russians on pilgrimage to Jerusalem in black habits, humble and shy; sailors in white dress uniforms – God only knows what religion they are, when today, Tuesday, is their Sunday!

Involuntarily we have made our way forwards, pushing through humanity into the middle of the bridge – which takes

28

fifteen minutes to traverse. Suddenly the crush from all sides
is so great that we can't catch our breath. Because they have
opened the bridge to allow a schooner into the inner military
port, the stream of people has halted, and at that same moment
a steamer from Scutari has spilled out hundreds more people
onto the same spot. But it's only a moment, and then we can
once again move 'freely,' elbowed and trodden on from all sides.

Jan Neruda, *Pictures from Abroad* (1870)
translated by Ray Furlong

❊ ❊ ❊

*Writing just a few years after Neruda, Edmondo de
Amicis paints an even more detailed and vivid picture
of the river of humanity – in all its variety – continually crossing the Galata Bridge.*

To see the population of Constantinople, it's a good idea to go
upon the floating bridge, about a quarter of a mile in length,
which extends from the most advanced point of Galata to the
opposite shore of the Golden Horn, facing the great Mosque of
the Sultana Valide. [… ..]

Standing there, one can see all Constantinople go by in an
hour. There are two never-ending currents of human beings
that meet and mingle from sunrise to sunset, presenting a
spectacle compared to which the marketplaces of India, the
fair of Nizhni Novgorod and the festivals of Peking fade into
nothingness. To see anything at all, you must choose a small
portion of the bridge and fix your eyes on that alone; otherwise
in the attempt to see everything one ends up seeing nothing.
The crowd goes by in great multicoloured waves, and each
new group represents a new populace. The most extravagant
types may there be seen in a space of fifty yards and within
ten minutes. Behind a crowd of Turkish porters who run past,
bending under enormous burdens, a sedan chair comes along,
inlaid with ivory and mother-of-pearl, with an Armenian lady

looking out; on either side of it a bedouin wrapped in a white mantle and a Turk in muslin turban and sky-blue kaftan, beside whom canters a young Greek gentleman followed by his dragoman in an embroidered jacket and a dervish with his tall conical hat and camel-hair tunic, who makes way for the carriage of a European ambassador, preceded by a footman in livery. All this is glimpsed rather than seen. Before you've had time to turn round, you find yourself in the middle of a crowd of Persians, in pyramid-shaped hats of astrakhan fur, who are followed by a Jew in a long yellow coat, open at the sides; a frowzy-headed gypsy woman carrying her child in a sling on her back; a Catholic priest with a breviary and staff; while through a confused throng of Greeks, Turks and Armenians a fat eunuch rides on horseback, crying out 'Make way!' in front of a Turkish carriage, painted with flowers and birds, and filled with the ladies from a harem, dressed in green and purple, and wrapped in large white veils; behind the carriage comes a Sister of Charity from one of the hospitals in Pera, an African slave carrying a monkey, and a professional storyteller wearing a necromancer's robe. What is quite natural, but appears strange to the newcomer, is that all these different people pass each other without a second glance, like a crowd in London; no one stops for a moment, everyone is in a hurry. [...]

It is amusing to look down at the passing feet and see all the footwear in the world go by, from that of Adam down to the latest fashion in Parisian boots – yellow Turkish babouches, red shoes for Armenians, turquoise for Greeks, and black for Jews; sandals, great boots from Turkistan, Albanian gaiters, low-cut shoes, richly coloured gambados worn by horse merchants from Asia Minor, slippers embroidered with gold thread, Spanish *alpargatas*, shoes made of satin, rope, rags, wood, so many that while you look at one you catch a glimpse of a hundred more.

Edmondo de Amicis, Constantinople (1877)
translated by Stephen Parkin

* * *

Taking up de Amicis' description of the variety of footwear to be seen crossing the Bridge, Geert Mak gives us a twenty-first-century version as part of his portrait of present-day Istanbul.

Almost one hundred and fifty years later I see an endless flow of sports shoes passing by, those of merchants, tourists, gamblers, pickpockets. I see waiters' black lace-ups. The dingy loafers of a porter lugging a huge basket of vegetables. The pavement photographer's white Pumas. The gold winkle-pickers and silver sandals of two self-conscious girls parading about in fashionable turquoise and orange dresses, their headscarves bright and colourful. The tanned bare feet – with black oil stains – of a glue sniffer. The no-nonsense clogs of a fundamentalist couple in black. The high-topped trainers in which a schoolgirl – bobbed hair, 'Life' T-shirt, satchel slung over one shoulder – gambols along. The silver slippers of a miniscule Mardi Gras prince, a little boy who is today celebrating his circumcision. The perfume vendor's worn leather brogues.

Edmondo de Amicis had to take care not to be knocked over, that's how busy it was on the bridge in his day. [...]

Today the activity on the bridge has been channelled: there is the tramway for the middle class, the road for the wealthy and the would-be rich, and the pavement for the losers, the tourists and dissidents. The pace of pedestrian traffic has slowed to something more like traipsing or strolling. And the fishermen never budge, an unthinkable phenomenon on de Amicis's lively bridge. In his day almost no one fished from the bridge, there were plenty of other places in the city where one could scoop the fish straight from the water. It was only in the 1980s, when the city was again confronted with mass unemployment, that the bridge became a popular fishing spot.

Geert Mak, *The Bridge:*
A Journey Between Orient and Occident (2007)
translated by Sam Garrett

* * *

And finally, a brief moment of watery happiness for a resident of the city ...

We got out of the taxi in front of the fish restaurant boats moored at Yeniköy. We chose one of them and sat at a table on deck. The weather was cool, but it was also kind of sunny. Freighters passed us in the distance. Every time they did, we enjoyed the rocking of the little boat caused by the waves that came a bit later. On the seaside road, there was a calmness that led one to think that this Sunday would last for ever and ever.

Tuna Kiremitçi, *The Way of Loneliness* (2003)
translated by Jak Korı

"The cloister of the whirling Dervishes ... lay on our way"
Hans Christian Andersen

Travellers' tales

Byzantium – Constantinople – Istanbul ... Over many centuries travellers have filled thousands of pages with accounts of their visits to this most desirable of destinations. We sample the experiences of travellers of many nationalities – American, Australian, British, Canadian, Czech, Danish, Dutch, French, Greek, Italian. Let's start with the ever-enthusiastic Italian, Edmondo de Amicis, who agreed with the steersman of the ship which brought him into the city that to 'come into Constantinople on a fine morning' is truly 'a great moment in a man's life.'

On the towers of the Seraskerat and of Galata, on the old bridge and in Scutari, I asked myself over and over again: 'How could you fall in love with Holland?" Not only that country, but Paris, Madrid, Seville, all now seemed to me dark and melancholy places where I couldn't have lasted a month. Then I thought of my poor attempts to describe them and said to myself bitterly: 'You wretch! How many times have you wasted the words "beautiful", "immense", "splendid". And now what will you say about this spectacle?' It already seemed to me that I would be incapable of writing even a single page about Constantinople.

Edmondo de Amicis, *Constantinople* (1877)
translated by Stephen Parkin

* * *

Despite the above claim of writerly humility in the face of the city's glories, de Amicis went on to write one of the most detailed descriptions of the Ottoman city.

The emotion I felt on entering Constantinople almost made me forget everything I had seen in my ten days' voyage from the straits of Messina to the mouth of the Bosphorus. The blue Ionian Sea, motionless as a lake, the distant mountains of the Morea tinted rose-pink by the first rays of the sun, the islands of the Greek archipelago glowing in the sunset, the ruins of Athens, the Gulf of Salonika, Lemnos, Tenedos, the Dardanelles, and many persons and events that had amused and interested me during the voyage, all faded at the sight of the Golden Horn; and now, if I wish to describe them, I must work more from imagination than from memory. But in order that my first page starts out warm and alive, I must begin on the last night of the voyage, in the middle of the Sea of Marmara, at the moment when the captain of the ship approached me and my friend Junck, and putting his hands on my shoulders said, in a thick Sicilian accent, 'Gentlemen, tomorrow at dawn we'll see the first minarets of Stamboul.'

Ah! Reader, full of money and ennui – you who, a few years ago, when on a whim you felt like visiting Constantinople, filled your wallet and packed your case and within twenty-four hours had left as if taking a short trip to the countryside, uncertain up to the last moment whether you shouldn't go to Baden-Baden instead! If the captain had said to you, 'Tomorrow morning we shall see Stamboul,' you would have answered phlegmatically, 'I'm glad to hear it.' But you need to have nursed this wish for ten years, to have passed many winter evenings sadly studying the map of the East, have inflamed your imagination with the reading of a hundred books, have wandered over one half of Europe in the effort to console yourself for not being able to see the other half, to have been nailed for one year to a desk with that purpose only, have made a thousand small sacrifices, calculated and recalculated, built many castles in the air and gone through many domestic battles; finally you need to have passed nine sleepless nights at sea with the immense and luminous image of the city before your eyes, so happy that you even feel a pang of remorse at the thought of the dear ones you've left behind at home; and then you might understand what these words mean, 'Tomorrow at dawn we'll see the first minarets of Stamboul'; and instead of answering quietly, 'I'm glad to hear it,' you would have done as I did and struck the ship's rail with your fist in excitement.

Edmondo de Amicis, *Constantinople* (1877)
translated by Stephen Parkin

❋ ❋ ❋

More than a century before de Amicis' pæen to the city, Lady Mary Wortley Montagu – wife of the British ambassador to the Ottoman court – also wrote very appreciatively (though with more brevity) about the city in her letters home. As well as giving vivid details, she demonstrates great open-mindedness and a true fascination with a culture very different from her own – and some startlingly modern attitudes for an English woman of her class and time.

I am now preparing to leave Constantinople, and perhaps you will accuse me of hypocrisy when I tell you 'tis with regret, but I am used to the air and have learnt the language. [...]

I am more inclined, out of a true female spirit of contradiction, to tell you the falsehood of a great part of what you find in authors; as, for example, the admirable Mr Hill, who so gravely asserts that he saw in St Sophia a sweating pillar very balsamic for disordered heads. There is not the least tradition of any such matter, and I suppose it was revealed to him in a vision during his wonderful stay in the Egyptian catacombs, for I am sure he never heard of any such miracle here. 'Tis also very pleasant to observe how tenderly he and all his brethren voyage-writers lament on the miserable confinement of the Turkish ladies, who are, perhaps, freer than any ladies in the universe, and are the only women in the world that lead a life of uninterrupted pleasure, exempt from cares, their whole time being spent in visiting, bathing or the agreeable amusement of spending money and inventing new fashions. A husband would be thought mad that exacted any degree of economy from his wife, whose expenses are no way limited but by her own fancy. 'Tis his business to get money and hers to spend it, and this noble prerogative extends itself to the very meanest of the sex. Here is a fellow that carries embroidered handkerchiefs upon his back to sell, as miserable a figure as you may suppose such a mean dealer, yet I'll assure you his wife scorns to wear anything less than cloth of gold, has her ermine furs and a very handsome set of jewels for her head. They go abroad when and where they please. 'Tis true they have no public places but the bagnios, and there can only be seen by their own sex. However, that is a diversion they take great pleasure in.

I was three days ago at one of the finest in the town and had the opportunity of seeing a Turkish bride received there and all the ceremonies used on that occasion, which made me recollect the epithalamium of Helen by Theocritus, and it seems to me that the same customs have continued ever since. All the she-friends, relations and acquaintance of the two families newly allied meet at the bagnio. Several others go out of curiosity and I believe there was that day at least two hundred women. Those that were or had been married placed themselves round the room on the marble sofas, but the virgins very hastily threw off their clothes and appeared without other ornament or covering than their own long hair braided with pearl or ribbon. Two of them met the bride at the door, conducted by her mother and another grave relation. She was a beautiful maid of about seventeen, richly dressed and shining with jewels, but was presently reduced by them to the state of nature. Two others filled silver gilt pots with perfume and begun the procession, the rest following in pairs to the number of thirty. The leaders sung an epithalamium answered by the others in chorus, and the two last led the fair bride, her eyes fixed on the ground with a charming affectation of modesty. In this order they marched round the three large rooms of the bagnio. 'Tis not easy to represent to you the beauty of this sight, most of them being well proportioned and white skinned, all of them perfectly smooth and polished by the frequent use of bathing. After having made their tour, the bride was again led to every matron round the rooms, who saluted her with a compliment and a present, some of jewels, others pieces of stuff, handkerchiefs, or little gallantries of that nature, which she thanked them for by kissing their hands.

I was very well pleased with having seen this ceremony and you may believe me that the Turkish ladies have at least as much wit and civility, nay, liberty, as ladies amongst us. 'Tis true the same customs that give them so many opportunities of gratifying their evil inclinations (if they have any) also puts it very fully in the power of their husbands to revenge them if they are discovered, and I don't doubt but they suffer sometimes for their indiscretions in a very severe manner. [...]

I am well acquainted with a Christian woman of quality who made it her choice to live with a Turkish husband, and is a very agreeable sensible lady. Her story is so extraordinary I cannot forbear relating it, but I promise you it shall be in as few words as I can possibly express it. She is a Spaniard, and was at Naples with her family when that Kingdom was part of the Spanish dominion. Coming from thence in a felucca, accompanied by her brother they were attacked by the Turkish Admiral, boarded and taken; and now how shall I modestly tell you the rest of her adventure? The same accident happened to her that happened to the fair Lucretia so many years before her, but she was too good a Christian to kill herself as that heathenish Roman did. The admiral was so much charmed with the beauty and long suffering of the fair captive that as his first compliment he gave immediate liberty to her brother and attendants, who made haste to Spain and in a few months sent the sum of £4000 sterling as a ransom for his sister. The Turk took the money, which he presented to her, and told her she was at liberty, but the lady very discreetly weighted the different treatment she was likely to find in her native country. Her Catholic relations, as the kindest thing they could do for her in her present circumstances, would certainly confine her to a nunnery for the rest of her days. Her infidel lover was very handsome, very tender, fond of her and lavished at her feet all the Turkish magnificence. She answered him very resolutely that her liberty was not so precious to her as her honour, that he could no way restore that but by marrying her. She desired him to accept the ransom as her portion and give her the satisfaction of knowing no man could boast of her favours without being her husband. The Admiral was transported at this kind offer and sent back the money to her relations, saying he was too happy in her possession. He married her and never took any other wife, and (as she says herself) she never had any reason to repent the choice she made. He left her some years after one of the richest widows in Constantinople.

Lady Mary Wortley Montagu, *Turkish Embassy Letters* (1716)

✳ ✳ ✳

By the nineteenth century, Constantinople had clearly become one of the 'must see' places for European travellers from many countries. In 1841, renowned Danish writer Hans Christian Andersen made a trip to Constantinople, publishing The Poet's Bazaar *the following year – a work from which the next extract is taken, translated for this anthology by novelist Mikka Haugaard.*

On the left Constantinople greeted us, on the right Galata, and further up Pera whose round tower stretched high into the sky among the drifting clouds. Huge ships made a forest of masts in the wide bay. A chaos of boats, most of them narrow and thin like the canoes of savages flew past like arrows – the rowers and the passengers lying at the bottom. There was a yelling and shouting, a right roaring Babel compared to which the noise in the bay of Naples would have seemed almost funereal.

Ancient Turks, their skin a golden brown, their arms naked, huge brightly coloured turbans on their heads, were shouting at one another and waving their oars to invite us on board. I had my clothes thrown down, got in myself and then with rapid strokes of the oars we approached a coast cluttered with ships and small boats; we had to walk across them to get to dry land. We were standing on the jetty and I offered the man who had done the rowing a silver coin, the value of which I didn't myself really know. He shook his head, took a really tiny coin out of his pocket and showed it to me, insisting that he wasn't

39

entitled to anything more. That's how honest the Turks are and every single day I was there I was given further proofs of their honesty. The Turks are the most good natured and honest people there are.

A ruddy brown, muscular Arab offered to carry my clothes. Quickly he tied a rope round my suitcase, travelling bag and hat-box, threw it all on his shoulders and wandered off – whenever I mentioned the name of the hotel where I wanted to stay, he just nodded.

We entered a street that curved this way and that, full of nooks and corners, every house was a shop offering herbs, bread, meat or clothes. We met people from every corner of the world. We entered Pera through the narrow gate of Galata. No one asked us for passports. A road as narrow and as badly paved as the one we had just left ran steeply up hill. We passed a guard, some young, golden brown lads in tight blue trousers and jackets, white bandoliers and red fezzes who were lying almost flat on their stomachs along the street, saying their prayers. An hourglass was standing next to them.

In the moat, by the tower of Galata, there were flayed horses lying all covered in blood. We passed Turkish cafés with fountains splashing inside. The cloister of the whirling Dervishes (where, above the entrance gate, there are inscriptions in gold from the Qur'an) lay on our way. We were travelling along the main street which is very narrow. The houses are two or three storeys high and all of them have porches. The side streets are even narrower, and the buildings seem to meet in the air so that I don't think one would ever need an umbrella, should it rain.

What a swarm of people there was! And in the middle of this swarm a Bulgarian peasant was doing a dance. He had a red close fitting hat on his head, miserable sandals on his feet, and was wearing a sheepskin. He danced like a bear standing on its hind legs. Another Bulgarian was accompanying his dance on the bagpipes. Some haulers were dragging huge marble blocks attached to poles; there were about six to eight of them, brown, muscular fellows. They kept shouting to make people get out of their way. We met some Armenian priests, black crêpe fluttering from their hats. Suddenly the quiet murmur of a song reached us, a young Greek girl was being buried. She was lying in an open coffin, all decorated with flowers, in everyday clothes and her face uncovered. Three Greek priests and two small boys, carrying lit candles, were walking in front.

What a crowd there was and what chaos and confusion! Gaily coloured vehicles, like small four-poster beds on wheels made out of card, gilded all over and with long flapping curtains, through which veiled women peeped, went bumping along the uneven stone bridge. Horses and donkeys carrying beams and planks of wood that dragged behind them along the road were trying to make their way through the crowds.

Finally we reached Hotel de la France and were greeted by the proprietor, Mr Blondel.

Hans Christian Andersen, *The Poet's Bazaar* (1842)
translated by Mikka Haugaard

❊ ❊ ❊

The vibrant and teeming variety of this city that stimulated all the senses elicited an extraordinarily vivid recreation of the city's life from Czech writer Jan Neruda – another extract translated for this anthology.

Loping past, a cavalcade of European travellers, who have taken themselves on a trip across Stamboul, onwards 'towards the seven towers.' The riders are of varying qualities, with white veils on their hats and cheerful smiles on their faces. Behind each of them runs the owner of the horse, a lanky, barefoot fellow, the blue tassel of his dirty fez swinging to and fro and his stick constantly beating the horse's bony rump. Two burly Turks morosely gaze at the cavalcade, clearly rich men. They walk alongside each other without talking, their figures – not large, but thick set – moving casually, as if to inform any with a sharp eye: 'I am still the master here!' […]

'Bana bak!' (Watch out!), a baritone voice calls out and a Turkish Talika clatters by. It is a coach built like a see-saw, covered on top, at the front and at the back, open at the sides; its boot usually tends to have the shape of a ball sliced in half. It is always painted in gay colours, with flowers, arabesques and so on bursting forth from dark earth. Several women are seated within, veiled, and gazing curiously at their surroundings. And again, 'Bana bak!' A second, slightly longer coach, almost an omnibus, with a roof on columns; seated within, about another ten women. This kind of coach is called an 'arba,' with two oxen harnessed to it, which have been washed and colour-fully decorated; a long, thin pole extends from the yoke on their necks, high into the air and bending back over their tails, adorned with red, yellow and blue tassels. 'Guarda – guarda!' The calls ring out. Bulgarian and Armenian bearers, 'hamals,' pass by with steady foot, a mountain of goods on each of them, several quintals in weight. Among them, one hamal carries a huge greasy pile of suckling pigs, decorated with strips of pink crêpe. And 'guarda – guarda!' With quiet, majestic step an entire train of camels, loaded with crates and baskets, makes its way forward. And behind the camels a train of mules; one of them is hauling logs on its back, tied in a bundle over its neck, another carries baskets of gravel, a third bricks, a fourth stones – even stones are sold by weight here. The tiles must be brought from far away, a six hour journey, and there are neither roads nor carriages. And suddenly the ear-splitting cry of a pack of urchins whistles through the air, the boys shoving through the crowds to offer Turkish, Greek and French newspapers hot off the presses.

Jan Neruda, *Pictures from Abroad* (1870)
translated by Ray Furlong

* * *

*And now a rather different emphasis from the creator
of* Madame Bovary *as* Gustave Flaubert *writes home
to his friend Louis Bouilet.*

Constantinople, November 14, 1850

Regarding Constantinople – I arrived yesterday morning –
I won't say a word just yet, except that I've been struck by
Fourier's idea that, at some point in the future, it will be the
capital of the world. It is utterly amazing – a human anthill. It
gives one the impression of being crushed and overwhelmed,
just as on one's first visit to Paris: it really gets inside you as
you rub shoulders with so many unknown men, from Persians
and Indians to Americans and the English – just so many individuals who, in their terrifying mass, make you feel extremely
small. Moreover, the city itself is vast. You get lost in its streets,
which seem to have no beginning and no end. The cemeteries
are like forests in the middle of the city. As you look out, from
the top of the Galata tower, over all the houses and mosques
beside and between the Bosphorus and the Golden Horn, both
crammed with ships, the houses themselves seem like ships –
a motionless fleet with masts formed by minarets. (A rather
long-winded sentence: do ignore it.) We walked through (and
only walked through) the street given over to male brothels. I
noticed male prostitutes buying sugared almonds, with bugger
money, no doubt – the anus thus about to provide for the
stomach rather than the reverse, which is more normal. I heard
the sound of an ill-played violin coming from some ground-
floor rooms where a Greek dance was being performed. These
young boys usually are Greeks: they wear their hair long.

Gustave Flaubert, *The Letters of Gustave Flaubert 1830–1857*
translated by Erica King

* * *

The next extract combines observations from a writer of the late twentieth century, journalist and author Jeremy Seal, with references to the nineteenth century French adventurer Pierre Loti, whose well-known association with the city is still referenced in modern Istanbul.

The slope fell sharply away below where a jumble of brambled and broken graves gave way to the road and the water beyond it. A rim of still scum lacquered the waterline in a ruff of black flecked with mercury. Beyond it lay a palette of putrid greens, greys, and browns. Fishing boats lined the waterfront and occasional freighters lay broken-backed in the mud, seeping coiled gouts of rust. To the west, where hills hemmed in the water on all sides, mud-banks shrugged out of the murk to punctuate the poisoned shallows. Far to the east, the water eddied into the Bosphorus and lapped at the fringes of Asia. But I could not see so far, only a succession of bridges shrouded in mist, whited-out echoes of bridges that bound Istanbul across her legendary waterways, each like a fainter impression of Turkey herself spanning land masses, continents, even beliefs.

I was looking down at the western extent of the fabled Golden Horn which was known to the Ottomans as the Sweet Waters of Europe. In the eighteenth century, there were tulip shows along these banks where the Sultan's guests wandered through the gardens and along the marble quays drinking sherbet, while candle-bearing tortoises clambered among the flowerbeds, throwing lumbering flickers of light. Now, there was a cold, snow-laden wind, and a shepherd driving his sheep through a graveyard to the butchers, and all those who had seen the tulips and the tortoises were dust at my feet. I remembered a line from Pierre Loti: 'In no other country have I seen so many cemeteries, so many tombs, so many dead.'

Loti, a young French romantic and adventurer, often returned to this sprawling, hilltop cemetery in the late 1800s to dream of an Orient that even then was fast disappearing. The tulips and the tortoises were long gone, and cobwebs were beginning to ravel up the Ottoman Empire in a cocoon of decay as the last of the Sultans languished in their palaces while the great powers collected at the deathbed of the Sick Man of Europe.

At the top of the hill, Loti's memory had been press-ganged into service at the Pierre Loti Shop, Bazaar, and Café. Where once he had sat and conjured up quixotic visions, the modern world had wreaked vulgar revenge until all that remained of him was now swathed in trinketry. [...]

I walked through the colourless winter grass and among the headstones. Some were chipped, cracked, and broken; others ran green with lichen and brown with rust. Squat stones arched to a rounded point while minor mausoleums were ringed with low rusty chain fences. There were delicately engraved tablets and tall cylindrical steles, topped off sometimes by stone turbans gathering lichen, but mostly by Mahmud II's innumerable stone fezzes. They were everywhere, these fezzes, large and small, some with carved tassles, some tapering dramatically to the crown. A number of stones had been decapitated so that the fezzes lay in the mulch at their feet or had rolled away until the trunk of a cypress tree or another headstone had finally brought them to rest above the remains of another.

Jeremy Seal, *A Fez of the Heart* (1995)

* * *

After the great procession of visitors recording their impression of the city throughout the nineteenth century, the first half of the twentieth was mainly occupied with wars and their aftermaths. The fall of the Ottoman Empire and the establishment of the Republic under Ataturk in 1923 meant the whole country was less likely to be visited by the kind of people seeking the 'exotic'. But one visitor in the late 1950s was French writer and philosopher Simone de Beauvoir.

Istanbul at night looked deserted. Next morning it was teeming with life. Buses, automobiles, handcarts, horse-drawn carriages, bicycles, porters, people walking, the traffic was so thick on the Eminonu bridge that one could scarcely cross the road without risking certain death; all along the wharves, there were clusters of ships: steamships, tugboats, tenders, barges. Their sirens were wailing, their engines hiccupping; on the road, overloaded taxis rushed up, skidded, screaming, to a stop, then drove away again in a series of minor explosions; there was the clanging of metal, yells, whistles, a vast discordant uproar reverberating inside our heads already battered by the violent bombardment of the sea. It was like a sledgehammer, yet no reflections spattered the blackish waters of the Golden Horn, cluttered with old tubs and pieces of rotting wood jammed between the warehouses. In the heart of old Stamboul, we clambered up dead streets lined with wooden houses more or less in a state of collapse, and along others with shops and workshops opening off them. Shoeshine boys, cobblers, crouching inside with their gear in front of them, gazed at us with hostility; we got the same looks in the wretched bistro where we drank our coffee at wooden tables; was it Americans they hated, or just tourists? Not a woman in the place; almost none in the streets; nothing but masculine faces, and not one wearing a smile. The covered bazaar, bathed in a flat grey light, made me think of a vast hardware store; everything about the markets in the dusty streets was ugly – the utensils, the stuffs and the cheap pictures. One thing roused our curiosity: the quantity of automatic scales and the number of people, often quite poverty-stricken, who were prepared to sacrifice a coin to weigh themselves. Where were we? These jostling crowds, entirely male, were a sign of the East, of Islam; but the colour of Africa and the picturesqueness of China were missing. It felt as though we were on the fringe of a disinherited country, and of some dismal Middle Ages. The interiors of Santa Sofia and the Blue Mosque lived up to all my expectations; I had seen and liked smaller mosques, more intimate and more alive, with their courtyards, their fountains and pigeons circling overhead; but there was almost nothing left in them of the long-extinguished past. Byzantium, Constantinople, Istanbul: the town did not live up to the promises of these names, except at that hour when its domes and their slender, pointed minarets were silhouetted along the hilltop against the glowing sky at dusk; then all its sumptuous, bloodstained past appeared through its beauty.

Simone de Beauvoir, *Force of Circumstance* (1963)
translated by Richard Howard

✻ ✻ ✻

By the early 1960s, Istanbul had become an important staging post on the hippie trail to the East, and visitors in search of 'otherness' began to flock to the city once more. Acclaimed travel writer Rory Maclean recreates that time.

In the early sixties, the first Intrepids began arriving in Istanbul in small numbers, finding a sweet, melancholy city of ramshackle wooden and crumbling city walls, without tourists or touts. Old men in baggy trousers idled away afternoons in backstreet coffeehouses. Taxi drivers wore ill-cut Western suits, chewed gum and drank opiate wine. Fearsome razor-sellers worked the piers. Diesel smoke rose from weathered freighters. The oily air smelt of charcoal and mackerel. Along the cobblestone pavements, pedlars stirred steaming cauldrons of sweet corn cobs. Tailors slithered on the heels of their slippers, bent under the weight of dozens of leather jackets. The bazaar – where public letter-writers typed on Coronas – wasn't yet a gift-shop warehouse. Sultanahmet hadn't become a sightseers' ghetto. The neighbouring slopes and hills were still bare of buildings. With rainbow patches on their jeans or maple leaves on their backpacks, the travellers hung out at the first hostels, played guitars together on the steps of the Blue Mosque, smoked hubble-bubbles under the cypress trees before driving their battered VW Campers and Morris Minors on to the rusty Bosphorus ferry.

Rory Maclean, *Magic Bus* (2007)

✽ ✽ ✽

In Just As Well I'm Leaving, *Michael Booth attempts to follow in the footsteps of Hans Christian Andersen. In this short extract he reminds us of some of the other famous visitors to the city who have stayed in its famous Pera Palace Hotel.*

My hotel, the Pera Palace, is legendary in these parts, boasting Hemingway, Agatha Christie (who wrote *Murder on the Orient Express* in the room next to the one I was given), Garbo and the spy Mata Hari as former guests (although, you have to wonder, if everyone knew Mata Hari was a spy, how did she actually get to do any spying?). It was built by the Orient Express company for their passengers but these days it is the very definition of faded grandeur. The bar in particular is awash with period atmosphere. It is the kind of place where arms dealers rub shoulders with impecunious eastern European royals seeking funding for a revolution; where caviar smugglers do deals with Russian Mafiosi in exchange for pink diamonds and Volga virgins; and where dishevelled backpackers live out absurd Graham Greene fantasies.

Michael Booth, *Just As Well I'm Leaving* (2005)

✽ ✽ ✽

And here's Dutch travel writer Geert Mak on the Pera Palace Hotel, too.

I stay at the Pera Palace, an antique hotel built in 1892 as an extension of the Orient Express, a cool resting place after the exhausting train trip through the Balkans. The building breathes a nostalgic chic, an ancient lift creaks up and down all day, right through the middle of the stairwell. Gold and marble glisten in the immense halls. In the big, flaking bathrooms you can sit on the same toilet as Greta Garbo, stare out of the same window as Empress Sissi of Austria, and lie in the same bed as King Zog of Albania. The TV is turned up loudly in the room where Trotsky slept: 204.

The loveliest suite here is held eternally for Mustafa Kemal Pasha – known from 1934 as Kemal Atatürk, the 'father of all Turks'. A porter takes me by the hand, lets me peek around the door. It is a small, silent sanctuary: a bed, a bathroom, two easy chairs, a desk with a couple of photographs and some papers. So this was the Istanbul pied-à-terre of the military dictator, this hero of the First World War who reined in the chaos of the collapsing Ottoman Empire, drove out the foreign occupiers and led the country powerfully and energetically into the modern age.

Geert Mak, *In Europe:*
Travels Through the Twentieth Century (2004)
translated by Sam Garrett

❊   ❊   ❊

Back to Michael Booth. We join him as he wanders,
observing, reflecting upon and enjoying some of the
quirkier sights the city offers him.

After the modern concrete wasteland of Izmir, it was satisfying to be back in a city so evidently layered with history as Istanbul. Wandering around the steep side streets of Pera and Galata (modern-day Beyoğlu) the next day, the nineteenth-century Constantinople Andersen described was still much in evidence. Here were the traditional Turkish gravestones that he drew, as well as the ancient churches and Italianate balconies – many of them clinging on by their fingertips – he described.

Pera and Galata used to be the Italian and Jewish quarters of the city. Foreign visitors have traditionally stayed here since the early nineteenth century, and many European embassies and consulates remain here as a reminder of that time. The area's main landmark is still the Galata Tower, a fat, round fourteenth-century lookout tower, a bit like the cardboard core of a toilet roll, with a conical roof. These days there is a lift that takes you to the top floor – now a nightclub, which, though empty when I visited, was instantly recognisable as the type of place where middle-aged men with gold jewellery and double-breasted suits dance awkwardly with women old enough to be their first wives.

As I lolloped further down the steep Galata hill towards the Atatürk Bridge, I passed a man pushing a trolley laden with elaborate, cream-filled desserts for sale, and another carrying trays suspended by chains and loaded with tumblers of Turkish tea. Just before the bridge were stalls piled with bananas, rubber bands, TV remote controls and mountains of pistachios (the entire city is carpeted with their shells). I bought a pastry from one of the glass-sided carts that you see throughout the city. It seemed to have been made, not from a mixture of flour, eggs and water, but an inedible by-product of the construction industry. I placed a sample in an envelope and posted it to NASA for possible use in the space programme.

The incessant hawking of goods continued on the bridge itself, where fishermen traditionally drape their curtain of lines into the Golden Horn – the modern equivalent of the iron chain that once stretched across the Bosphorus to keep out enemy fleets. Surely no fish can pass beneath this bridge alive.

The fishermen were vying for pavement space with men selling cigarettes, mobile phone cases and pirate copies of Office 2000. One enterprising soul was pushing a photocopier on a hostess trolley, powered by a generator on the lower shelf. Kebab grills, roasting chestnuts and candy-floss machines provided the olfactory backdrop – along, of course, with the choking fug of diesel fumes.

Down by the harbour-side small boats contravened every fire safety rule imaginable with skillets of frying fish balanced precariously over open fires as they rocked in the wake of the elderly passenger ferries that ply non-stop from Europe to Asia. Watching this I was accosted by the rapacious postcard sellers who cling like limpet mines to tourists as they wait for the ferries. Some people simply will not take a 'Look, please, I do not want to buy any postcards, I have already bought loads of postcards, now will you please fuck off and leave me alone before I kill you NOW!' for an answer.

Walking on I passed a man tending to a large white rabbit on a small folding table. Beside the rabbit was a tombola. What in God's name was this all about? I stood and watched for a while. He was raffling the rabbit! I bought a ticket, but the rabbit and I were not to be. A short while later a man walked past dressed in a comedy convict's costume, replete with black-and-white stripes and a ball chained to his leg. Not one passer-by batted an eye. Then, a street-cleaning machine drove past. Nothing unusual in this, except that it was driven by a woman in her early twenties in full make-up and dressed in platform heels, a long fur coat and sunglasses. It was as if she had been en route to a party, but had decided to tidy the place up a bit on her way.

Michael Booth, *Just As Well I'm Leaving* (2005)

❊ ❊ ❊

Travellers' tales of Istanbul include those of Turks themselves, coming to the city from elsewhere in the country. An extract from a novel by Tuna Kiremitçi (b.1973), one of Turkey's best-selling novelists.

For the next few hours, I walked around. I meandered, looking at street stands selling trinkets, flowers and half priced books. I passed my time losing my way and enjoying doing so in the streets of Kadiköy, streets that often required one to walk uphill. What made losing one's way so attractive was that in fact it was impossible to do so. When one went down the narrow streets, just like Ertugrul said, one ended inevitably at the seaside. The ease of finding one's way, allowed the traveller the luxury of being lost. I hung up my famous non-erring sense of direction ingrained in me since childhood. I did not read the street-signs. I wasn't trying to learn the names of the streets I was walking in. I did not look at shop windows, at trees or at dog turds as signs that would be useful to find my way back, but just at windows, trees and turds, and forgot about them instantly.

The area to be explored was much too large for me, though. There was too much detail, enough to make one give up and return. It was so difficult to take in everything around me that it seemed pointless to go faster. After a while, even walking seemed pointless. So I stopped.

From where I stood I could see the large mosques on the other side, the seaside that connected Moda Cap to the ferry terminal and the large freighters anchored at sea. I needed time even to take in and absorb just this view. I was not a good tourist. I could not pick out what I really needed to see. Everything that came into my field of vision was equally important. The tea garden, or the Suleymaniye mosque, the Topkapı Palace or the Caferaga Sports Arena, it was all the same. For me all of them were new, matchless, and startling.

Tuna Kiremitçi, *Leave Before I Fall In Love With You* (2002)
translated by Jak Korı

* * *

One of the experiences some visitors opt for is a visit to the 'hamam' – the Turkish baths. Australian writer Marian Edmunds tells it as it is ...

Cok kirli.

'Sorry?'

I know he said *cok* which is 'very' but very what?

'You very dirty,' said the hamam attendant.

I laughed for it was the truth. I was *very* dirty, carrying with me to Istanbul residue from the travertines of Pamukkale, the sulphur baths of Lake Koyceğiz, and the mud baths of Dalyan. On which note I warn, don't wear pale clothes there. The mud gets into the stitching and the smell never leaves.

I like to wear nothing but a towel when I'm at the hamam, except for when there's a large group of tourists, or teenage boys. Mind you, I can't help thinking youths should see adult bodies in the flesh, if only as a warning against keeping terrible hours and eating junk food.

The simple checked cotton towel I knot around me could just as easily be spread out on a field beneath a picnic of bread and cheese. Pinned to it is the key to the cubicle where my possessions have been left.

I walk by the central slab below the dome, and sit on the side bench in the most steamy room. A blurry figure leans against the opposite wall. In the segments of other rooms I can see, a couple of abstract figures complete their ablutions. One reclines on the bench. A tap drips, then after a while, drips again into a marble sink, and again. Bright plastic bowls are stacked to one side. I fill one with water, and pour it down my back, and repeat.

Like an inhalant, the steam catches my throat.

After a while perspiration and dirt have mixed to a sludge that cloys in every one of my pores. It feels disgusting.

The attendant leans towards me directing me across to the

slab to where he wants me to lie down. Another attendant and bather are on the other side of the hexagon. The two attendants compare notes.

My attendant has deftly arranged my towel to cover me. He picks up a coarse mitt in his hand and starts scraping it across my skin. I grit my teeth. With each stroke, a sludge of dirt, sweat and dead skin forms into tiny rolls. It's this which sparks his 'very dirty' comment.

He fills a large fabric bag with water and soap and fluffs it out and turns it up as if piping suds across me. I must look like a giant meringue from neck to toe.

He pats me on the side to sit up, and brings up the now soaked towel about me.

People speak little in the hamam, except for tourists who chatter on, and on, diverting their nervousness from what's about to happen to them. I only tell them on a need-to-know basis, and there is not much they need know. Better just to let the experience wash over them. I learned this during my first Turkish bath when an Australian woman said, a nanosecond before it happened to me, 'Here comes the big neck crack.'

'Sit,' says the attendant, and turns to a sink where he fills a huge bucket. With an easy swing of his arms he empties it all over me. Icy water. It's a shock but oddly welcome too. He refills the bucket and pours it over me twice more then goes to bring fresh towels. I wrap one around my body, and enclose my hair in another.

My skin feels like that of a newborn, silken and soft. Yet all I can think about are my teeth. They feel so unclean, so unlike the rest of me. I've forgotten my toothbrush and toothpaste again.

I cover my baby skin with grown-up clothes and head out into the evening towards a bar that I know.

Marian Edmunds, 'Don't forget your toothbrush' (2011)

✳ ✳ ✳

And the perspective of a Greek male on the same experience ... popular writer Yiannis Xanthoulis (b.1947).

A large number of attendants work at the hamams; at the end, when you're ready to go out again into the dirty outside world, they ask, with their eyes, for baksheesh, even if they haven't needed to attend to you. One of them for drying you with the big towel, another for bringing an even bigger dry one, another for the little ones, another for ordering tea or Ariani (a yoghurt drink), another for giving you your shoes, which mandatorily remain outside the room, another for sprinkling you with lemon perfume, another for opening the door for you, expressing a hope of seeing you again, with the words '*Görüşmek üzere*'. See you.

But the basic ruler over your body is the man who will loosen the knots of weariness. He who will use his strength and technique to defeat even the suggestion of dirt, the one who will reach to your soul with well-studied movements of an ancient wisdom. Holding the '*kese*', the hard cloth tool for exorcising the sebum of your hide, he leads you to the '*sıcaklık*', his hot fief, where he leaves you to wander about for a bit, as you wish, in the misty cellophane of the moisture.

Taking care not to take a false step, with a slightly uncertain walk, I slumped down next to a simple marble bowl, very different from the first one, laden with the ornamentations of 'Turkish bath aesthetics', as Ferhan commented next to me, as he too was thoroughly amusing himself with the prurience of certain hairy fellow-customers. The prurience had to do with the cleanliness of the 'secret' parts of the body, and its culmination was an elegiac shave in special booths. The razors, as I understood, are used without hesitation by anyone who wishes to be rid of the pubic hair, as the conclusion of self-cleansing.

I shuddered at the idea of this depilation; some preparations for serious surgery flashed through my mind. I closed my eyes to recover the hedonistic logic of the hamam, to isolate myself before being wrapped in the lace of the soap suds. Both I and Dr Ferhan seemed to be made of different stuff from the rest of the very few bathers, though only one of those present could have been described as a 'Turk with three moustaches'.

They weighed us up from time to time with the sidelong Turkish glance, now recognisable, and continued to wrestle with their sweat, the repeated hair-washings or the brushing of their teeth, fortunately not with a toothbrush in common use.

While we were waiting for our masseur-torturer, I tried to render myself independent of Ferhan, who was a torrent of comments and encyclopaedic information, a little unsuitable in the sudatorium and on the hot marble. Thus I learnt that, with very few exceptions, the hamams were supplied with their marble from the Marmaronisia of the Sea of Marmara. The marble is off-white to grey, without any particular beauty. Just enough to reflect the heat, to be pleasing to the touch and to lend to the place the necessary sense of cleanness, which was the prime desideratum. He saw that my eyelids soon drooped, while the gaze of both of us had taken on the bluish limpidity of fish.

'Dream, but don't go to sleep ... ' is the rule, he told me. 'Those who go to sleep take with them some slices of hell.'

I didn't fully understand what he meant, and so I entered into the philosophy of the baths, which from time to time have kindled occasions for misunderstandings of every kind, and into the paradoxical conservatism of Islam, which, on the one hand, produces men and women believers with obsessions about the exposure of bodies, and, on the other, welcomes nakedness in these collective vaulted places with such generosity as to shock the progressives from the opposite, 'Western', bank. I agreed in silence, swallowing my sweat, salt with the texture of an antibiotic in capsule form.

'All this is splendid, but I'm afraid that by the time we die, and before very long, there will be fewer than ten hamams left in the City as sacred temples of tourist curiosity ... The Cağaloğlu Hamamı, the Çemberlitaş, which was built by Sinan, the Galata Seraï, more or less adjoining the Greek school, the Zografeio, and one or two others ... .'

Yiannis Xanthoulis, *The Istanbul of My Disrespectful Fears* (2008)
translated by Geoffrey-Alfred Cox

✳ ✳ ✳

*French traveller Daniel Rondeau loves the view from
his hotel balcony.*

The balcony of my hotel room looks out over the strait. In the morning I open my curtains and look out. The water, the boats, the air, the light – everything is constantly moving and changing. The liquid pathway of the strait is decorated with hypnotic and circular patterns. Seas and continents converge there, as if brought together by the current, and seem to be the gateway to the whole world. I cannot tear myself away from my balcony. One day I change hotels and make for Hagia Sophia. Once I've got visits to that area of the city over with, I allow myself to rush off towards the Sea of Marmara and turn back towards the Bosphorus. From the Pointe du Serail, the view is good – absolutely perfect.

The mouth of the Bosphorus – one lip Asian, the other European.

Daniel Rondeau, *Istanbul* (2002)
translated by Erica King

✳ ✳ ✳

*To end the section, a night out in Istanbul with
American visitor David Byrne.*

Upon returning to the hotel, I rendezvous with a group of Turkish expatriates (who now live in Belgium, New Jersey, and Chicago) and upon the arrival of a Kazakh gentleman, we depart for the Sulukule neighbourhood to eat, drink, and be entertained by low rent belly dancers. This gypsy neighbourhood, a thousand years old, is almost all run-down houses and tea shops filled with people hanging out on the semipaved streets in the cold night air. Sadly, the whole neighbourhood is threatened with demolition now, as it's coveted by real estate developers.

Our friend from Kazakhstan knows which house we're heading for, so we ignore the kids who swarm over the car urging us to stop at their families' establishments and we proceed to 'Chez Moi.' We're met by more Kazakhs – bankers, they claim, although one wonders exactly what sort of 'banking' these fellows do – and then a group of bleach-blond babes with rouged cheeks dressed in bulky sweaters. The house mother, a short woman in a house dress (is she pregnant?), leads us to 'our' room, upstairs, where we will be entertained and, we have been forewarned, fleeced.

This is the polar opposite of Sakıp Sabancı's mansion, in the extreme. As the room is stone cold, 'Mom' carries in a bucket of glowing coals from outside and plonks it down in the middle of the linoleum floor, which is pretty ripped up in spots. Our Kazakh friend begins to negotiate while we get settled. The room is almost completely bare, except for the mismatched chairs that line the walls. A kid brings in a kind of folding card table. Four musicians (two percussionists, a tambourist, and a man with a Turkish banjo) seat themselves opposite us and begin to tune up.

The dancers, still in their winter sweaters, enter briefly and then leave. Mom takes drink orders – beer for the expats and me, raki for the Turks, and vodka for the Kazakhs. A Kurdish gentleman, who might be part of our party, sits near the musicians. He doesn't drink.

The musicians start to wail. They sound great, full of vigour and emotion that explodes in sudden bursts of intense and beautiful sadness. The sadness of the world is in this music. I don't care if they're just playing for us to make a quick buck; it's deeply moving anyway. I'm transported. A kid circulates and takes 'donations'. Cheese, grated carrots, and pistachios appear and eventually even a dancer, who makes the rounds before she starts asking for more donations (small bills seem to do). She takes off her sweater and plops it on a chair, revealing not a costume, but her bra and a pair of tights, rolled down just enough to reveal the arches of the top of her panties. She begins to dance. Not belly dancing really, but whatever it is, it's got some spirit. Everyone, whether from the cold, the drink, the music, or the whole situation, is in great spirits, laughing and toasting one another.

The dancer makes the rounds again, and bills are stuffed in her bra this time. Occasionally she does a sort of very basic lap dance. She sits on someone's lap (male or female, it doesn't seem to make a difference) and bounces up and down. It's more funny than it is sexy. It's all pretty tame, and it's not really belly dancing, but everyone's having a great time.

David Byrne, *Bicycle Diaries* (2009)

"Like so much in Constantinople, Topkapı Palace ... owes its existence to Mehmed the Conqueror"

Philip Mansel

The glorious past

The legendary glories – and horrors – of the Ottoman Empire are very much part of the modern city's personality. Architecture, literature, artefacts, and food all carry the residue of the time when Constantinople was the sumptious seat of power for an extensive empire. The only multinational capital in Europe, Constantinople was named differently by more languages than any other city. Russians, Bulgarians and Serbs knew it as Tsarigrad (city of Emperors). Armenians called it Gosdantnubolis (the city of Constantine). In everyday language Greeks called it (and some still do) just 'polis', the city. Its official name in Greek had been Constantinoupolis Nea Roma, after which Ottomans called it, on coins and official documents, Kostantiniyye (also its name in Arabic). In the literary version of Ottoman it was called Der-i Sa'adet (the House of Good Fortune). In Persian it was Astihaner (house of state). But in everyday spoken Turkish, even before the conquest, its name was a corruption of the Greek phrase for 'into the city', eis teen polin: Istanbul.

In Unto the Tulip Gardens: My Shadow, *Gül İrepoğlu (b.1956) recreates some of that glorious past.*

Grand Vizier İbrahim Pasha's waterfront palace gardens in Beşiktaş had, for many days now, been the site of much excitement. Painted, wooden galleries had been set up, facing each other. They looked like miniature amphitheatres, narrow shelves going down in steps. The palace folk tried to determine what purpose they would serve; the master had only divulged his plan to the craftsmen making these structures, and under strict orders to keep the secret they were.

It was the middle of the most promising month in the year: April raises hopes and brings joy to the heart. The yalı was preparing to entertain the emperor of the universe that evening. The host didn't want the surprise show to be spoiled; he would take such delight in amazing Ahmed Han, and a pleasant treat it would be.

Countless tulip vases, glass and silver, had been carried outdoors as the evening drew on: a slender flute, only wide enough to take a single tulip stem, and with a broad base for balance. It was impossible to count how many they were, there were so many. Each carried a single tulip, picked from the rarest, and only the freshest buds.

İbrahim Pasha personally oversaw the arrangement of the

tulips in colour harmony, and commanded many to switch places with others, so the bright flame red tulips were followed by shades of red that became lighter, all the way into the corals. Tulips from the palest pink to the deepest fuchsias were ranged on a different shelf; all the colours waved in shades deep and pale. The shelves facing those bore tulips from the palest lilac to the deepest purple, and in between were the yellows, from the most searing sunbright to the coolest metal. The pasha had the purples and the yellows arranged in the middle to best display the divinely contrasting harmony of these two colours. Lace-like variegated tulips marked the colour changes. Those precious white tulips called 'unique pearls' lined up on the bottom and top shelves.

Coloured crystal globes were hanging from the shelves on fine chains between the tulip vases. These globes would reflect the light of the lanterns on the bottom shelf. Coloured lanterns hung from the trellises in the garden.

It was beginning to get dark and the hour set for the arrival of the most valued guest approached. Kaftans lined with sable would stave off the evening chill; the wind was but a light breeze. İbrahim Pasha bade the lanterns be lit.

As the imperial caïque drew up at the pier, Sultan Ahmed got to his feet in the royal box of carved and gilded posts and a velvet baldachin. He was looking forward to going ashore to begin to enjoy the feast İbrahim Pasha had laid on; no need to hide his impatience.

The emperor of the universe couldn't believe his eyes when he stepped onto the garden, once, that is, appropriate responses had been given to the florid phrases of welcome; he walked through his crowded entourage. It was as though the gardens of paradise had alighted on the earth: tulips shining in the settling dark. A thousand and one beams of light, splintering off the cut crystal, were reflected on the flowers nestling in brilliant silver vases, creating a scene that defied instant comprehension. The light breeze made the tulips and the crystal globes sway gently, heightening the effect.

The emperor slowly walked between the rows of tulips and reached the high seat in the small, open-fronted tent erected as protection against the evening chill, and the music began. The princes who had been allowed to accompany their father were most delighted by the goldfinches, canaries and nightingales in silver cages hanging from the branches.

Sinuous dancers would come on once the delicacies in the gilt bowls were consumed. Grand Vizier Damat İbrahim Pasha had created a fresh, lively and sparkling world for his master.

Gül İrepoğlu, *Unto the Tulip Gardens: My Shadow* (2004)
translated by Feyza Howell

✳ ✳ ✳

Exploring the theme of the Ottoman garden further,
here's historian Philip Mansel on the subject.

The prevalence of gardens distinguished Constantinople from other water cities like Lisbon and Venice. Swathes of green stood out against red-tiled roofs and grey stone mosques. The Slav proverb 'Where the Turk trod, no grass grows' is a slur. If the physical image of heaven for Christians is a shining city on a hill, for Muslims it is a garden of delight, with ever-flowing springs and rivers. […]

Ottomans created many different styles of garden in Constantinople: the inner paradise garden with flowerbeds; the pleasure garden outside a house; terraced gardens shaded by trellised vines; fruit and kitchen gardens known as *bostanlar*; sunken gardens, dug in the earth, for cool in the summer. In 1690 a French visitor, the historian Jean du Mont, was impressed by the garden of the Grand Vizier's *kaimakam* (deputy): 'The paths are sanded and bordered in some places by orange trees and in others by fruit trees. The squares of the gardens are not laid out like our parterres, but only separated by boards and filled with flowers which the Turks love very much.' Trees also grew in the streets and walls of Constantinople. Vines and wisteria were, and are, draped over houses, and trailed across streets on ropes – making even the poorest districts less squalid than slums in other cities. […]

One form of garden was peculiar to Constantinople: the flowering graveyards stretching across the hills and valleys outside the city. Cypresses, flowers and creepers grew between Ottoman tombs, or out of holes carved in the middle of them. The tombstones, of which there were said to be enough to rebuild the entire city, were scattered haphazardly rather than arranged in orderly rows. The funerary flowerbeds were so agreeable that they became a favourite picnic resort for families on Fridays. Cafés were built in, or overlooking, graveyards. […]

Jasmine, irises, roses, lilies, carnations and hyacinths were favoured in the gardens of the capital. No flower, however, was more Ottoman than the tulip: it was particularly cherished since the letters of its Turkish name, *lale*, are the same as those of Allah. The Ottoman Empire was scoured for tulips for the gardens of Constantinople. In 1574 Selim II wrote to an official near Aleppo: 'I need about 50,000 tulips for my royal gardens. To bring these bulbs I send you one of the chiefs of my servants. I command you in no way to delay.' In 1577 Murad III ordered 300,000 tulip bulbs from the Crimea. They were given names like Dwarf's Purple, Glitter of Prosperity, Beloved's Face, Rose Arrow; their colour, stalks and stamens were subjects of discussion and emulation. Pointed petals are a characteristic of Turkish tulips. A perfect tulip was described as 'almond-shaped, needle-like, ornamented with pleasant rays, her inner petals like a well, as they should be; the outer petals a little open, thin too, as they should be'. In summer they might be shaded with linen to prevent scorching by the sun. From Constantinople in the sixteenth century tulips spread to central and western Europe.

Philip Mansel, *Constantinople:
City of the World's Desire, 1453–1924* (1995)

* * *

In Ottoman times, the weekly procession associated with the Muslim holy day (Friday) is recreated in A Momentary Delay *by Reha Çamuroğlu (b.1958).*

'7th Infantry Battalion! Attention!'

'Parade rest!'

'Yes, Sir!'

'At ease!'

'Forward! To the Hamidiye Mosque! March!'

Every Friday morning, the district of Beyazıt resounded with these salutes. The mounted troops went out of the barracks in Davutpaşa and Maltepe. The military bands preceded them, and the entire procession crossed the Galata Bridge, passed through the districts of Karaköy and Tophane, and eventually reached Yıldız.

High ranking officers and civil pashas wearing all of their badges and medals, esteemed scholars, all types of religious leaders, ambassadors from Europe and Asia, ministers, diplomats with different degrees and areas in various coaches competing in decoration and flamboyance followed this military procession while travellers who wanted to observe this splendour, curious tourists, various artisan lodges, workers, jobless people, in short, Istanbulians from each and every class crowded the Yıldız Square.

The Royal Orchestra would take their place next to the main entrance gate of the palace; the palace employees and gunmen surrounded them, and thousands of ears concentrated on the Hamidiye Mosque and waited. The noon prayer was the first and foremost signal. After this signal was received, everyone forgot about his ears, and this time, thousands of eyes stared at the two wings of the heavy iron gate.

As soon as the gate was open just enough, the Royal Orchestra started playing the Hamidiye March, the ears got wide open again, all soldiers in the square stood at attention, and Sultan Abdulhamid II, the 'Sultan of the Ottoman Land', the 'Sultan of the Sublime State' and the 'Caliph of the Entire Muslim Community,' appeared in a coach with a halfway folded tag in his grey-coloured greatcoat and huge fez. The imperial flank guards walked on both sides of the coach, and next to them walked the pashas.

Three or four broughams, which usually carried the ladies of the palace, followed the Royal Coach. Since the distance between the main palace gate and the Royal Lodge of the Hamidiye Mosque was rather short, thousands of soldiers and civilians who waited without breathing for His Majesty to appear finally decided to exhale unanimously and shouted: 'Long live the Sultan! Long live the Sultan! Long live...'

While the European diplomats and tourists stood amazed for witnessing once again on a Friday how the people of the 'Sick Man of Europe' that had so many problems to solve hailed the Red Sultan with such joy and sincerity, the Sultan himself always passed by in solemn dignity or sometimes blew through like the wind, raising dust.

Meanwhile, hundreds of officers, privates and gunmen who were responsible for the Sultan's security as well as hundreds of civil agents and civil officers scanned the crowd incessantly with piercing eyes while at the same time they silently said all the prayers they knew, imploring God Almighty for this Friday ceremony to come to an end without a calamity.

The women passed out and regained consciousness over and over again, and some citizens whose 'identity cards had worn out' suffered lethal heart attacks.

As all this took place, the Sultan descended a flight of stairs of the mosque consisting of eight or maybe ten steps and disappeared in his private lodge. He stayed there for half an hour, performed the ritual prayer, and then upon leaving, he did not take the coach that had brought him there but another one, which he usually drove himself. This time he entered the palace grounds very fast from the main gate and disappeared out of the sight of the onlookers, who never knew that a totally different activity went on inside: animals were sacrificed to thank God that the Sultan was able to return to his home without trouble while the pashas responsible for the security of the Friday procession to the mosque were granted gold coins.

As the military troops in the square prepared to return in the most ordely manner, the crowd started disbanding, and often formed clusters around more than a hundred street vendors in the square. According to the season, they rushed to buy either various sherbets, *boza* or *sahlab* or gulped down meatballs, *kokorec* and rice dishes with chickpeas.

Reha Çamuroğlu, *A Momentary Delay* (2005)
translated by Çiğdem Aksoy

✳ ✳ ✳

Philip Mansel again – on another fascinating aspect of Ottoman life: clothes.

Costume was another code conveying the grandeur of the Ottoman sultanate. There was a saying of the Prophet: 'Do not drink in vessels of gold or silver and do not dress in silks or brocade, for they belong to the infidel in this world and to you in the next.' In the palace, however, the lure of the kaftan was more compelling than the words of the Prophet. Kaftans were single robes, cut straight from the neck to the feet, often with a flare at the waist. They were made of velvet, satin or brocaded silk. Costume was one of Constantinople's principal industries. By 1577 there were two hundred and sixty-eight looms in the city, of which eighty-eight were 'attached to the palace'; only they were allowed to make 'cloth of gold'. At times the mint threatened to run out of gold and silver since so much went in the making of gold and silver thread. In vain the Sultan issued edicts forbidding their use in clothes: his orders were rarely obeyed.

A collection of a thousand kaftans survives in Topkapı palace, owing to the Ottoman custom of putting a dead Sultan's belongings in wrappers, sealing them with his name and storing them either in his mausoleum or the palace treasury. Most of the kaftans are monochrome and unpatterned (like the black silk kaftan often worn by Suleyman the Magnificent). However some are decorated with flowers and trees in vibrant colours, tulips falling in undulating crimson streams, and golden leaves swirling in an unseen wind. Other kaftans are more original. A kaftan of gold spots and stripes on scarlet satin, made for a seventeenth-century Sultan, another with a pattern of white triangles on deep crimson satin, possibly of the eighteenth century, seem to leap-frog time. Like Coptic textiles or Biedermeier silver, they look as if they could have been designed for Paris in the 1920s.

As with the number of minarets permitted on a mosque, costume was governed by dynastic priorities. Whereas his predecessors had worn Camelot or mohair, Suleyman wore cloth of gold. Although in theory it was reserved for the Sultan alone, as a special favour he permitted his beloved Grand Vizier, İbrahim Pasha, to wear 'gold brocade and on campaign a suit of cloth of gold'. The Sultan and his viziers would sometimes wear three kaftans, so that the contrasting fabrics and colours, peeping out under sleeves, could be admired. Three centuries before uniforms began to appear in Western courts, the colours of officials' turbans and robes on ceremonial occasions were regulated by law. The *ulema* wore purple, viziers green, chamberlains scarlet. In such costumes, Ottoman writers noted with pride, the Sultan's servants resembled a parterre of tulips.

Worn mainly on ceremonial occasions, kaftans were as important to the Ottoman honours system as knighthoods to the British. Ambassadors judged their standing in Constantinople by the number and quality of the kaftans they received when they paid their respects in the imperial palace. [...]

Fur was a second language of splendour for the palace. Winds from the north can make the city bitterly cold. Furs were useful as well as sumptuous and their purchase in Russia by the Ottoman treasury became an affair of state. Sultans alone wore black fur. Other furs were worn by the Sultan and his officials in a special timed sequence: ermine in autumn, followed by an interval of squirrel, and sable in winter. The day the Sultan changed fur, the Grand Vizier and the pashas followed suit.

The palace combined colour, deference, silence and majesty. Ottoman historians recorded that foreign ambassadors or princes were 'astonished, bewildered, stupefied and completely enraptured' by the sight of the Sultan and his train. The Imperial ambassador Baron de Busbecq wrote: 'Everywhere the brilliance of gold, silver, purple, silk and satin ... No mere words could give an adequate idea of the novelty of the sight. A more beautiful spectacle was never presented to my gaze.' [...]

Heads and feet, as well as names, demonstrated the city's multinational character. The inhabitants of Constantinople, whatever their religion, generally wore simple robes or tunics, like those of Gulf Arabs today, but of darker colours. Over the tunic they wore a dolman of satin or linen, padded with cotton in winter, and a sash. They laughed at western Europeans who spoiled their clothes with trimmings, pleats and slashes.

Until the nineteenth century, in order both to demonstrate Muslim superiority and to foster national rivalries, the Ottoman government enforced distinctions of dress between the different communities. Only Muslims could wear white or green turbans and yellow slippers. Greeks, Armenians and Jews were distinguished respectively by sky blue, dark blue (later red) and yellow hats, and by black, violet and blue slippers. The rules governing the costume of religious minorities were regularly reasserted. In 1580, for example, 'considering that their attitude from the point of view of the *sheriat* [Muslim holy law] and of logic should be humility and abjection', Jews and Christians were formally forbidden 'to dress like Muslims', to wear silk, fur, or red shoes, and instead were enjoined to wear dark colours or blue. They were also repeatedly forbidden to live near mosques, to build tall houses or to buy slaves.

Such reiterations show that the rules were often flouted: the status of Muslims was so attractive that the minorities' desire to resemble them was irrepressible.

Philip Mansel, *Constantinople:*
City of the World's Desire, 1453–1924 (1995)

❊ ❊ ❊

The world-famous Topkapı Palace is one of the glories
from the city's past. Philip Mansel again ...

Constantinople was synonymous with imperial splendour. Its source lay in the palace built on the eastern end of the peninsula, where the Bosphorus, the Golden Horn and the Sea of Marmara meet. Set on the edge of Europe, the palace had a commanding view into Asia. It was a site suitable for the 'World Conqueror'.

On land and sea, the palace was enclosed by a high battle-mented wall. Most of the sea wall has been destroyed. However, the land wall still climbs from the Sea of Marmara, across one of the hills on which Constantinople is built, down to the Golden Horn. In the middle of the wall, a towering portal of grey marble, the Imperial Gate, leads the visitor out of the tumult of the city into the peace of a tree-lined courtyard. It is the first of three courts around which the palace is built.

Like so much in Constantinople, Topkapı Palace, as it is now called (from one of its gates, the *top kapı* or cannon gate), owes its existence to Mehmed the Conqueror. Begun in 1459, the palace was finished in 1478. Since he had already built one palace in the middle of the city, its official name was the New Imperial Palace.

Until the departure of the Sultan and his household in the nineteenth century, the first courtyard contained the outer offices of the household: a weapons depot, housed in the ancient Byzantine church of St Irene, dedicated to peace; stables for four thousand horses; the mint; a hospital; a kiosk for scribes receiving petitions and dispensing the Sultan's decrees or firmans. Like palace precincts in Western capitals, the first courtyard was open to all, even foreigners. From across the Golden Horn, the palace appeared as a peninsula of pavilions, surrounded by trees and gardens cascading down to the sea: the windows were compared to imperial eyes watching the world outside. Inside this courtyard, however, the palace looked like a medley of buildings, which most visitors considered unworthy of the Sultan. The sole visible elements of splendour were the size of the courtyard and the presence of large numbers of richly clad soldiers – and exotic animals, including the occasional leopard or elephant.

Only the Sultan was permitted to ride a horse through the next gate, the Gate of Salutation, into the second courtyard. Filled with fountains and cypresses, it is both courtyard and garden and is so spacious that people on one side are inaudible on the other. The visitor is surrounded by a series of low, arcaded, wide-eaved buildings. Reflecting the Ottoman obsession with rules and boundaries, each building was conceived separately for a specific function, like a series of tents. They contained living quarters for different groups of household servants, for example the 'tressed halberdiers', who attached long ringlets to their hair to prevent them from glimpsing the women when they delivered firewood to the harem. The buildings are on a human and domestic, rather than palatial, scale, in contrast to architectural unities built to impress like the Louvre, the Doge's Palace in Venice, or the imperial mosques.

Philip Mansel, *Constantinople:
City of the World's Desire, 1453–1924* (1995)

* * *

In Unto the Tulip Gardens: My Shadow, *Gül İrepoğlu,
as well as telling a good story, fills in many fascinating
details about life in the glory days of the Ottoman
Empire. Here she explains the practice of* devşirme.

The unique practice of 'devşirme' had formed the backbone of
the Ottoman Empire for hundreds of years. The purpose was
to select and train future janissaries – the foundation of the
Ottoman military, servants of the emperor and state officials.
Male children, between the age of eight and twenty, were picked
every three to five years, as needed, from Christian families resident in the vast lands of the empire. Recruiting officials of the
relevant province would pick healthy, strong boys, who would
be converted and taken into public service. As members of the
merchant class, Jewish boys were exempt. The number of boys
each province had to supply would be determined beforehand.
The appointment of collecting official bestowed the mark of
the Porte's complete trust in the recipient. Traditionally, a janissary officer would be so appointed. His assistants would be
masters of the emperor's hunting dogs or janissary colonels,
and a clerk.

The recruiting officials picked one boy out of every forty
homes with more than one son. They took pains to select the
strongest and finest looking in the family. Only families of high
standing in the community qualified. The sons of cowherds or
shepherds, for example, were not eligible. Also excluded were
boys with physical disfigurements like baldness and hydro-
cephaly, and with congenital conditions such as beardlessness
or hypospadias. Sons of the chief steward of the village were
exempt to avoid compromising law and order in the area.

Boys who had already learned a trade were similarly excused;
a primary condition in the practice was that all, including
Islam, be taught after the boys entered service to the Ottoman

state. Regardless of aptitude, teachings of the earlier life were not considered 'positive'. If a gem, then uncut; if a stone, at least whole!

There was no room for chance in this system, which had been worked out down to the finest detail ... The boys would be examined by the *Commander of the Janissaries* upon their arrival in Istanbul. Circumcision and Muslim-Turkish names would follow. Those picked for court duty would be educated in one of three palaces: Edirne, Galata or İbrahimpasha. Topkapı Palace, the imperial abode, awaited the best; the biggest joined the imperial guard and the rest became cavalry servants of the Porte.

Lay emotion aside a moment if you can, and admire the internal consistency of the system. The Ottoman state implemented its own rules as it adopted the children, raising them in a one-way boarding school. The state would be their only family; who came from where might have mattered at first, but in time, that terrific, centuries-old tradition would erase any trace of the past. The boys became true-born sons of the August Ottoman State: the inexorable power that was the janissaries, before whom all infidels trembled; the veteran statesmen who held the fine balance between the West and the East; the force that was the emperor's most trusted ağas, who guarded his life and possessions and the artists who elevated Islam and the Ottomans with their peerless masterpieces.

Some, who had been gathered at an older age and so remembered their families well, would seek them out many years later. Some tried to send help surreptitiously. Powerful men, like Sokollu Mehmed Pasha, had less difficulty re-establishing relations with their families. They could even move their birth families to Istanbul. This famous grand vizier of Süleyman, the most magnificent ruler of the sixteenth century, the most magnificent of all Ottoman eras, used a cognomen that ever evoked his origins: of Sokol, a Serbian. But even these names only served as mementos. The most important identity of the recruit – his Muslim Ottoman one – always took precedence over any relationship. Thus was it that the majority would learn to content themselves with their new lives, not looking back.

Gül İrepoğlu, *Unto the Tulip Gardens: My Shadow* (2004)
translated by Feyza Howell

❊ ❊ ❊

An eighteenth-century visitor writes home about the excellent shopping in the city.

The exchanges are all noble buildings, full of fine alleys, the greatest part supported with pillars, and kept wonderfully neat. Every trade has their distinct alley, the merchandise disposed in the same order as in the New Exchange at London. The Bedesten, or jewellers' quarter shows so many riches, such a vast quantity of diamonds and all kind of precious stones, that they dazzle the sight. The embroiderers' is also very glittering, and people walk here as much for diversion as business. The markets are most of them handsome squares, and admirably well provided, perhaps better than in any other part of the world. I know you'll expect I should say something particular of that of the slaves, and you will imagine me half a Turk when I don't speak of it with the same horror other Christians have done before me, but I cannot forbear applauding the humanity of the Turks to those creatures. They are never ill used and their slavery is in my opinion no worse than servitude all over the world. 'Tis true they have no wages, but they give them yearly clothes to a higher value than our salaries to any ordinary servant. But you'll object men buy women with an eye to evil. In my opinion they are bought and sold as publicly and more infamously in all our Christian great cities.

Lady Mary Wortley Montagu, *Turkish Embassy Letters* (1716)

❋ ❋ ❋

*Although an Ottoman emperor wielded great power
and enjoyed great wealth, the position did come with
some drawbacks ...*

The limitations on the emperor's life most impacted upon
the one aspect of it in which everyone believed him to be the
most free: women. He could not select the women to join his
own harem. This honour was reserved for girls selected by
the sultan's mother or sisters, presented to the emperor by a
general as spoils of war or purchased as a very young girl by
some official at certain parts of the empire; in that last instance,
the girl would have to excel at something during her education
first. True, he was at liberty to pick whom to bed; but he could
never be left truly alone with the woman he had so picked: a
lady steward had to stand behind the drapes of the bed, both
for his own safety, and the proof of paternity for any issue of
the coupling. So there were no secrets concerning whom he
had bedded. It was possible to get accustomed to this, certainly,
provided one did not examine it all that deeply.

Another limitation concerning his women was that they
should not be present at entertainments attended by his male
friends – and all his friends were male.

Gül İrepoğlu, *Unto the Tulip Gardens: My Shadow* (2004)
translated by Feyza Howell

❋ ❋ ❋

*But what led to the eventual fall of the Ottomans?
Of many possible contributing factors, William
Dalrymple suggests an important one.*

The achievements of early Ottoman Constantinople were built
on the foundation of religious and ethnic tolerance. The great
majority of senior Ottoman officials were not ethnic Turks,
but Christian or Jewish converts. At a time when every capital

in Europe was ablaze with burning heretics, according to the exiled Huguenot M. de la Motraye there was 'no country on earth where the exercise of all Religions is more free and less subject to being troubled, than in Turkey.' It was the gradual erosion of that tradition of tolerance under the tidal wave of nineteenth-century nationalism that as much as anything finally brought down the Ottomans.

William Dalrymple, *From the Holy Mountain* (1997)

❊ ❊ ❊

Yashar Kemal (b.1923) is one of Turkey's most renowned writers and is published in thirty languages. His first novel, Mehmet, My Hawk *(1955) is still one of his most famous, but the extract below, from the much later* The Birds Have Also Gone, *movingly uses an ancient tradition to document and comment upon a changing society.*

Ever since ancient Byzantium, through Ottoman times to this day, these tiny birds, coming no one knows whence and going no one knows where, have sojourned here, on Florya Plain, from October to the end of December. And ever since, the people of Istanbul town have set all kinds of snares to capture them. They capture them, and then sell them, in front of churches if they are Christians, synagogues if they are Jewish, or mosques if they are Moslems. 'Fly little bird, free as the air, and meet me at the gates of Paradise.' And so, all over Istanbul town, the sky will be swarming with little birds delivered from captivity by those who wish to ensure a place in Paradise cheaply. Children especially, and also the very old ...

Many years ago, it must have been when I first came to Istanbul, I had seen in Taksim Square a very old gentleman, wearing a fur-collared coat, and a little boy of six or seven. From a barefooted youngster they were buying tiny wild-eyed birds and casting them up into the air. They would take it in turns, first the old gentleman, then the little boy, and at every throw the three of them would cry out in pure joy. And there was that cat huddling in the bushes under the plane trees ... Every now and again, one of the small birds, unable to take wing, would fall to the ground and flutter off into the bushes. No sooner there than that monster of a cat would pounce on it, tear it apart with claws and teeth, and devour it greedily. Then, licking its chops, the cat would lie in wait, quite still, its eyes on the air, for its next prey.

Nowadays, it is only in the courtyard of Eyüp Mosque that children manage to sell a bird or two to be set free. So they prefer to take them to the bird market in Eminönü where the dealers select a few of the finest out of hundreds, in order to sell them at a high price to bird fanciers. And the children go back home, weary, disappointed, toting their cages filled to the brim, wondering what to do with all these birds.

If the chroniclers of Istanbul city neglect the history of these birds and of the fowlers on Florya Plain, then their work, according to me, will not be worth much. Indeed, it will all have been in vain. The joy of millions of little birds set free in front of churches, synagogues and mosques for hundreds of years, and the joy of so many people too ... Is that an adventure of small importance? One day, I know it, some person, imaginative, wise, pure of heart, will come forward and write a fine history, full of hope and gladness, of the birds of Florya Plain, and then Istanbul city will be a more beautiful, a more enchanting place. Is the magic of Istanbul only in its sea and sky, its rivers and monuments?

Yashar Kemal, *The Birds Have Also Gone* (1978)
translated by Thilda Kemal

"Wind coming off the Black Sea ... at three o'clock
it grows dark. I await the snow"

Daniel Rondeau

A city for all seasons

*Which is the best season for a visit to Istanbul? There
are enthusiasts for all four – even the inconvenience
of a snowfall can create an unforgettable atmosphere.
Let's start with January – though the weather in that
month isn't always as ideal as it is depicted in this first
little extract.*

The climate is delightful in the extremist degree. I am now
sitting, this present 4th of January, with the windows open,
enjoying the warm shine of the sun, while you are freezing over
a sad sea-coal fire, and my chamber is set out with carnations,
roses and jonquils fresh from my garden.

Lady Mary Wortley Montagu, *The Turkish Embassy Letters* (1716)

78

✻ ✻ ✻

For some residents, one of the joys of springtime are the flowering Judas trees, as in this extract by much-loved, award-winning writer Oya Baydar (b.1940) who published her first novels while still in high school.

I had forgotten it was the season of the Judas tree. When it was the end of April or beginning of May, we used to go to the old wooden mansion in Beylerbeyi copse to watch the Judas trees. That house was the one my father loved the most and used the least. It was almost at the top of the copse. It was far away and the road was difficult. My mother used to find all sorts of excuses not to go there; my school was too far, the house was badly maintained and damp, it didn't heat well on cool April days and it was in a very lonely place. And when she gave in to my father's insistence and we did go, she would want to get back right away. Perhaps this was because she missed her young lover. In the garden which was full of trees, Judas tree flowers would fall on the white cloth covering the table, on my mother's black hair, on our shoulders, on the ground, and the garden paths would be covered with a carpet of Judas tree flowers. It was so beautiful that I wanted to lie on the ground and eat the pink-purple flowers by the handfuls, filling myself with the beauty which left me helpless.

Oya Baydar, *The Gate of the Judas Tree* (2004)
translated by Stephanie Ateş

✻ ✻ ✻

And a little more on spring, from Esmahan Aykol (b.1970), best known for her detective fiction.

It was May when Petra called for the second time. The magical Istanbul spring was about to turn abruptly into summer. I would have liked Petra to see Istanbul in spring: to drink tea under the shade of ancient pine trees in the gardens of magnificent Ottoman palaces, to walk along mimosa-scented streets, to shiver in the dampness of the Byzantine underground reservoirs, to light a candle in one of the churches as the muezzin chants the call to prayer, to stretch out in the warm spring sunshine on grass damp with early morning dew looking at the Hippodrome and the Sultan Ahmet fountain, to eat artichokes prepared in olive oil at Hacı Halil Restaurant ...

Esmahan Aykol, *Hotel Bosphorus* (2010)
translated by Ruth Whitehouse

✳ ✳ ✳

The outdoor life of the summer city is captured, in passing, in a short story by Sema Kaygusuz (b.1972), who has published novels as well as several collections of short stories.

It took place on a suffocating summer day. A Sunday ... The smell of grilled meat was wafting in the air as families gathered under the laurels in the park and laughter rose from men drinking beer in the cars parked by the sea. Istanbul people love the streets. When the weather is nice, a flood of people descends to the shores of the Bosphorus as if they had some old account to settle with the city. They turn the area into a fairground, with their fishing lines, picnic baskets and baby buggies. Seeming to play out old memories of distant homelands by flowing waters, they stretch out wherever they find the smallest patches of grass, or flowers, or in the verdant areas around the ancient city walls. This is why the Istanbul landscape is just an allusion to somewhere else. The joyful mourning of what has been lost is being performed with this site as a backdrop. Those who experience the real city are those who dare to see the city without any allusions. A couple of people who can control their sorrow, who unlike others don't rely on the eclectic architectural beauty of the Dolmabahçe Palace to cover the sewage smell spreading in fine waves from Dolmabahçe. A noisy, crowded city ...

Sema Kaygusuz, 'A Couple of People'
translated by Carol Yürür, in The Book of Istanbul (2011)

❋ ❋ ❋

Well-known short story writer Füruzan (b.1935) vividly recreates the atmosphere of a summer Saturday afternoon in the city.

It was around the end of August; the air seemed to vibrate with the most oppressive waves of heat.

'It's too hot,' said the woman. 'But you know you can never count on Istanbul's weather – suddenly it may get cold. Don't they say if one half of August is summer the other half is winter?'

The woman was dressed in a dark, wine-coloured, two-piece outfit in a style that was the fashion quite a few years ago. This made her look rather ridiculous. She was about thirty years old. The handbag she carried looked like a small suitcase; its colour had vanished under several layers of dirt; there was a little snakehead attached to its clasp, showing that the handbag had once been bone colour. Somehow, that snakehead with its glass-bead eyes had not lost its original colour but had just turned a little yellow and was the only proof that the handbag was made of snakeskin.

'If it turns into an Indian summer it may last till the end of November ... This is Istanbul ... You can never tell ... '

The afternoon vendors showed up at the pier. The simit-seller putting his portable, glass-topped simit-box on his back, came out of the shadows of the acacia trees where he had gone to protect himself from the sun, and got ready to meet the ferry's passengers. The water-seller quickly rinsed his glasses in the water poured from the spout of his portable brass vessel.

When they were wet, the glasses sparkled and seemed cleaner. The cheap, bright, artificially coloured candies of the candy-seller had melted in the heat. Two shoeshine men, side by side, worked furiously at their jobs. One was busy shining the shoes of a navy man. He shined the old, misshapen shoes so thoroughly that all the creases in the leather stood out like peaks and valleys. The navy man, with an absent-minded smile on his face, waited patiently.

This Saturday in the month of August was like the other Saturdays of the summer. And the people who came to the pier were more or less the same people.

The woman thought: 'It's always the same people. The military men on leave. The old women. The children. The old men just like old women. They walk with small steps like women. They talk in low voices. They're always munching something.'

The old people ate up everything their grandchildren left behind when they went to play, saying, 'We'll eat later'; they picked at their dentures from time to time to remove the food particles underneath. Perhaps the people who came to the pier every day weren't exactly the same people. But, somehow, in the carefree abandon they seemed identical, and could be discerned as separate only after dark when they went home. They were a uniform crowd of people, with their loose clothes hanging from their shrunken shoulders, their coarse skins and blue cataracts gradually covering their eyes.

The woman thought: 'Old people are so patient. Look at that one the blond brat is pestering. She is doing nothing, just smiling. If she'd smack him in the face he wouldn't dare bother her. Poor woman came here to warm her tired bones in the sun; she hasn't got the strength to deal with him. We sacrifice everything for our children. But is it worth it? Mine is well-behaved; a little stubborn, but she's still a child.'

She looked at the little girl who sat beside her quietly. She was around six or seven years old and very thin. She wore rubber boots. Her dress was quite short and faded – it did not cover her thin legs. She covered her knees with her hands. Her hair was cut short. Her neck bones stuck out. She had her large dark eyes fixed on the water-seller. She was watching his activities. She was interested in what was going on around her and looked happy. Her lips were parted and this gave her face a dumb expression. A smell of perspiration came out of the child's rubber boots. Both the mother and the daughter had grown used to this smell. The child had invented a name for it: 'The car smell.' She loved cars. The mother and the daughter had never taken a ride in a car. Perhaps the mother had – a long time ago – but the child didn't know about it. In hot weather their greatest fun was to walk all the way to the pier.

Füruzan, 'In The Park By The Pier', in Parasız Yatılı (1972)
translated by Nilüfer Mizanoğlu Reddy

✳ ✳ ✳

But all too soon the summer is just a memory ...

By midmorning they were on the ferry. The sea was rough, and the town, when they got there, was deserted. The grey waves washing up against the old Ottoman ferry terminal seemed less real to Jeannie than the smooth blue sea in her mind's eye. As they walked through the windswept town, past shuttered shops and houses, she thought back to the lost summer crowds, and the flurries of waiters, and the children on bicycles, the maids beating carpets, the creaking and clopping of horses and carriages, the warm stench of manure rising from the tree-lined streets.

They climbed the hill, passing houses so wet and so grey that she could no longer imagine them any other way. They walked down into a mist and when they came up the other side, they had arrived at the Greek monastery. The church was locked, but from the courtyard they could see the Marmara nestled in a bed of clouds. The rain was not quite with them yet, so they carried on. The first drops hit them as they were passing the sodden, shuttered shack that became a teahouse during the summer.

Maureen Freely, *Enlightenment* (2007)

* * *

Istanbul is famous for its winds. Dutch travel writer Geert Mak names them.

In the same way that other parts of the world have a dozen or more words for rain, snow or fog, this city knows at least thirty varieties of wind, and the fishermen have named them all. When the Pleasant Storm, the Storm of the Blackbirds or the Storm of the Cuckoos comes blowing in from the west, the spring will be mild and dry. Easterly winds with their morning mist, like the Storm of Fish, provide relief from the heat of summer and bring rain all year round. The Black Wind – which comes from the east as well, but only in winter – powders the city with snow. Now everyone is braced for the spring storms, the Storm of the Swallow and the Storm of Swans. The tourist season has started. They've planted three million tulips, even atop the bridge's control booths they stand swaying in the cold wind, fat plastic bubbles of red and yellow.

For the moment, however, all the weather still comes from the Black Sea, it's the Boreas that is blowing and showers fall incessantly. The fishermen have decked themselves out in sheets of plastic, worn tarpaulins and old fertiliser bags. The ferries putter back and forth in the greyness, gulls dive past, shiny black umbrellas go trundling across the bridge, its far end hidden behind a foggy white wall. The sonorous motors of the *Professor Aykut Barka* and the *Mehmet Akif Ersoy* are idling along the northern quay, queasy black smoke shoots from their stacks, an abrupt turn of the rudder and the two ferries are off. […]

The Wind of the Stars has come up. It is one of the city's stranger natural phenomena: great booming gusts of wind that come hurtling in off the river. Suddenly the waves have grown nasty little whitecaps, the ferries steam and puff to stay on course, on the terraces the place settings begin blowing off the tables, pavement signs slam to the ground, sand bites the eyes.

Geert Mak, *The Bridge:*
A Journey Between Occident and Orient (2007)
translated by Sam Garrett

✳ ✳ ✳

German writer Kai Strittmatter meditates upon the winds' qualities in an extract translated for this anthology.

A city of winds. The *Karayel*, bitterly cold, the one out of the northwest, which the poet sends gliding across the coast like a scythe. The *Poyraz*, the one from the northeast. For centuries, together with the current, it blocked the passage of sailors from the Mediterranean through the Bosphorus up into the Black Sea. A welcome visitor today, it brings longed-for coolness to Istanbulites in the oppressive summer, blows the veil away from their eyes, lets the continents slide closer together. All at once the nighttime lights on the opposite side appear to be engraved with a laser in the slope of the shore, so fresh and clear. The *Poyraz*. Fishermen name their boats after it, and some their sons.

Not one boat or man in this city is named *Lodos*. *The storm.* *The Lodos. So passionate. So hot.* The *Lodos* caught the prisoner Nazım Hikmet in his cell, it forced those verses from him. The greatest poet of the Turks, this Nazım Hikmet, and a Communist as well. *So passionate. So hot.* It attacks from the southwest, the *Lodos*. Makes cats mangy, this wind, makes windowpanes crack and caged-in men burst with longing and lecherousness. *In the air/the scent of female skin/the heat of bulging ovaries.* It makes the sea crazy and people as well, the

Lodos. It is said that the *kadis*, the Ottoman judges, were at one time forbidden to decide on a verdict during the *Lodos*. It blows out one's reason, piles foam on the shore as high as a minaret. Then the ships lie still. And many people. One individual has pain in his head and limbs, others feel vertigo and nausea, some even smell the 'acidic breath of the sinful dead.'

Yet the *Lodos* doesn't just wash seaweed and sorrow, migraines and dead jellyfish onto the shore. It also brings the scent of the sea into the city, lays sea salt on skin and lips. On the morning after a storm, with day breaking and the water clear to the sea floor, the *Lodos*-runners used to set off, looking about with sharp eyes for washed-up objects that they could sell. They hoped for the good luck of that poor fisherman who, according to legend, once found the famous Kaşıkçı Diamond, the biggest precious stone in the Ottoman treasure vault. They swore that they would be more clever than that fisherman, who traded his find for three wooden spoons.

This wind is a moody intruder which brings rain and mist and leaves behind melancholy and sadness. Confronted with the *Lodos*, ships take early refuge in the safe harbour of the Golden Horn. And people? *The heart a large black hole.* In her *chanson* 'Istanbul Istanbul olah', the incomparable Sezen Aksu calls up the *Lodos* for a girl lying on a rock on the Bosphorus, mourning the betrayal of her lover. *Now I need a Lodos and a rudder.* To tear apart the pain, to drown it. *Ah! Istanbul never saw such sorrow/Since it came to be Istanbul.*

Kai Strittmatter, *User's Guide to Istanbul* (2010).
translated by Susan Thorne

❋ ❋ ❋

A powerful short story by Feryal Tilmaç takes up Kai Strittmatter's observation that the wind known as the 'lodos' can make people behave in uncharacteristic ways.

86

Perhaps all of this still would have happened, even if the city hadn't been caught up in the tempestuous lodos that night. But the truth is, that frantic wind, spinner of its own mysteries, provided justifiable motive for aggression. Strange, droning, lukewarm, the lodos keeps in its thrall not only the city, but the souls of its people as well. And Cavidan Altan was one of those people. Perhaps what would occur later hadn't even remotely crossed her mind when she left home that day. I say 'perhaps', because we can never know for sure what's on a woman's mind. Now, I could pretend that I knew, but I don't want to taint the authenticity of the story by adding to it something I'm not sure about. We can safely assume the same about Tolga Güçel, and say that he, too, never would have guessed that he would experience the things he did that evening, or any evening, for that matter. [...]

That evening on his way home from work, as he passed Zincirlikuyu and made a right onto the road to Levent, he was listening to the radio programme *Women Sing Jazz*. '*Dear listeners, we continue with Ethel Waters's "Stormy Weather"* ... ' There couldn't have been a more fitting selection. He tapped along on the steering wheel. The invasive wind whistled and shook the coloured lights on the trees. Who knows, maybe everything would have panned out in another way if the weather had been different; say, if it had been snowing. After all, the New Year spirit calls for snow; and for love, hope, new beginnings, packages of presents, angels hanging on trees, the cinnamon-spiced scent of mulled wine. But it didn't happen, it didn't snow. Instead, a crazy, wayward wind kept the area convulsing for days on end, making the city slave to its whim. Though the majority suffered only mild headaches and a little shortness of breath in the aftermath, at the time, melancholy ran like a viscous liquid through the streets.

Tolga, for his part, did something he never would have done otherwise: compelled by the sorrowful music and the feeling of benevolence that the New Year's spirit aroused, he pulled up to the curb, where a woman with shopping bags was trying to flag down a taxi. The woman, Cavidan Hanım, had just finished her shopping at the mall in Levent. On the window behind her, 2007 was written in cotton balls, and adorned with wreaths of mistletoe, yellow, green, and red lights, gold-lacquered pine-cones, and red stars. She was a woman of a certain maturity; she held her hand in front of her face as she tried to protect herself from the wind. Perhaps hitching a ride wasn't her inten-tion at all. Still, when she stooped and saw Tolga, she opened the back door, dropped her bags in the car, and settled into the passenger seat without hesitation. [...]

'If you drop me off in front of Akmerkez, I can walk from there.' A sudden gush of wind rattled the windshield, and shook the car even more, or so it seemed to them.

'With all those bags? Out of the question! I'll drive you to your door.'

The young man's polite, soft-spoken manner emboldened the woman. 'I love going to the shore and watching the sea during the lodos. How about you?' [...]

They passed Bebek Hotel, Starbucks, Divan bakery, and then the grocery store. Even if the whole world were to go haywire, the colourful fruit-packed trays of that grocery store would be enough to restore the illusion that everything was A-OK. Cavidan Hanım, turning to her right, pointed to the olive oil speciality shop and asked: 'have you ever shopped there?'

'No,' said Tolga, laughing.

Brightly lit windows, the headlights of standing cars, people going in and out of restaurants and liquor stores on both sides all blended together into one big blur; a single, gigantic organism quivering in the wind. They stopped again, where the waterfront houses ended and the sea began. The coats and the scarves of people crossing the avenue were flying in the wind. An old man laughed as he pressed down on his fedora. Now *that's* a retiree, Cavidan Hanım thought. She was happy, giddy; she'd never felt younger. The whistle of the lodos blew in one window and out the other.

An increasingly contented Tolga pointed to a man selling fish on the shore. 'Beautiful, isn't it? How bright and colourful they are, even in this weather ... ' [...]

Beaten black-and-blue by the wind, the sea churned and foamed. The bus in front of them let out a hiss as it lurched forward, and they followed. Launched from the terrace of one of the seafront houses, an umbrella, a remnant from summer, blew over the road and toward the water. Spared, by the grace of God! The incident brought them closer; it was that special affinity shared by people who have survived an accident together. [...]

'Should we keep going? Is there any particular place you'd like to stop?' For the first time in his life he felt the comfort of being with an assertive woman, a woman in charge, a woman who made decisions for him. But then, there were many firsts in store for him that evening. Feeling submissive to the core, he waited for an answer.

'There's a parking lot by the water, across from the grave-yard. Let's go there. It's always deserted after dark.' The traffic abated. She unzipped the jacket of her jogging suit a little further, just to get some air. The medallion hanging from her neck glinted for a brief second, catching the young man's eye; Cavidan Hanım promptly took notice. The lodos was blowing through the giant trees along the roadside. [...]

Tolga slowed down next to the cemetery, turned on his right-turn signal, then parked by the water. The headlights illuminated the sea one last time before going out; the seagulls, caught in the circles of light, flitted about the sky like giant snowflakes.

Feryal Tilmaç, 'Hitching in the *Lodos*' (2008) in *Istanbul Noir*, edited and translated by Amy Spangler and Mustafa Ziyalan

* * *

The famous Istanbul wind again – here vividly described by Gaye Boralıoğlu (b.1963) in the novel Syncopated Rhythm.

An unrelenting wind violently whipped the city. Giant ships rolled on the waters of the sea like rowboats, and fishermen's boats, moored askew, struggled to take refuge in secure harbours. The entire shore road was drenched by the sea's waves. Those travelling on the city's boat lines disembarked with queasy stomachs and puked onto the piers. The electrical lines which ran from one end of the city to the other shivered ferociously. Ceramic shingles from the roofs of poor neighbourhoods descended onto muddy roads. The signs of upscale stores in rich neighbourhoods swung right and left, in a series of vehement cracks and bangs. The hats and umbrellas of the hatted Istanbulites bearing umbrellas flew up, up and away; the rich did not run after them, the poor reaped the harvest of the wind. Skinny little Istanbulites grabbed on to poles so as not to be swept away. Those who were cowards hid in stores. Not a single one of the stray cats or the dogs sporting municipality tags as earrings, who commonly strutted the streets as if they and they alone owned the city, were anywhere to be seen. And there was no sign of the giant seagulls, whose bountiful diet of garbage made them look more like plump turkeys. Apartment rats, their lineage traceable back to Byzantine times; termites, the insidious inhabitants of derelict houses; adolescent cockroaches – that is, the entirety of Istanbul's creatures had burrowed into the deepest holes they could find.

And Halil, who had just lain down on the bed where Güldane slept, was no different from the Istanbul moaning beneath the weight of the *lodos*. All of his nerves shivered ferociously, the shingles in his brain were dashed about, the signs squeaked and squealed, damaging his ear drums. Waves of anxiety rose and rolled in tides of turbulence, away from his heart, beating against his soul; his stomach was queasy, he felt he might puke.

Gaye Boralıoğlu, *Syncopated Rhythm* (2009)
translated by Amy Spangler

✳ ✳ ✳

Even when the weather is bad, however, there can be sudden moments of glory.

As they passed Şişhane, clouds parted momentarily. Above the Süleymaniye Mosque, sunshine gushed as if from a sluice through a massive, single-hued, nearly translucent cumulus cloud, the likes of which appeared in old miniature paintings. The entire city had become the opulent and ornate décor for a fairy tale of sorts, or a Scheherazade fable. He exited the taxi at Galatasaray. Under the pure, make-believe golden light, he at first wanted to walk up toward Taksim Square. But in the dread of running into an acquaintance, he turned back. He walked toward Tepebaşı. There he entered a small bistro. The rain had quickened again. Through the dirty window, he stared at the rain pelting the façades of the apartments opposite, pondering the immense radiance he'd just witnessed.

Ahmet Hamdi Tanpınar, *A Mind at Peace* (1949)
translated by Erdağ Göknar (2008)

✳ ✳ ✳

Elif Shafak (b.1971) gives us an Istanbul downpour in her world-wide best-seller, The Bastard of Istanbul.

Rain is an agony here. In other parts of the world, a downpour will in all likelihood come as a boon for nearly everyone and everything – good for the crops, good for the fauna and the flora, and with an extra splash of romanticism, good for lovers. Not so in Istanbul though. Rain, for us, isn't necessarily about getting wet. It's not about getting dirty even. If anything, it's about getting angry. It's mud and chaos and rage, as if we didn't have enough of each already. And struggle. It's always about struggle. Like kittens thrown into a bucketful of water, all ten million of us put up a futile fight against the drops. It can't be said that we are completely alone in this scuffle, for the streets too are in on it, with their antediluvian names stencilled on tin placards, and the tombstones of so many saints scattered in all directions, the piles of garbage that wait on almost every corner, the hideously huge construction pits soon to be turned into glitzy, modern buildings, and the seagulls ... It angers us all when the sky opens and spits on our heads.

But then, as the final drops reach the ground and many more perch unsteadily on the now dustless leaves, at that unprotected moment, when you are not quite sure that it has finally ceased raining, and neither is the rain itself, in that very interstice, everything becomes serene. For one long minute, the sky seems to apologize for the mess she has left us in. And we, with driblets still in our hair, slush in our cuffs, and dreariness in our gaze, stare back at the sky, now a lighter shade of cerulean and clearer than ever. We look up and can't help smiling back. We forgive her; we always do.

Elif Shafak, *The Bastard of Istanbul* (2007)

✽ ✽ ✽

Just a little more rain and wind ...

And then, winter arrived. Autumn had gathered its stuff without us noticing, and during one night, had fled far away like a dry leaf fluttering in the wind. When we woke up, we were greeted by a rain that didn't look like rain any more, and a wind that slapped one in the face.

Tuna Kiremitçi, *The Way of Loneliness* (2003)
translated by Jak Korı

✽ ✽ ✽

No wind, no rain – just a foggy night in Istanbul.

There was a dense fog outside. And the street lamps were out. The apartment ·blocks across the way that I was used to seeing from this angle were rendered invisible by the fog and the darkness. I waited in vain for a car to pass through the avenue, finally giving up hope. I knew that Monday nights were the most boring, deadest time of the week in this city. When I opened the window to get some fresh air, my throat was attacked by a cold, smoky darkness that seared my nasal passages. I closed the window. I leaned my legs against the radiator, trying to get warm. But the radiator was quickly growing cold. I couldn't decide what to do next.

Murat Gülsoy, 'Marked in Writing'
translated by Amy Spangler, in *The Book of Istanbul* (2011)

✻ ✻ ✻

And then winter ...

Wind coming off the Black Sea. It can bring storms and snow and can harden the winter. The Bosphorus has even frozen over in the past. Let's not exaggerate, though – it was only a dozen times in two thousand years (according to Mamboury,[1] in 763, the icebergs were so huge that they formed a barrier and damaged the city walls). Lunch at Çırağan (a creamy risotto); at three o'clock it grows dark. I await the snow.

Daniel Rondeau, *Istanbul* (2002)
translated by Erica King

✻ ✻ ✻

Mehmet Zaman Saçlıoğlu gives a more detailed account of an Istanbul winter, in the context of its framing seasons.

---

1 Ernest Mamboury (1878–1953) – a Swiss scholar devoted to the study of Turkish cities, particularly the Byzantine art and architecture of Istanbul. (Ed.)

After autumn has played games with summer, it sits on Istanbul's throne with the great power of the Lodos (the southwest wind). Quince yellow, pomegranate red, red ivy leaves, the faint smell of rotting fruit, the coolness of rain. The moss on the paving stones, the shortening days, all decorate this throne and suddenly the day comes when, without your knowing it, it hands over the throne to winter and steps aside. [...]

When autumn realises that it will lose its throne to winter, a wind which the fishermen call Yıldız (North Star) is felt in the north. Determined, reliable, it comes from the Black Sea. With its right side it touches the Anatolian shore, with its left side it touches the European shore, and with its chest it weighs on the Istanbul Bosphorus. Without faltering it proceeds along the Bosphorus where it darkens the waters and searches the mansions, talks to the boathouses and seeps into the side streets. It hits the walls of the old wooden houses. It shakes the windows where the putty has dried. It gets through the walls and plays with the curtains.

When cats feel the north wind they look for shelter. Their fur puffs up, their eyes narrow. The north wind picks up the last remaining leaves, swirls them around the road and throws them into nooks and crannies. It is no longer that idle October, November wind which plays with the leaves. Like an angry wing it passes along the Bosphorus shaking small fishing boats, causing the ropes of anchored yachts to hit the poles. When it sees Topkapı Palace, Hagia Sophia, the Blue Mosque and old Istanbul in front of it, it gets confused and tries to turn in front of Sarayburnu. This sudden change in direction causes turmoil in the Sarayburnu Sea, strengthening whirlpools and frightening the young girl waiting to throw herself into the water.

The girl has come from an eastern town. Staring absently into the dark waters with a far off, sad expression, it is obvious that she is just one of the many who came to Istanbul without hope, where, once in Istanbul, this hopelessness grows and causes her to lose her way. How many people have jumped into the whirlpool sea, how many people have disappeared? The north wind, like an inquisitive, restless bird, turns, stops at the historic peninsula, turns to the opposite shore or takes off towards the Marmara Sea. Now with the strengthening north wind, autumn takes a back seat – although Lodos will show itself at every opportunity, as if to say, 'I will not give up Istanbul for any season, I am Lord of this town.' It will surprise the fish, people, birds, by softening even the harshest winter weather and all living things will be happily drunk and dazed.

Both winter and autumn are ignorant of the calendars of humans. That is why autumn does not know that it has to give up Istanbul, and the entire northern hemisphere, to winter on the first of December. If one year this handover is early, the next it is late. In the end, the duration of the seasons' reign is the same.

At the beginning of December, a few days early or a few days late, we enter winter with the storm of the Pleiades. Following that, other storms make sudden appearances. The Zemheri (intense cold), Karakış (severe winter), Karansolos and Ayandon (St. Anthony's Storm). The wind, sometimes fierce, sometimes soft, but always persistent, fuels winter until the coming of the Cemre (an increase in warmth in February). [...]

As January approaches, New Year excitement starts in Istanbul. With a tradition left over from the days when Jews, Greeks, Armenians and White Russians all lived together in harmony, everyone prepares for the New Year. Nişantaşı, Beyoğlu and Bağdat streets are lit up with New Years' trees, flowers and decorations, Father Christmas, presents, cotton wool and snowflake shapes stuck on shop windows, glitter, beads, all marking a change of year. [...]

Even if January is harsh, the most problematic month is February. It may be short, but if one said that each day is worth two days of any other month, one would not be exaggerating.

It generally snows in this month in Istanbul. The most severe winter in previous years was in 1954. On 24th February the Istanbul Straits were covered in ice. You could walk from one shore to the other. In this cold the fish became disorientated and came to the surface of the water and were collected by hand. There are few winters like this in Istanbul's history. Another such winter was the winter of 1929, which only the very elderly remember. Istanbul's Golden Horn froze over; people walked from one shore to the other. Birds on electricity wires and chickens in their coops froze. The wise street cats of Istanbul waited for the birds to fall from the wires. [...]

During Istanbul winters, the bachelor rooms are the rooms where winter is harshest. These are Istanbul's cheapest boarding places. Some have not even been plastered, some have no heating, others, a small brazier to warm the room; sometimes there are bunk beds and sometimes there are mattresses on the floor. There is a melancholy camaraderie among the poor who have come from far away villages with hope, and who share the same problems. They can put up with this in the summer. However in these rooms where the winter cold, rain and wind coming through the broken windows covered with plastic bags attempt to break down these men, at night dreams that no one can imagine are dreamt. The paths of those living in bachelor rooms cross in markets, construction sites and while collecting rubbish. Next to the rubbish bins, the runny nosed street cats with their chests hunched over their front legs against the cold, settle and wait. They have a quiet agreement with the rubbish collectors. The cats wait for the food that lies under the rubbish, away from the 'rubbish children'. In better off areas, gypsies selling flowers by the roadside, wearing layers of colourful jumpers, resemble the flowers they sell. On very cold days, if there is a fire burning behind the stall, you can be sure there is a baby sleeping inside a box or in an old pram. The gypsy flower sellers are the colour and aroma of Istanbul's streets.

Istanbul with its diverse faces, looks at different people in different ways. To some she smiles, to some she frowns. Some cry out with pleasure and some with pain. The discrepancies increase in winter. The cold increases the distance between these different faces. [...]

Towards the end of February the cemres (increases in warmth, supposedly falling from the sun) are awaited. It is believed that cemres are fires which fall to earth. First they fall into the atmosphere, and the world warms up, but this is temporary. Winter resists a little more, another fire falls, this time into the water. The world is revived a little more, movement starts under the earth. In the end the earth pulls towards it a third fire, which will bring it to life. When the cemres end it will be the end of winter.

Mehmet Zaman Saçlıoğlu, 'Winter' in
Four Seasons Istanbul from 1000 Feet (2010)
translated by Hatice Ahmet Salih and Joan Eroncel

" ... the molasses-thick and bracingly bitter Arabian coffee"

Anya von Bremzen

'The imam fainted'

Turkish food – yes, it can be delicious enough to make even an unworldly imam faint with pleasure ('the imam fainted' is actually the name of a Turkish dish made with aubergines). In this section we taste some of the culinary pleasures that await the visitor to Istanbul. First, food writer Anya von Bremzen gives us a whistle-stop tour of some of the typical dishes and eating places to be enjoyed in the city.

With its succulent kebabs and simple grilled fish, its healthful vegetable stews and bright salads, along with all manner of mezze (small dishes), from stewed white beans to stuffed

98

mussels, Istanbul's food is easy to love. The local cuisine has much in common with the cooking of the Middle East and the Balkans: a reliance on yogurt, an emphasis on braising or grilling, a skill with stuffed vegetables, and a penchant for eggplants, legumes, bulgur, and rice. But Istanbul's food has its own unmistakably urban identity, too. Its patchwork of flavours and eating styles reflects both Turkey's shared nomadic heritage and the city's past as the capital of the cosmopolitan, multicultural Ottoman Empire, which attracted vast waves of migrants. [...]

Sultan Mehmet the Conqueror [...] equipped his Topkapı Palace with a domed kitchen so vast it could have been mistaken for an imperial mosque. Delicate and refined, Ottoman court cooking was also highly specialised; separate guilds of chefs were assigned to the making of particular genres of dishes: köfte (meatballs), kebabs, pilavs, or, say, halva. Today, Istanbul's eateries reflect that specialisation: you have skewered lamb at *kebabçı* (kebab joint), fish at a *balıkçı* (fish house), börek – the savoury pastries fashioned from layers of paper-thin yufka, a phyllo-like dough – at a *börekçi*, and boza, a thick fermented-bulgar drink, at a *bozacı*. Alcohol? The city's secular-minded bohemians do their drinking – plus plenty of eating – at *meyhanes*, raucous taverns traditionally run by non-Muslim minorities. [...]

Like other *Istanbullus*, I develop a stubborn, irrational devotion to particular joints and food rituals. Each morning I practically sleepwalk to my local *çay bahçesi* (tea garden), where Cihangir's intellectuals crowd around tables laid out beneath tree branches and grape arbours, all shadowed by our green neighbourhood mosque. At a *çay bahçesi*, you order your tulip-shaped glass of sweet çay (black tea) and are free to linger forever. I usually take along a breakfast of feta, cucumbers, olives and simit, a sesame-crusted, ring-shaped bread sold as a snack by street vendors all over the city. Two hours later, when the wood-burning oven is fired up at the corner dive, I'm back at the tea garden with my midmorning lahmacun: a pliant, smoke-tinged oval of dough topped with a faintly spicy smear of ground meat, sprinkled with lemon juice, and rolled around parsley springs and tomato slices.

For lunch, I dash across the traffic-choked intersection for mantı (dumplings) at Özkonak, a worn storefront wedged between trendy cafés. Over tin bowls of red lentil soup, a trio of cops are talking soccer. Greek-speaking ladies, remnants of Cihangir's once substantial Hellenic community, order their usual kabak graten (zucchini under a blanket of gratinéed béchamel). My mantı arrive: tiny, toothsome meat dumplings (versions of which appear across Turkey and Central Asia) bathed in tart yogurt and enriched with a flourish of chilli-and-mint-infused butter. Özkonak belongs to a cardinal genre of Istanbul eatery, the *esnaf lokantası*, a rudimentary merchants' canteen offering sustenance to shopkeepers and city workers. The esnaf setup rarely varies. There's always a guy who hails you with a loud '*Hoşgeldiniz!*' ('Welcome!'). Always a portrait – or six – of Mustafa Kemal Atatürk, the stupendously photogenic, sartorially splendid founder of the Turkish Republic. Ordering is easy: just point to the cold cases and steam tables and nod.

For a truly encyclopaedic selection of *esnaf lokantası* fare, I go to a place called Kanaat, near the ferry landing in Üsküdar, a bustling working-class district on Istanbul's Asian shore. In a big, sombre room that seems lost in the 1970s, I tour the food displays, ravenously plotting my lunch. Everything one wants to know about Turkish cuisine is here, somewhere. I find zeytinyağlı – green beans, artichokes, celery root, or other vegetables braised in olive oil until luscious and spoon tender – and every kind of stuffed vegetable: cabbage, peppers, eggplant and grape leaves filled with meat or sweetly spiced rice. In the glassed-in kitchen, cooks made Uzbek lamb-and-carrot pilaf, stewed white beans, all types of köfte, and yahni, earthy stews of lamb, tomato and eggplant. By the entrance, sweets glisten in their dark amber syrup. Fragrant quince chunks, bread pudding with sour cherries – it's a trauma to choose. [...]

A pillar of Istanbul's foodways is its *kebabçı*, or kebab joints; indeed, most visitors consider grilled meats and their tangy accompaniments to be among Istanbul's native foods. But spicy skewered lamb, chillies, hummus, and other Middle Eastern fare are actually fairly new to the city, the consequence of a vast influx of migrants from southeastern Turkey in the early twentieth century. [...]

Kebapçi meals usually follow a strict progression. Strong tulum cheese and puffy breads give way to içli köfte, torpedo-shaped bulgur shells filled with spiced lamb. Then come lahmacun and, finally, skewers of meat accompanied by a pomegranate syrup-laced salad of tomatoes and herbs. Our minced lamb Urfa kebab is salty and coarse, but everyone loves the eggplant-and-meatballs skewers and the ciğer şiş, which alternates liver cubes with crisp but plush nuggets of sheep tail fat. In the Eastern tradition, we lubricate our meal with ayran, a refreshing yogurt drink. The best lands last: künefe, a miraculous, syrup-drenched cheese-and-shredded wheat pastry served with mirra, the molasses-thick and bracingly bitter Arabian coffee.

'No, no! Don't put your mirra cup down!' Soner cries. 'Urfans say that if you do, you'll have to fill it with gold or marry the server!' The server is sixteen and no pop star, so I just wave my cup in the air.

Anya von Bremzen, 'The Soul of a City' in *Saveur* (April 2009)

✳ ✳ ✳

Although the once commonplace 'pudding shops' are now a rarity, the milk-based foods served in them are something any 'foodie' should know about.

Twenty years ago in Istanbul they were everywhere, and there are still a few around – special little shops with a couple of marble-topped tables and Thonet chairs, not there in the name of fashion, but simply because that was when the place was last refurbished. A white-aproned waiter hastily wipes a table to make room for another customer. In a way these shops are as much a part of Istanbul life as cafes are in Vienna, though the food and the concept are entirely different, and there is not the same panache, of course. These simple shops offer only one specialty: milk puddings. Called *muhallebici*, they are pudding shops – milk parlours, if you like – and they operate quite separately from restaurants and patisseries.

Muhallebi is a sweet, milk-based cream, thickened only with starch (unlike custards and *crème pâtissière*, it contains no eggs), and it is a familiar dish from the Crimea to North Africa, from the Balkans to India. Even the name varies little from place to place. Only in Europe is it unknown, or perhaps forgotten.

In Turkey *muhallebi* forms part of everyone's diet, from babies to grandmothers, for it is wonderfully nourishing. It has two essential ingredients: pure starch – whether from the flour of rice, wheat, corn, or potatoes – which is entirely digestible; and milk, which is rich in protein, calcium, and vitamins.

In the distant past, before ready-made rice flour existed, and corn and potatoes were waiting to be discovered in America, rice flour was made at home. Whitened, short-grain rice grains, which contain more starch than long-grain rice, were ground or pounded and sifted to the desired fineness. To obtain the pure starch – *nişasta* in Turkish – the powdered rice was washed in hot water and filtered through layers of muslin.

The consistency of the *muhallebi* varies according to taste. Personally, I prefer a fairly creamy, rather than a dense, texture. You can obtain a thicker cream by increasing the ratio of rice or other flour to liquid. One kind of *muhallebi*, known as *taş* (or stone) *muhallebisi*, not surprisingly, is pretty solid. [...]

An entire food culture grew up around *muhallebi*. The special heart-shaped silver spoons with the maker's stamp that you find in antique shops are just one reminder. When the puddings had cooled, it used to be the custom to cover them with a paper stencil and shake powdered cinnamon over them. When the stencil was removed, the puddings might bear – in stylised calligraphy – the words *Afiyet olsun* ('*Bon appétit*') or 'Long live the Sultan' or some such greeting. Later, under the Republic, they were replaced by a cinnamon crescent and star. Today, only the sprinkling of cinnamon remains.

I vaguely remember in my childhood seeing these stencilled crescent and stars in *muhallebi* shop windows. Less blurred is my memory of dozens of china dessert bowls, some delicate, others plain, all filled with *muhallebi* left to cool on the table in my grandmother's kitchen. Later I would be served with my own bowl with my initial, B, in cinnamon. My grandmother had cut a stencil for every one of my cousins, too.

The first mention of the dish as a dessert dates from 1473, when the imperial kitchen accounts of the Ottoman sultan Mehmet the Conqueror record that he and his retinue were served *muhallebi*. This is the very same dish that we know today. But *muhallebi* was not always such a simple affair. Medieval Arab cookery books give recipes for a dish of the same name that was a complicated confection of milk, rice, almonds, saffron, and chicken breast or other meat. This bears a striking resemblance to the medieval English *blancmanger*.

Berrin Torolsan, 'The Milky Way'(2002)

✻ ✻ ✻

Travel writer Rory Maclean tells us about one particularly famous pudding shop.

I'm at the Pudding Shop, the first meeting point on the trail. In 1957, two brothers from the Black Sea, Namık and İdris Çolpan, opened the *Lâle Pastanesi* across from Istanbul's Blue

Mosque. For a couple of years, well-to-do Turks stopped by for frothy black *kahve* and honey-soaked *baklava* topped with green pistachios. Then, the tiny, open-fronted patisserie attracted the attention of the early overlanders, both because of its central location and their sugar-craving munchies. Overnight, the travellers made the *Lâle* their place, renaming it the Pudding Shop. Outside its door, London double-deckers and fried-out Kombis parked along the Hippodrome. Pop music played in its garden. The well-to-do Turks stood outside, their mouths agape, watching their sons and nephews – among them Ersin Kalkan – drink coffee with paradise-bound freaks in Apache headbands and paisley waistcoats.

Today the cafeteria is indistinguishable from a dozen of its neighbours, apart from a few faded sixties photographs tacked on the rear wall. Beneath them, a handful of Lycra-clad Danish civil servants procrastinate over desiccated pizzas and *köfte* meatballs. At the next table, a sunburnt Englishman nurses an early Troy Pilsner.

'In your book you can write that the hippies discovered Turkey,' Adem Çolpan tells me a few minutes later.

'And that Turkish tourism started in our *pastane*,' adds Namık, as he and his nephew join me at my table.

'Our country had no tourism policy, no telephones, no information in those years,' Adem explains, turning his neat, twirling moustache with long, manicured nails. 'My uncle and father, because of their personalities, wanted to help our young guests to find their way. So they stuck announcements on the wall about the nearest Turkish bath and the next boat to Antalya.'

'Our noticeboard was the first signpost along the trail,' confirms Namık.

On it, kids traded travel advice, found the address of the Iranian Embassy and checked out the safest route through Afghanistan. 'Gentle deviant, 21, seeks guitar-playing chick ready to set out for mystical East,' read one message. 'Anyone know where to crash in Kabul?' asked another. At times the notices were so thickly layered that nails rather than tacks had to be used to post them on the board. Today, the messages themselves, as the first scribblings of an oral tradition, are nearly lost.

'We in return are grateful to the hippies,' concedes Adem. A mild sweetness has been instilled in him by a lifetime of serving desserts. 'Because they taught us how to make Nescafé, delivered by bus drivers who refilled the tins for the return journey with hands of Afghan Black or Lebanese Gold.

'The hippies didn't want to drink Turkish coffee,' he goes on, with no hint of irony. 'They wanted to eat ice cream and macaroni.'

'And *sütlaç*,' I reminded him. Sweet baked rice pudding.

'My father always said to me, "If we don't live our dream, why live?" That is why we are still here.'

By 1969, the Pudding Shop was so popular that a refectory and an authentic-looking wooden façade were added. The self-service counter was introduced in the seventies. As travellers morphed into tourists, the Çolpans started writing bus tickets and making hotel bookings, charging a dollar for each service, pioneers of a national industry which now serves twelve million visitors every year.

Rory Maclean, *Magic Bus* (2007)

❊ ❊ ❊

If you have a stomach for things considerably stronger than milk puddings, you might like to try a dish described by Kai Strittmatter.

The Turks love grilling more than anything: meat over an open fire, the fragrance of the steppes. They grill the finest sea bass here and the tenderest kid. And sometimes they take two or three sheep intestines, wrap them around a long skewer and grill that, too. Then it's called *Kokoreç*. '*Kokoreç* is the tastiest form that sheep's intestine can assume,' it says in the Sauren Dictionary, an alternative cultural website. 'Anybody who doesn't like it is crazy.' I don't like it, but then I am the exception in Istanbul. They have even dedicated a hit tune to the *Kokoreç*: *My smouldering love/I will never forget you/ Kokoreç, Ko Ko Ko Ko Kokoreç*. That was a few years ago, at a time when rumours were circulating in the country that the European Union wanted to ban the *Kokoreç* on hygienic grounds: *Strangers have parted us/Your flavour still on my lips/Kokoreç, Ko Ko Ko ...* Those rumours had roughly as much truth to them as the rumour that Europe wanted to take away the Tigris and Euphrates rivers and move them to Brussels, and after a while the excitement died down.

Kokoreç is also made into a sandwich. The ready-grilled intestines are chopped finely and mixed with chilli and salt. *Kokoreç* grillers like to stand with their wagons on the parking lots for the Istanbul ferries or push them along the Bosphorus promenade. Wherever the *Kokoreç* is found, the *İskembe* – tripe soup – is often close by. They share a second livelihood as nighttime dishes: when the drinkers of the city have had enough of *Meze* and raki, discos and bars, when the dawn and hangovers are not far away, then they come to the tripe soup kitchens and *Kokoreç* grills for a sobering-up meal. The best *Kokoreç* in the city is served by Mustafa Güneş in Üsküdar (or so says Mustafa Güneş from Üsküdar): 'I use only the entrails of milk lambs. No older than three or four months. And I only buy these from February to May. Later on the lambs start to eat grass, and then the intestine tastes different.' Yet there are a few Istanbulers who wholeheartedly detest *Kokoreç* : 'Disgusting' is the assessment of a long-established Istanbul society lady: 'You didn't have such things here in the past,' she snorts, 'before these Anatolians invaded our city.' However *Kokoreç* didn't originate in Anatolia. Rather it's from the Balkans and from Greece, where it is known as *Kokoretsi* and has been passionately loved and consumed even after that country's entry into the European Union. *Ko Ko Ko Ko/Kokoreç, we can't do without you/ Kokoreç Ko Ko Ko Ko ...*

Kai Strittmatter, *User's Guide to Istanbul* (2010)
translated by Susan Thorne

      ❋ ❋ ❋

Maureen Freely tells us what we might expect for breakfast and how Turks take their tea.

The hardest part of living in a foreign country must be getting used to what they eat for breakfast.

What they eat here is toast (not so strange in itself, I know, but the bread is a different consistency, springy with hard, thick crusts, and never comes sliced). They eat the toast with butter, jam, cucumbers, tomatoes, green peppers, a thick slice of white cheese, and milkless sugary tea they serve in tiny curved glasses rimmed with gold.

They drink tea in these glasses all day long. If you go to the Covered Bazaar to buy a carpet, a boy rushes out and brings the teas back on a swinging copper tray, and no one can take a car ferry across the Bosphorus without their glass of tea, although there is often more sugar in it than water.

Maureen Freely, *Enlightenment* (2007)

      ❋ ❋ ❋

And then there are the coffee shops, which have a long history here – Jan Neruda writing in 1870.

The house on the corner, behind the kiosk, has a ground floor coffee shop. In front of it, Europeans and Turks sit on low straw chairs drinking Turkish coffee, which is drunk without sugar and without milk and with the dregs, and everyone smokes from a nose warmer or the Nargile (water pipe). Coffee houses are, for the Oriental, more important than the tavern for us. And yet there was a time when there was not a single coffee house in all Constantinople. In retribution, that the uprising against Osman II began in one coffee house, his brother, Murad IV, had all five hundred coffee houses destroyed. The same also outlawed the smoking of tobacco, walked in disguise among the common people in search of secret smokers, and put them to death with his own hands. In the bazaars, in the name of God, it is still forbidden to smoke anywhere. So often has smoking been forbidden in Constantinople; sometimes it was not allowed to smoke at all, at other times only from a pipe. But in Constantinople any order lasts no longer than three days; by the fourth nobody pays it any further regard. Nowadays every man has a nose warmer in his mouth, every woman and every boy a cigarette, and on the local steamers there are special servants who must constantly carry hot coals and kindle the water pipes.

Jan Neruda, *Pictures from Abroad* (1870)
translated by Ray Furlong

* * *

And an evocative piece on some of the contemporary coffee shops.

The coffee shops are so different during winter in Istanbul. The chairs which had been in front of the door in summer are now inside, the open windows are closed and the heaters set up. The coffee shop coal heater in the middle of the shop, sometimes with the smell of smoke, sometimes with the smell of tangerines, is the black sun of the coffee shop.

In the early morning the construction workers, porters with cheese sandwiches made at the corner shop, sipping their tea from water glasses, sit at tables near the stove, chat, and try to get their fill of human kindness, which they will need throughout the day. Without it, it would be difficult to face the merciless cold or the unpredictable reactions from the people they are working for.

When they leave, it is the turn of the neighbourhood's retired. After having breakfast at home, scarves on their necks, caps on their heads, wearing long old coats, they come to play cards or backgammon. After being used to going to work early every day, they now make their way to the coffee shop, making their adaptation to retirement easier. Of course we must not forget the women who chase them away from their homes, saying 'get out from under my feet'. Around noon the retirees go home for a lunch break. During this break the coffee shop is aired. However, just as it is impossible to rid the table cloths of cigarette burns, it is impossible to rid the coffee shop of the smell of cigarettes, the dampness of the tea maker, the smoke of the fire. Towards evening when the coffee shop is well and truly hot and the windows steamed up, those who went to work in the morning start to return. They have either had bread and soup at the restaurant down the road, or if the day has gone well, they have eaten a good meal, or they will once again make do with cheese and bread. As the fatigue of the day weighs on their eyelids, after a few cups of tea, they stagger to the bachelor rooms a little way down the road. Once more they have survived a day in Istanbul. God help them tomorrow.

Mehmet Zaman Saçlıoğlu, 'Winter' in
Four Seasons Istanbul from 1000 Feet (2010)
translated by Hatice Ahmet Salih and Joan Eroncel

✳ ✳ ✳

Good Turkish food is wonderful, but a hungry Michael Booth warns against choosing the wrong kind of restaurant.

Having checked in at around eleven at night, I hit the streets, desperate to find somewhere to eat. So desperate was I that all my usual restaurant criteria were rashly cast aside. I headed up a steep side street opposite the hotel and into the first restaurant I could find: a hideous one-room joint, with bizarre

Portacabin-style plastic cladding on the walls. *Who Wants to be a Millionaire?* was playing on a fuzzy, wall-mounted TV screen in one corner, and around it were gathered most of the staff. Another waiter arrived shortly after me, carrying food for them all, which he had bought from a nearby takeaway. Not the most encouraging sign.

There was no menu, and my Turkish being rather rusty, it seemed that I would have to be satisfied with getting what I was given. This turned out to be a bowl of deep-fried breaded fish – more like bait actually. These were not quite small enough for me to comfortably crunch the whole, yet neither were they large enough for de-boning to be a practical option. I asked for bread; the owner laughed.

If the restaurant had been full I would have paid and left at that point, but I was the only diner, sitting in full view of the staff and owner, all of whom were watching me intently.

Millionaire built to its climax and to enliven the atmosphere I started shouting out random answers. By coincidence, I got the first four questions right, despite not having a clue what they were about and the staff began to regard me with a mistrustful awe. Following a quick calculation, I reckoned I could have walked away with a tidy sum of no less than two pounds eighty.

I gave up on the fish about a quarter of the way through – if I wanted to eat skinny pin cushions I would … actually I don't know what I would do if this were the case, but the whole scenario is pretty unlikely, so let's just say I had little confidence that any of the waiters could administer the Heimlick manoeuvre, and leave it at that. I asked for a receipt; the owner laughed. It had been one of the worst restaurant experiences of my life (and that includes the time vomit came out of my nose after a rogue knickerbocker glory in the Haywards Heath Wimpey *c.* 1977).

Michael Booth, *Just As Well I'm Leaving* (2005)

* * *

He might have done better to go for some of the 'street food' on offer.

They walked out of the restaurant into an exquisite Bosphorus landscape sparkling under the late winter sun. They put their hands over their eyes to block the sun. Both took a deep breath and knew instantly that spring was in the air.

Having no better plans, they strolled through the neighbourhood, buying something from almost every street vendor they came upon: boiled sweet corn, stuffed mussels, semolina halva, and finally, a large package of sunflower seeds. With each new treat, they launched on a new topic, talking about many things, except the three customary untouchables between young women who were still strangers to one another: sex, men, and fathers.

Elif Shafak, *The Bastard of Istanbul* (2007)

* * *

Some winter 'street treats' – and necessities – described by Mehmet Zaman Saçlıoğlu.

In the past each season came with its fruit and vegetables. Even though every fruit is available, certain foods and drinks on the stalls and in the streets announce with joy the coming of the seasons. The coming of winter is announced by chestnuts. As the weather gets colder, the numbers of chestnut sellers increase. The coal burning in a small brazier is both the seller's heater and his trade. A small set of scales stands next to the stall, a fifty gram weight on one tray and a hundred gram weight on the other. There are also paper bags which take exactly that amount. In any case no one buys more than this. Chestnuts are not meant to fill you up, they are only for taste. They are a friendship ... it should fit into your palm so that by the time you get to the cinema your hands are warmed. Most customers turn

111

a blind eye to a seller who, with sleight of hand, puts a wormy chestnut into the packet first. What is he to do, he doesn't know, he is not inside the chestnut! ... If one chestnut in the paper bag is wormy, no one says a word, but if two or three are, then the customer may turn back to have them exchanged. As the seller knows this, he treats everyone equally. One wormy chestnut in a fifty gram packet, and two in a hundred gram packet, does not annoy anyone, and the seller doesn't lose out either. Some customers ask if the chestnuts have protein in them. It is a joke, but is also a warning not to give them wormy chestnuts. This doesn't make a difference though since no one can change the way sellers work.

Now that we are in the month of January, we are used to the quinces. They have been in the grocers for two or three months. They are plentiful in the markets. In the old days they would say that if the quince was plentiful then winter would be harsh, but now in Istanbul the saying doesn't hold true. Apples and pears have been with us quite some time. Tangerines and oranges have also been in the big markets for months, but it is only now that they are tasty. They have found their season. Half of the tarhana pickles, tomato and peppers pastes which have come from Anatolia, on buses to Harem, in October and November have been used up in most homes. In the cold winter tarhana soup is a necessity. And after dinner, tahini and grape molasses are a treat. A small cup of grape molasses drunk by children in the morning on their way to school not only gives them strength but protects them from the cold as well. [...]

If the chestnut sellers are the harbinger of the coming of winter, the boza sellers are the portent of the winter becoming harsher. On the ferryboats and motorboats carrying Istanbul residents from one shore to another, as well as serving tea and coffee, there are other drinks available in winter. One is salep (a drink made from powdered orchid root), another linden. Linden is first seen near the end of autumn.

The changes in the seasons in Istanbul bring with them colds and flu. The whole city starts to cough and sneeze. It is then that the queen of herbs, linden, takes her place in homes, coffee shops and on ferryboats. As for salep, due to the reduced number of orchid roots and salep powder becoming more expensive, it is now so watered down that you feel like exclaiming 'where is the old salep?' It is reinforced with milk and smothered in cinnamon to make it tasty and, even if it is not as good as before, it is still beneficial to cold hands and chests. The coffee shops are where salep, linden tea and black tea are consumed among friendly conversations, the sound from backgammon boards, jokes and curses.

Mehmet Zaman Saçlıoğlu, 'Winter' in
Four Seasons Istanbul from 1000 Feet (2010)
translated by Hatice Ahmet Salih and Joan Eroncel

* * *

Although well-known for her fantasy stories, Çiler İlhan (b.1972) gets down to the very real business of eating out in Istanbul – the place that taught her to love food.

I like the fact that this city has more restaurants than I can find time to get to, to sample, however less than filling, high quality or delicious the fare offered by some. I love eating in Istanbul; it was in this city I learned to love food. Istanbul leaves a Cabernet Sauvignon taste in my mouth, sharp, rounded after many years in the private cave of a wealthy and intellectual connoisseur who, having given up his business interests, has dedicated himself to wine. This domineering red that always gives me a headache if I consume more than a couple of glasses reminds me of the fragility of life: fine in moderation, harmful in excess. That fine red line. That single breath that separates life and death. The superiority of sailing the Bosphorus in an elegant *gulet* and the menace one feels wandering at three a.m.

the side streets of Tarlabaşı, supposedly 'gentrified', the consequence of an infinite optimism. Istanbul constantly reminds one that he or she is alive. Istanbul constantly reminds one of the fragility of life.

When it comes to food, I, like many other people, pick not only the restaurant, but the location and atmosphere. It would be desirable for the restaurant to be airy, spacious, bright and somehow blessed with a view ('The Bosphorus', 'the city', 'the park', or by other *ways of seeing* 'overlooking the ugly masses of property development sited over burnt forests', 'overlooking the concrete jungles heaped over one another' or even 'overlooking a huddle of stunted plants not even meriting the definition of a park or even a garden.') The next thing I'm picky about is the food. If we're going for something ethnic, I defer to my husband, whose palate is far more sophisticated than mine. If it's breakfast, then it has to be Emirgan or Bebek. If it's seafood, it has to be Yeniköy, Tarabya, any one of the Hisar or Asian side villages or the tiny bays in Beylerbeyi. And for reading-writing-daydreaming, Asmalımescit. Here I go again, only writing of districts, instead of the food. The way to my stomach obviously goes through the district and the atmosphere; food feeds my soul, instead of serving the flavour of the morsels I put into my mouth, this much is clear. In any case, my tastes are far too ordinary to support a claim of sophistication; I've never once, for instance, wanted to eat snail paté.

I might as well come clean: my problem is with drinking, rather than eating. Please take a moment before you pronounce smugly, 'There you go, yet another dipsomaniac of a writer.' It is water I am addicted to above all. Then, black tea. Then, green tea. Other drinks I like: espresso (only when appropriate, occasionally a small one, occasionally decaffeinated,) and red wine (what a limited portfolio, huh?). Give me the drinks, the food can come later. As for groundnuts though, call them peanuts or whatever, I never had another one since that time. I must have

114

stuffed my face enough to feel bloated. But I have made new discoveries! The tiny ice cream shop in Bebek. I'm not much of a one for ice cream, (that's just the way I am) but I do like that one. Perhaps it was the immediacy of slipping down to the road in comfy slippers of an evening, stepping out of the house that overlooks the Bosphorus. Here we go, diverging from food once more. Now we're talking of belonging, of peace, the ice cream but an excuse.

Çiler İlhan, 'Groundnut Sky Cake' (2011)
translated by Feyza Howell

✳ ✳ ✳

French visitor Daniel Rondeau describes the food and atmosphere in ordinary working-class restaurants.

It's difficult to ignore them for long, Galatasaray and Fener-bahçe – the two football teams with their clubs of supporters, the UltraAslan (Ultralions) and the Canaries, who occupy pride of place in the life of the city as once upon a time the two factions of the Hippodrome did in the daily lives of the inhabitants of Byzantium. In order to take the pulse of the city and measure its sacred passion for football (the only religion encouraged by Kemalist secularism, some say), you only have to take yourself to one of the countless working-class restaurants where, every evening, thousands of people get together to eat and have a good time: smoky cheap restaurants belonging to a chain known for its charcoal-grilled meat; fish restaurants; the brasseries of Beyoğlu; local pubs, like those around the 'women's market' (Kadınlar Pazarı, a village of wooden houses between an aquaduct and the fire station, where olive oil, honey, pistachios, herb cheese, vegetables and sides of meat are brought each morning from farms in the east of the country). In all these establishments, television sets are on continually, though no-one pays any attention to them (even the goings-on of the Turkish version of 'Big Brother' don't attract a single glance).

The 'show' is no doubt there on the plates, where meatballs with cumin and garlic are sending up wafts of odour alongside aubergines in tomato sauce, the most popular dishes at the tables – tables onto which clamber young women in clingy trousers, without even waiting until after the desserts of rice pudding or crystallised quince, and dance between the empty glasses, something never to be seen on the television screen. But all that changes on match evenings. The room is divided in two. The clients arrange themselves mentally into one of the two camps, their eyes glued to the television sets (as are those of the waiters, making it better to hold back until half time or breaks in play to give orders), and shouts of distress or joy punctuate the stages of the match, while outside, until the final whistle, the streets stay strangely silent.

Daniel Rondeau, *Istanbul* (2002)
translated by Erica King

"One rainy afternoon the bookseller, who sees and hears everything, gave Onur and myself a short lecture on the sociology of the bridge"

Geert Mak

Stamboullus

No matter how beautiful or interesting a city might be – its location, its buildings, its history – its character is largely determined by the people who live there. We start with a 'God's-eye-view' of the city's people waking up, from Elif Shafak.

It is almost dawn, a short step away from that uncanny threshold between night-time and daylight. It is the only time in which it is still possible to find solace in dreams and yet too late to build them anew.

117

If there is an eye in the seventh sky, a Celestial Gaze watching each and every one from way up high, He would have had to keep Istanbul under surveillance for quite some time to get a sense of who did what behind closed doors and who, if any, uttered profanities. To the one in the skies, this city must look like a scintillating pattern of speckled glows in all directions, like a firecracker going off amid thick darkness. Right now the urban pattern glowing here is in the hues of orange, ginger, and ochre. It is a configuration of sparkles, each dot a light lit by someone awake at this hour. From where the Celestial Gaze is situated, from that high above, all these sporadically lit bulbs must seem in perfect harmony, constantly flickering, as if coding a cryptic message to God.

Apart from the scattered twinkles, it is still densely dark in Istanbul. Whether along the grimy, narrow streets snaking the oldest quarters, in the modern apartment buildings cramming the newly built districts, or throughout the fancy suburbs, people are fast asleep. All but some.

Some Istanbulites have, as usual, awakened earlier than others. The *imams* all around the city, for instance; the young and the old, the mellow-voiced and the not-so-mellow-voiced, the *imams* of the copious mosques are the first ones to wake up, ready to call the believers to morning prayer. Then there are the *simit* vendors. They too are awake, headed to their respective bakeries to pick up the crispy sesame bagels they will be selling all day long. Accordingly, the bakers are awake too. Most of them get only a few hours of sleep before they start work, while others never sleep at night. Every day without exception, the bakers heat their ovens in the middle of the night, so that before dawn, the bakeries in the city are thick with the delicious smell of bread.

The cleaning ladies are also awake. These women, of all ages, get up early to take at least two or three different buses to arrive at the houses of the well-off, where they will scrub, clean,

and polish all day long. It is a different world here. The wealthy
women always wear makeup and never show their age. Unlike
the husbands of the cleaning ladies, the husbands in suburbia
are always busy, surprisingly polite, and somewhat effeminate.
Time is not a scarce commodity in suburbia. People use it as
lavishly and freely as hot water.

It is dawn now. The city is a gummy, almost gelatinous entity
at this moment, an amorphous shape half-liquid, half-solid.

Elif Shafak, *The Bastard of Istanbul* (2007)

❉ ❉ ❉

At the opposite end of the day, when the last late-
nighters have finally gone home, those who feel out of
tune with the modern city can find a place to revisit
the familiar past. From a short story by Hikmet
Hükümenoğlu (b.1971).

In her youth, Cemile Abla used to love to walk to Bebek and get
a cherry-vanilla ice-cream cone, sit on a park bench with a dog-
eared Sait Faik book, and just relax. But nowadays, in front of
the ice-cream stands stood long lines of bronze, blonde-haired
girls, pot-bellied boys, and odd, shaggy dogs of a sort she had
never seen before. Cemile Abla had begun to feel like a stranger
in her own land, as if at any given moment she might be caught
and deported. But instead of worrying herself over nothing,
she'd made a resolution not to venture beyond the cemetery,
the boundary of white marble separating Rumelihisarı from
Bebek, during normal waking hours. She would go for walks
in the wee hours of the night, once the fancy dining high-lifers
and the bar brawlers had hopped into their cars (which were
usually parked on the sidewalk and nearly toppling into the
sea) and gone home, once all the apartment lights had been
turned off, once all the dogs had stopped howling.

What she liked most about these walks was the fishermen.
Because of the wall of wedding boats blocking the shore,

not many fishermen, other than Captain Hasan, stopped by these parts anymore. But there were a few who, as if by some unspoken agreement, would draw their boats ashore in the shadow of Hisar on moonlit nights and, if they happened to be in the mood, reminisce about the old days for hours on end. Sometimes they'd lean on the old cannons at the base of the towers. It made Cemile Abla happy to see them as she walked along the deserted sidewalks and the asphalt roads now devoid of passing cars. She'd join them when invited; there was no need to insist. She would join them not because she couldn't say no, but because their conversations reminded her of her father. She'd sit down on the old blanket they'd have spread out on the ground, sticking her legs out to the side and bending them just so, and then she'd cover her knees with the edge of her topcoat and sip on the half-full tea glass of undiluted *rakı* that they'd offer. It was during those hours that the fishermen, so reticent during the daytime, would wax talkative; they'd discuss sea currents and schools of fish, they'd tell stories about the adventures of Ali Reis, ask Cemile Abla how she was getting on, and then, when dawn began to break, they'd get back into their boats, their minds at ease, knowing that they had done their duty and tended after the daughter of the great man who preceded them. Then they would head out into the foggy waters of the Black Sea.

Hikmet Hükümenoğlu, 'The Smell of Fish'
from *Istanbul Noir* (2008)
translated by Amy Spangler and Mustafa Ziyalan

✻ ✻ ✻

In this extract from Hotel Bosphorus, *Esmahan Aykol introduces us to a place where different social strata of Stamboullus can be seen together – and shows what is possibly a common locals' reaction to a visitor's enthusiasm!*

We strolled along the tree-lined road, full of exhaust fumes, which led to the tea gardens in Ortaköy, chatting about German cinema, without any mention of the film or its director. With some *simits* from a street seller and mature *kaşar* cheese from a corner shop near the square in Ortaköy, we went to sit in the tea garden nearest to the sea. Ortaköy is an interesting district. The gulf between classes, which is glaringly obvious in Istanbul, is just as evident here but somehow doesn't oppress people. For instance, we were sitting in a fairly cheap municipal tea garden, yet just behind the garden we could see luxury chauffeured cars queuing up at the doors of the former Esma Sultan Palace for a society wedding. Ortaköy is one of several districts in Istanbul where the jet-set and ordinary people can live and enjoy themselves in close proximity.

As soon as the waiter left us alone, Petra started relating what she had done the day before. It was the first time since she arrived that she'd had an opportunity to look round Istanbul and, like all normal tourists, she had visited Sultan Ahmed. Until that city tour, my friend had probably thought the beauty of Istanbul consisted of the view of the Bosphorus she could see from her hotel window. She started to describe with surprised excitement the wonders of Topkapı Palace, Hagia Sophia, the Underground Reservoir and the Sultan Ahmed mosque, which she had visited during her tour of the historical peninsula the day before. But I interrupted her: I'd spent the last thirteen years, as well as my first seven, in Istanbul and had had frequent visitors who all told the same stories, with the same expression of enthusiasm and wonder. I found it nauseating.

Esmahan Aykol, *Hotel Bosphorus* (2004)
translated by Ruth Whitehouse

✳ ✳ ✳

For most of its history, Istanbul has been a multi-ethnic, multi-faith society in which differing peoples

*and cultures were not only able to co-exist in reason-
able peace and safety but were encouraged to make
positive contributions to the life of the city. Yashar
Kemal describes one particularly diverse district.*

Ali Şah lives in Dolapdere. And this Dolapdere is by far the
most enchanting quarter of Istanbul, a bustling hodgepodge
of a place. Istanbul is immense, the city seems to stretch on
and on infinitely, its populace teems like ants, but the limits
of this multiformity, this hugeness, are well-defined. Dolapdere
is small, but it is a universe in itself, boundless in its variety.
One can confidently assert that it is unique in the world. A
labyrinth of streets and alleys, of shanties, brothels and ill-
famed hotels, yet chaste and pure at heart ... Dirty enough to
engulf all of Istanbul, yet its dwellings scoured clean as a new
penny ... A pageant of humanity, garage mechanics, odd-job
men who can repair oil lamps, sailors' lanterns, people who
can produce a brand-new bicycle out of a couple of old wheels,
rebuild a car, devise some new kind of outboard motor or even
an original watercraft ... Cobblers hammering in hobnails,
weavers, lottery-men and people drawing for lots, vendors of
black-market cigarettes, hard-drinking carousers who know
how to hold their drink, blind-drunk boozers – you can run
across all kinds in Dolapdere. All the failures, the wash-outs
of the universe seem to have taken refuge here and found an
anchorage. In Dolapdere, vice and turpitude, corruption and
treachery are rampant, but so are friendship and love. Indeed,
it is a magic town. Whatever his origin, whether he comes from
the mansion of a bey or the tent of a gypsy, the man who has
once lived in Dolapdere will never again escape from its slime
and hurly-burly, not if you offer him the whole world. Kurd
or gypsy, English, French, Laz, Turk or Turkoman, Arab or
Persian, once a man has settled here, wild horses cannot drag
him away.

All kinds of languages are spoken in Dolapdere. Swarthy gypsies, fair-haired immigrants, tall Kurds, beautiful-eyed Georgians, and countless others have brought with them their thousand and one songs, their thousand and one dialects. Not in the whole of Istanbul is there a place to match Dolapdere. In fact, I defy anyone to show me another like it in the whole world.

Yashar Kemal, *The Birds Have Also Gone* (1978)
translated by Thilda Kemal (1987)

❉ ❉ ❉

A Turkish author writing in German, Emine Sevgi Özdamar (b.1946) reflects the cultural complexity of the city in this extract from My Istanbul, *translated for this anthology.*

When I was a child, four hundred thousand people lived in Istanbul.

Back then our neighbour Madame Atina ('Athena'), an Istanbul Greek, used to pull her aging cheeks back behind her ears and stick them down with sticky tape. My job was to help her. She said to me: 'I'm a Byzantine like the Hagia Sophia church which was built in the time of the Byzantine Emperor Constantine the Great, in A.D. 326. It was a basilica with stone walls and a wooden roof. The Byzantines believed that they were nearer to God in the Hagia Sophia than anywhere else, and I too believe that I'm nearer to the moon in Constantinople than anywhere else on earth.' With the sticky tape behind her ears Madame Atina would go to the fruit shop. I went with her. With her ears pulled back she looked young, so I walked quickly. She tried to walk as quickly as me but sometimes she fell over in the street. The owner of the fruit shop was a Muslim and he joked with Madame Atina: 'Madame, a Muslim angel came along, he stuck his finger in a hole in a pillar and turned the Hagia Sophia to face Mecca.' I loved the Hagia Sophia, its floor was uneven and on the walls you could see frescos of Christ without a cross, a muezzin sang the ezan from a minaret, and at night the moon shone down on Christ's face and on the face of the muezzin.

One time Madame Atina took the ship over to the Asiatic side with me. I was seven years old. My mother said: 'See, the Istanbul Greeks are the salt and sugar of the city.' And Madame Atina showed me her own personal Constantinople.'See that small tower by the sea. The Byzantine emperor, who had been prophesied that his daughter would be bitten by a snake and killed, had this Leander's Tower (Maiden's Tower) built near Üsküdar and hid her away here. One day the girl had a longing for figs so they brought her a basket of figs from the city and she was bitten by the snake that had hidden in the basket and died.' Madame Atina took my face in her hands and said: 'My girl, with these pretty eyes you will burn many men's hearts.' The sun lit up her painted red fingernails, and behind them I could see the Maiden's Tower by the sea.

Then Madame Atina walked across the Golden Horn Bridge with me. Back then, as I walked across the low bridge which moved in time with the waves, I didn't know that Leonardo da Vinci – the Ottomans called him Lecardo – had written a letter to the Sultan once, on 3 July 1503. The Sultan had wanted him to build a bridge over the Golden Horn, and in his letter Leonardo put his proposals to the Sultan. Another proposal came in 1504 from Michelangelo. But Michelangelo had a question: 'If I were to build this bridge, would the Sultan insist that I adopt the Islamic faith?' The Franciscan abbot who discussed the Sultan's proposal with Michelangelo said: 'No my son, I know Istanbul as well as I know Rome. I don't know which of these cities has more sinners. The Ottoman Sultan would never ask something like that of you.' But Michelangelo wasn't able to build the bridge after all, because the Pope threatened to excommunicate the artist. For centuries the Ottomans didn't build a bridge between the two European sides of Istanbul because Muslims lived in one part and Jews, Greeks and Armenians lived in the other part. Instead fishing boats took people from one side to another. Finally Sultan Mahmud II (1808–1836) decided to bring the Muslims and non-Muslims in Istanbul together and had the famous bridge built. When it was finished the fishermen banged on the bridge with sticks because it had deprived them of work. The bridge acted as a stage: Jews, Turks, Greeks, Arabs, Albanians, Armenians, Europeans, Persians, Circassians, women, men, horses, donkeys, cows, chickens, camels, they all crossed the bridge.

Emine Sevgi Özdamar, *My Istanbul* (2001)
translated by Lyn Marven

❊ ❊ ❊

A sad sight described by Ahmed Hamdi Tanpınar
– laid out on the pavement, the personal belong-
ings Stamboullus are being forced to sell, telling of
personal tragedies and changed fortunes in the teeming
city. Although set some years ago, such a sight is not
uncommon in cities around the world today.

Çardırcılar Street was bewildering as always. On the ground before a shop whose grate usually remained shuttered, waiting for who knows what, were a Russian-made samovar spigot, a doorknob, the remnants of a lady's mother-of-pearl fan so much the fashion thirty years ago, a few random parts belonging perhaps to a largish clock or gramophone, together with some oddities that had ended up here without breaking or crumbling to pieces somehow. A traditional coffee grinder of yellow brass and a cane handle made of deer antler were prominently displayed. Leaning against the shop's rolling shutter rested two sizable photographs in thick, gilt wooden frames: pictures of Ottoman-era Greek Orthodox patriarchs from the reign of Sultan Abdülhamit II or a little afterward. Their medals,

125

garments, and emblems were identical to those that appeared in the newspapers. From behind well-polished glass, through the vantage of time past, they gazed at the objects spread out before them and at the street crowds temporarily obscuring them at each surge. Perchance they were most pleased by the roar of life sounding so many years later – by the therapy of sun and sound.

Mümtaz wondered, *Did the photographer nudge and prod them the way the man who takes my photos does?*

He sought traces of such primping in the folds of their loose-fitting robes and in their expressions, which had striven for years to merge grace with representational grandeur.

Above them hung a handsome Arabic calligraphy panel in a kitschy plaster frame: *Hüvessemiulalîm*, 'the One who discerns and knows all.' The rigid plaster hadn't destroyed the vitality of the script. Each curve and curl articulated its message.

The peculiar quirks of this little street, however, weren't limited to just a few. A Nevâkâr song from a Darülelham conservatory record being played in a shop a bit farther down revealed and concealed its own numinous world like a rose garden under a deluge, while a fox-trot blared from a gramophone across the way. Mümtaz stared down the full length of the street, which seemed to rise vertically, searing his eyes under the midafternoon sun. Heaps of castoff items, bed frames, broken and worn-out furniture, folding screens with torn panels, and braziers were aligned and stacked atop each other in phalanxes along either side of the street.

Most regrettable were the mattresses and pillows, which constituted a tragedy simply by having ended up here. Mattresses and pillows ... the array of dreams and the countless slumbers they contained. The fox-trot dissolved in the snarl of an unwound spring and was immediately followed by an old *türkü* one would only chance to hear under such circumstances. 'The gardens of Çamlıca ... ' Mümtaz recognised the singer as Memo. The full sorrow of the last days of the reign of Sultan Abdülhamit II persisted in the memory of this singer, a cadet in the military academy, who'd drowned in the waters of the Golden Horn. His voice overspread these remnants of life like a grand and luminous marquee. What a dense and intricate life the alley possessed. How all of Istanbul, including every variety and assortment of its fashions and its greatest intimacies and surprises, flowed through here, composing a novel of material objects and discarded life fragments. Or, rather, everyone's quotidian life had gathered here entwined arm in arm as if proving that within our separate workaday lives, nothing new under the sun existed.

Every accident, every illness, every demolition, every tragedy that occurred in the city each day and each hour had cast these objects here, eliminating their individuality, making them public property, and forging an aggregate arranged through the hand-to-hand cooperation between chance and misery.

Ahmet Hamdi Tanpınar, *A Mind at Peace* (1949)
translated by Erdağ Göknar (2008)

※ ※ ※

In this extract from her novel The Colour Saffron, *İnci Aral (b.1944) depicts a resident of the city who has just started to personally experience what life is like for people in one of the poorer neighbourhoods.*

Eylem got off the dolmuş at the beginning of the street. She walked down turning right first and then left twice. With the apartment buildings lined side by side, the streets resembled cement walls. They had become even narrower because of the cars parked on both sides. Football shouts, arabesque songs, the exaggerated and affected sounds of old local films blaring from television sets turned on too loud were pouring out of open windows that never saw the sun. Even the banging drums of the music shop further along the road were not enough to smother the din which confused the mind at this time of the evening.

She had left her work place at six. Now it was almost eight. Her flat was certainly not easy to get to, but she had hired it because the rent was low and it was close to her sister. However, going to and from work took two hours every day because of the traffic and this was sapping her energy.

The empty street was drowned in the dull blue neon reflections of the water shop, the pastry shop and the grocer's. She saw the dark and handsome water distributor come to the door. She felt his eyes on her even after she had passed in front of him. She had moved to the apartment building on the other side of the road two weeks ago. She left every morning and came back in the evening. He was probably trying to figure out who this strange woman was. Or perhaps he was simply looking at her legs, because she had shortened all her skirts the week before.

She crossed the street, the sticky, dusty hum of the cool Indian summer evening getting louder in her ears. She was still living as a spectator and not as a participator in the neighbourhood. She observed emotionally, not deeply or with understanding. She felt intensely foreign and had an annoying suspicion of being followed. Even the children seemed unpleasant, insolent and repulsive at times. She thought that the look she gave them on such occasions probably carried a certain amount of violence and she felt ashamed.

Of course she was not blind. These people were living under difficult conditions and were fighting to hang on to life. They were too busy trying to overcome their fear of loneliness by being noisy, to be compatible with the rules of civilization, and to deserve their food, while quietly sharpening their endurance. They were not in the least interested whether or not 'the human quality, the cultural tissue of the city had deteriorated; a strange nomadic culture of the slums had become dominant.'

It was true, wealth and culture made everything beautiful, whereas poverty and ignorance deformed things as much as possible. She felt in her mouth the bitterness of the dark tea she had drunk at tea break that afternoon. Her thoughts did not match the reality of her own life. These were the worries of the well-heeled. What concerned her now was the fact that it would be difficult to get used to this neighbourhood filled with undeveloped, degenerate, fanatical people, where men in undershirts and women in headscarves sat at the windows and narrow balconies, and sounds of nose-blowing and throat-clearing and children screaming came from the light shafts. She would get accustomed to all this whether she liked it or not. The obligation of belonging would dominate and she would have to accept the place where she lived. For the time being, she didn't have the means to live anywhere else. For the time being? Who knew if there would be anything else?

As she opened her door, she wondered once again what her new life had in store for her. Would it be good to know? She wasn't sure. For a long time before becoming a mature person, one thought that the future consisted of a continuous spring, happy surprises, peace and illumination. One didn't think, or perhaps didn't want to think that it would also contain pains, sorrows, losses and great misfortunes.

As always the stairwell smelled of fried green peppers, burnt onions and of sewer. She entered her flat. She passed through the hall where the boxes with books were still piled up and entered the living room. She turned on the light and immediately closed the curtains. The most unpleasant thing about this little basement flat was that it could be watched easily, or at least, that was the impression it gave her. Fortunately it was only the living room that overlooked the street. The bedroom at the end of the corridor opened onto the unkempt back garden of the building which was full of wild weeds. Although the door with the iron bars did not give her much confidence, she planned to cut the grass outside and put a portable table there as soon as it was spring. If she didn't mind the upper back balconies full of old, rusty stuff where slave dogs barked constantly, she would have a small location where she could breath, drink her morning or afternoon tea every so often

İnci Aral, *The Colour Saffron* (2007)
translated by Melahet Behlil

❊ ❊ ❊

Life is hard for the city's stallholders, but even harder for those who have to make do with the markets' left-overs.

One of the most difficult jobs during winter is being a street market stallholder. Very early in the morning the trucks go to the street where the market will be set up. Some come at night, park their vehicles and sleep. The metal structures are constructed, the awnings are stretched, and the stalls set up. The morning customers are those who look for the best quality goods, those who have no money worries. In the afternoon, depending on how well sales are doing, the price reductions start. By evening, what's left on the stalls is half price. The stall-holders are now cold. Selling the few remaining kilos will not make them rich. It is then that the poorest go to the market. They pay almost nothing or get for free the withered fruit and vegetables from the stallholder.

In this way a few more kitchens will have been stocked. Evening comes; the stallholders get into their trucks, and set off for another area of the city. The streets are full of plastic bags flying around, remnants of fruit and vegetables, broken crates. Everyone awaits the rubbish truck for even this rubbish has takers. Before the municipality cleaners come, other cleaners come to the streets. In summer or winter at the top of the list of those who traipse the streets are the young rubbish collectors with their hand carts and massive sacks. Gypsy girls come. At set times their trucks wait in appointed places in the side streets to accept the collected rubbish. They empty the sacks and then rush back to the streets to fill up their sacks once more. It's said that the stones and dirt of Istanbul are gold, but somehow this gold looks like something else. Mostly it looks like dirt ... First the rubbish is collected and sorted by children, then the cats, crows, then what has spilled in the street is sorted by dogs, so there is little left for the municipality rubbish collectors.

Mehmet Zaman Saçlıoğlu, 'Winter' in
Four Seasons Istanbul from 1000 Feet (2010)
translated by Hatice Ahmet Salih and Joan Eroncel

✳ ✳ ✳

The protagonist of a short story by Barış Müstecaplıoğlu (b.1977) fondly recalls the city's old Gypsy neighbourhood.

It was still the middle of the night; in a few hours, the streets would be packed with vehicles bound for the Bosphorus Bridge. One of Istanbul's more fashionable neighbourhoods, Altunizade was home to modern office buildings with glass façades and shiny apartment complexes reserved for the upper crust, all surrounding the grandiose shopping centre, Capitol. The truck passed first by the apartment complexes, then by Capitol, then by the office buildings, before driving through an underpass and emerging at the top of a hill that led down to Üsküdar and the Bosphorus shore.

Ali knew this street well. When he was a kid, he used to come and visit his grandfather here, in a house in the Gypsy neighbourhood behind the riot police building. He was fond of his grandfather; in fact, Ali was the only person in his family whom the man really liked. A generous Istanbul gentleman with a dour face but a heart of gold, he had always had a big soft spot for his grandson. Disowned by his daughters, the old man had taken his final refuge in this neighbourhood. Ali would come here alone to see him, usually without even telling his mother. He felt safe, as if he belonged, there amongst the Gypsies, who sat on the sidewalk chatting, and amongst the slovenly children and the old, wrinkly faced women watching the passersby, and even amongst the trash that littered the street from one end to the next. Poverty had always had an allure for him; he felt more comfortable in run-down neighbourhoods like this one than he did in fancy restaurants or upscale hotels.

The avenue was every bit as fascinating now as it had been back then. It was like the crossroads of two civilisations, with police buildings situated like a border control between two different cultures, splitting the avenue almost right down the middle. Below the riot police building was the Gypsy quarter, which was always rowdy with weddings or brawls, while above it stood rows of two-storey houses, each with its own garden, all left behind by the Greeks, all still standing calm and silent amongst the centuries-old plane trees.

Barış Müstecaplıoğlu, 'An Extra Body' (2008)
in *Istanbul Noir*, edited and translated by
Amy Spangler and Mustafa Ziyalan

✳ ✳ ✳

The very poorest inhabitants of the city might find
themselves living in such places as that described by
Gönül Kıvılcım (b.1963) in her novel Razor Boy,
which reminds us how hard it can be just to exist in
a great city.

The new place was between the concrete platforms of a viaduct. Happiness villas! Above them, life streamed in the cars that drove at full speed. Sullen couples, lonely bosses, business women with leather briefcases drove their cars without being aware of the misery that prevailed under their tires. The 'other' residents of the city led a life in an invisible hole in the same city in the space between the legs of the bridge. The field below was entirely deserted, but all of a sudden, like in three seconds, a wooden ladder would be let down from beneath the bridge and some creatures would climb down. They took refuge in the empty concrete space that had been left under the viaduct for the electric installation and piping as if they took shelter under a parasol on a scorching beach.

Kunt caught sight of the unclaimed piece of land near the highway while he was touring around to find a place that would remain unnoticed by the police captain. He heard the sound of dogs and went under the viaduct, and as soon as he looked up, he knew it was his lucky day. The concrete platform promised a hole and a hope. The following day, Kunt stole a ladder from one of the shops in the area in order to carry out his expedition. He placed the ladder against the strange hole in the concrete, climbed up and sneaked in through the hole, and that's how he found the room that was big enough to make his friends sing happy tunes. The concrete space under the highway was a perfect shelter, which would, for sure, remain unnoticed. After they moved to their new place, the wooden ladder they kept hanging down and pulling up the concrete platform became their only connection with the world outside.

The place inside the viaduct was their kitchen, living room and also bedroom. They didn't have tables, chairs, expensive flowers, but they had mattresses they could sleep on in the winter, electricity they had illegally wired from the highway and walls on which everyone could hang the picture he wanted. Müslüm Baba greeted from the wall those who woke up in the frosty morning. What is more, they even had a black and white television set, a camping gas cylinder and dainty tea glasses. When they climbed upstairs, they took off their shoes as though they lived in a house that was cleaned every day.

Gönül Kıvılcım, *Razor Boy* (2002)
translated by Çiğdem Aksoy

* * *

A familiar sight in many great cities – youngsters touting flowers, hoping against hope that those rich enough to dine in restaurants will buy a rose or two. This next extract, from Gaye Boralıoğlu's Syncopated Rhythm, *gives an insight into the life of a young Istanbul flower-seller whose 'patch' is much more hazardous than eating establishments.*

On the wings of one of the flower-seller women from the neighbourhood Güldane flew to the place where she would be selling flowers. Together they landed on a street with heavy traffic, in Etiler, an upper class district of Istanbul. The older woman showed Güldane where she would hide her flower basket: one of the apartment building's custodians, or *kapıcı*s, was one of their own. He'd arranged a little spot behind the door for the basket. Then the woman placed three bunches of roses in Güldane's hand; as she did so, she made sure to pluck off the yellowed leaves. And then with the back of her hand she sprinkled some water on them. Though the rosebuds shined brightly, the truth was, none of them came even close to the magnificence that was Güldane. The woman placed Güldane amongst the cars on the street and left.

Güldane never forgot that day. She was going to sell flowers to the passing cars whenever the traffic jammed up; but the job wasn't nearly as simple as it seemed. There in the dust and the smoke, smothered by exhaust, trapped amongst cars heading straight towards her, Güldane's head began to spin. She'd never experienced anything like it before. She'd never experienced such dizziness, such befuddlement, such a desire to throw herself to the ground, such a wish to fly away; Güldane had never known the world like this before.

She couldn't tell when the cars would stop, when they would start, when they would slow down, when they would speed up. It was as if she'd fallen headfirst into a seething Devil's cauldron. How many times she barely escaped getting run over by one car, the brakes squealing to a halt, while trying to catch up with the next. How many times she had bouquets whisked away by a driver slamming on the gas as soon as traffic opened back up, without even getting her money. How many times side mirrors slammed into her chest. How many times the world spun around her, and she nearly crumpled. She stopped, she sat, she stood, she vomited, her eyes welled up with tears – she couldn't help it. But still, she didn't cry; at one point her ears heard a strange wheezing sound coming out of her mouth.

That day it was as if thousands of cars had run not down the street but right over Güldane.

By the time she got back home, she was on the verge of death. Without eating a bite, without drinking a sip, without saying a word to anyone, she went straight to her room and got under the covers; that night, she didn't go out at all. [...]

When she awoke at dawn, there was a strength within her, a strength resembling a thirst for revenge. She didn't eat a crumb, she didn't mutter a word to anyone, she snatched up her basket of flowers and threw herself onto the street.

When she arrived in Etiler it wasn't yet seven o'clock. The sun had only just risen and one by one people had begun to leave their homes. During those minutes, when traffic wasn't busy, Güldane left her basket at the stash and, without taking out a single flower, she stood there on the side of the street, which she set about scrutinizing from beginning to end. She took it all in: at what intervals the traffic lights changed colours. How the cars stopped and started, how they drew near to one another and then apart, where the spaces that could hide Güldane might form, exactly when a car that appeared at the top of the street would reach the end of it. All of these things she recorded in her mind, one by one.

Once she was sure she that she had gathered sufficient knowledge, she went to her stash, took out a few bouquets, and dived into the midst of the cars. She no longer stood so close to the traffic lights; that way, she'd have more time to stand next to the cars in her attempt to make a sale, since traffic would be jammed up until the light changed anyway. She never handed over any flowers until she'd got paid. She didn't get too close to the cars; that way, she avoided bumping into the sideview mirrors. She didn't move too quickly, and she didn't try to throw herself onto the sidewalk whenever she panicked; around the spaces that formed between the cars she wove, as if dancing.

Though she did experience a few minor mishaps now and then, by the end of the first week, Güldane had become completely fluent at her new job. She felt the rhythm of the street, every beat of it, inside her; she wandered amongst the cars as if wandering amongst the beats of Yunus's drum.

Once she'd got a grasp of this physical aspect of the job, she gradually began to develop sales techniques. For example, whenever the cars stopped, she would look at each driver, decide upon one, and approach him or her with determined steps. Without blinking she would look each one straight in the eyes, forcefully, boring into them, to their very depths. And, if possible, she never diverted her gaze until she had got her money.

She had begun finding tiny, alluring sentences to tempt drivers of every sex, age, and stripe, chosen accordingly. To the young men she would say, 'I've got beautiful flowers for beautiful young ladies. Do you know any?' To middle aged women, 'A pleasant smelling home is the perfect cure for a husband's wandering eye.' And to fat cat business men, 'Forget about your wife, buy some flowers for the other lady in your life.' And to those with children, 'The child deserves the chance to smell a rose, don't you suppose?'

She was flexible about the prices too. She raised her price for luxury autos and, for some reason, asked less of women without make-up. Still, no matter who the potential customer, she started off the bargaining by asking for twice the price she was willing to settle on. That way, the customer felt a sense of triumph, whereas it was really Güldane who was the vanquisher.

In a short time many people who necessarily took that route each day became regular customers of Güldane's self-confidence, spry body, vivacious eyes, and sharp tongue. [...]

It was an ugly Istanbul day, rainy. It was daffodil season. The sky was grey and murky, the ground muddy. The intoxicating fragrance of the daffodils was not enough to raise Güldane's spirits. Just a little way from where she worked, construction of a huge shopping centre had begun, and a gigantic pit of nearly abysmal depths had been gouged into the earth. The pit was surrounded by a barrier. It was impossible to see what was going on inside. Yet ever since that pit had opened, mud, that mucus of the terra firma, clung to the feet of every soul that passed by. High heels, leather boots, the wheels of luxury cars, all of them were framed in mud, as if they'd just been through Güldane's neighbourhood.

Güldane took a few bunches of daffodils and slithered into the traffic. Business was unexpectedly good. Güldane was being picky; she didn't approach every car, but every car that she did approach bought a bunch of daffodils from her, without exception. Yet Güldane's spirits remained low.

Fifteen minutes before sundown a black jeep appeared at the corner of the street. It grew closer. For a moment, Güldane's eyes met those of the driver. A man with dark black eyes, a slightly protruding chin, a moustache, and an odd gaze. The light turned red. The cars stopped. The jeep stopped too. As the driver of the jeep rolled down his window, Güldane's heart rumbled just like Yunus's *darbuka*. Güldane swallowed hard, silencing it. The man inside the jeep looked at Güldane.

'Come here,' he said.

Güldane didn't think about it, not even for a second; her soul went to the man first, followed by her feet. They began bargaining. At that moment, Güldane fell into a time that she had never experienced before. On the one hand, she wished that the moment would never end, that she could just stand there across from the man like that for eternity; she was overcome by an overwhelming desire to decipher him and the spell he had cast, to unravel the magic of the moment. On the other hand she felt time passing more swiftly than ever and this gave her incredible pain. A panic overtook her, and in that panic, she became oblivious, oblivious to how she had bargained, or even how much she had agreed upon. The only thing she perceived was that the man had said, 'Deal,' and how he then reached out towards her. She too reached out. Güldane felt as if she disappeared in the man's large, strong hands. Then, the cars began to move again. The driver of the jeep slammed his foot down on the gas, as if he weren't the same man who had just been bargaining with her. As Güldane stood there stunned, watching the jeep drive away, it stopped again. A strong, muscular arm extended out through the window. It motioned at Güldane for her to come over. Güldane hesitated for a brief moment and then, without giving it much thought, quickly ran up to the jeep. Just as she got there, the jeep took off again. Then it stopped again. Again, he motioned for Güldane to come. Güldane went over to him once more.

'Why do you keep starting and stopping like that? It's rather rude, don't you think?' Güldane said.

'We're just having a little fun now, what's wrong with that?' the man replied. And then he began bargaining again.

'But,' Güldane said, 'we already agreed on a price, I won't accept less. Besides, you've worn me out with all this running.'

'Alright then,' the man said, 'give me the flowers. I'd hate to hurt your feelings.'

Güldane held out the daffodils. She didn't realize that she had chosen the freshest, most beautiful bunch. She gave the daffodils to the man. The light turned green. The man leaned over as if to take out his wallet to pay her, before quickly shifting gears, slamming down on the gas and speeding away.

Güldane was left there, stunned, in the middle of the road. Cars were passing her left and right. She remained standing there, speechless, motionless. When she finally came to, her heart was aflame and there was no one to put the fire out.

A savage scream ripped from her throat as she slung all of the remaining daffodils into the air. The daffodils spun down to the earth, and the cars crushed them, one by one. Swallowing her tears, Güldane crouched down onto the edge of the sidewalk and watched the daffodils disintegrate, sink into the mud of the construction site and disappear. She was powerless to do a single solitary thing.

Gaye Boralıoğlu, *Syncopated Rhythm* (2009)
translated by Amy Spangler

✳ ✳ ✳

Hatice Meryem (b.1968) gives us a partly humorous, partly sad picture of the lives of some Stamboullus in It Takes All Kinds.

Some think that only women who live in the upscale neighbourhoods of Istanbul keep up with fashion trends; yet those who live in Kozluk and similar neighbourhoods – those which fall a bit beyond, a bit before, a bit to the left, or a bit to the right of the same city, but never ever in the centre of it – are fashion savvy too. Take the latest fashions in childbirth, for example. That's right, childbirth fashion trends! It was only up until five to ten years ago that the women of Kozluk considered home-birthing a respectful and necessary act, a kind of performance exhibiting a woman's strength and determination; now, however, faced with the onslaught of childbirth discounts offered by the private hospitals springing up like mushrooms on every corner, home-birthing has become a tradition on the brink of oblivion, and a rather degraded one at that. Even women of a certain age have reached a consensus on the dangers of home-birthing and have ceased to view the new custom as an act reserved for fussy daughters-in-law. Cesarian birth, however, has yet to gain their approval. Interfering in God's business, that's how they see it. Some find it blasphemous to expose a pregnant tummy just to learn the sex of the unborn, while others are put off by the apparatus known as 'the ultra-sound' and the sticky substance slathered on the stomach in order to use it. However, there's one thing firmly planted in the minds of all the women of Kozluk, something that the doctors stress with great importance, and that is breastfeeding, and plenty of it. And so they breastfeed, night and day, cooing, 'Suckle up, little lamb.' The little lambs of Kozluk guzzle milk from their mamas' breasts, and when they take to their feet and start climbing the walls, the mamas of Kozluk release them from their laps and into the second safest place they know: the streets. That is of course after having amply warned them of the dangers they are likely to encounter there. The little lambs of Kozluk, who quickly learn to disregard their mamas' warn-ings, head straight for the sewage streams, the treacherous irri-gation canals, or the perilous waters of the Bosphorus where (despite the noisy rage, and even detestations, of Istanbulites, who travel aboard the city ferries and lead benign lives) become marvellous swimmers.

Those same mamas of Kozluk, convinced that their little lambs are prone to crime and that the fear of God might subdue their rage a bit, send them off to a Koran course, or perhaps a sewing class. Yet the little lambs remain tantalized by dreams of bodybuilding, judo, and tae kwan do classes and shiny shop windows at the mall.

Thanks to plenty of training chasing after wedding convoys and holding their hands out for the traditional tip, the little lambs of Kozluk get a head start on business life and exhibit astonishing success at occupations such as washing car windows at red lights, and servicing dry throats with cold water in the summer and runny noses with tissues in the winter.

Most of the little lambs aren't able to get a proper education. Some of them find themselves behind bars for unheard of crimes; they become the bane of the prison system. Others wing their way through high school, and generally end up joining the ranks of those responsible for the homeland's security, as cops or soldiers. And that's when the clashes ensue! Those who rob the rich of their riches on the one side, and those who guard and protect the riches of the rich on the other.

Later, over the little lambs is cast the towering shadow of he who is considered the sole true representative of 'the real world' at home: their father. Thenceforth do the fathers of Kozluk, who up until then were acquainted only with the names of their wee ones, if that, undertake to set the lives of the little lambs in order, proclaiming that they want to see them promptly and properly hitched, and thus ordering for the immediate arrangement of a wedding.

Though some of the little lambs do their best to resist this first command, most suffer defeat in this first battle against the father. Sparing no expense, begging and stealing, the fathers of Kozluk go so far as to get invitations specially printed for the occasion. The household's smallest little lamb with the best handwriting writes the names of the invitees on the white envelopes into which the invitations are placed, until her arm falls weary and her fingers start to twitch.

The wedding inevitably falls upon a rainy day. The two little lambs of Kozluk, now referred to as 'bride and groom', turn into drenched rats by the time they make it, at a sprint, from the wedding car to the wedding hall. And with this rain the bride's ridiculously flamboyant hairdo, which took a whole afternoon to sculpt, the magic touch of each and every hairdresser employee making a unique contribution to the creative process, is ruined. Finally, all the friends and relatives gather together in stuffy, non-air conditioned basements and partake of wedding cake made with cheap margarine, down glass after glass of artificially coloured lemonade, and inevitably circle up for a *halay* dance or line up to do the *horon*. Because each wedding is essentially a kind of ritual get-together for people to see each other, mingle, and catch up with loved ones, and because the gift-giving ceremony goes on for hours, the bride and groom look on absently from the table where they sit in exhaustion, watching their own wedding like two strangers.

In no time the mothers and fathers of Kozluk embrace their eagerly awaited grandchildren, at which point they begin to speak of the afterlife as if it were the next street over. So much so that heaven and hell become their veritable next-door neighbours. That's why when they die, quietly, lying beneath heavy wool blankets, or in the dim hallways of state hospitals, not a soul takes notice.

Hatice Meryem, *It Takes All Kinds* (2008)
translated by İdil Aydoğan and Amy Spangler

❊ ❊ ❊

Geert Mak is given a 'sociology lesson' on some of the city's communities associated with the Galata Bridge.

One rainy Saturday afternoon the bookseller, who sees and hears everything, gave Onur and myself a short lecture on the sociology of the bridge. What he described amounted to a kind of economic compartmentalisation. The fishmongers, for example, all hail from the eastern city of Erzincan. Most of the professional anglers come from Trabzon, on the Black Sea. The rods and tackle, on the other hand, are sold generally by immigrants from Kastamonu and there's no getting around them. And if you're Kurdish there is no sense in trying to rent a space and fry fish, for that monopoly is in the hands of another group. On the other hand, though, you could move into the cigarette trade immediately. 'We are one family,' the cigarette boys say. 'When the police start hassling people we always help each other, we drag each other's wares along, hide other people's things for them; if we didn't do that we'd all be wiped off the street.'

Countless tightly knit immigrant communities exist in this way, all of them operating in isolation from the others and within the strict borders allotted them. Traditionally, the city has always been an amalgam of more or less closed urban villages and beneath the surface – and certainly among immigrants – those old demarcations continue to play a role. There are still, for example, two Armenian hospitals in Istanbul and eighteen Armenian schools. 'There are clubs for immigrants everywhere, tiny groups no one's ever heard of. And they all have their own newspaper,' says the bookseller. 'There are ten million people in this city, after all, which means there's a market for everything.'

Geert Mak, *The Bridge: A Journey Between Orient and Occident* (2007) translated by Sam Garrett

❊ ❊ ❊

In this extract from his novel Young Turk, *Moris Farhi (b.1935) reveals – among other things – one way in which Ataturk tried to meld a diverse nation into a more coherent one.*

This July of 1942, the people of Istanbul were insisting, was the hottest in living memory. Around Sultan Ahmet Square, where the Blue Mosque and the Byzantine monuments faced each other in historical debate, the traditional *çayhanes* had appropriated every patch of shade. The patrons of these tea-houses blamed the heat on *şeytan*: the land was fragrant with the verses and compositions of the young bards, and the Arch-demon, jealous of the Turk's ability to turn all matter into poetry or music, was venting his resentment. The narghile-smokers, mostly pious men revered as guardians of the faith, disagreed: such temperatures occurred only when sainted imams lamented the profanation of Koranic law; and, under this heathen administration called a 'republic', they had much to lament, not least the growing number of women who were securing employment – as well as equal status with men – in all walks of life. But down the hill, along the seaside *meyhanes*, where the solemn imbibing of raki engendered enlightenment far superior to that of tea or opium, the elders, veterans of the First World War, offered a more cogent reason. Pointing at the dried blood from Europe's latest battlefields settling as dust on this city, which Allah had created as a pleasure garden for every race and creed, they affirmed that man, that worshipper of desolation, was once again broiling the atmosphere with guns.

We believed the drinkers. Well, we either had just reached our teens or, like Bilâl, were at the threshold and knew, with the wisdom of that age, that old soldiers, particularly those who open their tongues with alcohol, never lie. Besides, Bilâl – actually his mother, Ester – had kept us apprised, with first-hand information, of the carnage devastating Europe. In Greece, where she had been born, Death was reaping a bumper harvest. Letters from Fortuna, Ester's sister in Salonica, were chronicling the atrocities. Though these accounts often verged on hysteria – and tended to be dismissed as exaggerated, even by some Jews – they were corroborated, in prosaic detail, by the family's lawyer. When, about fifteen years before, Ester had left Greece to get married in Turkey, this gentleman, Sotirios Kasapoğlou by name, had promised to report regularly on her family's situation.

It was in the wake of this lawyer's latest missive that Bilâl, Naim and Can, another gang member, approached me. You may have guessed, from my reference to Ester's concern for her relatives, that Bilâl – and, indeed, Naim and Can – were Jewish; and you may be intrigued by their Muslim names. There is a simple explanation: Atatürk, determined to distance the new republic from the iniquities of the Ottoman empire, had sought to instil in the people pride in their Turkishness. Consequently, by law, all minorities were obliged to give their children a Turkish name in addition to an ethnic one. Thus Benjamin had become Bilâl; Nehemiah, Naim; and Jacob, Can.

Moris Farhi, *Young Turk* (2004)

✳ ✳ ✳

Continuing the theme, Yiannis Xanthoulis vivdly describes one of the old Jewish areas of the city.

But at Balat, which was so named because it was next to the ruined Palace of Constantine Porphyrogenitus – and so '*palat*' or '*balat*', what's it matter? – things are more straightforward. Here you'll find some of the oldest synagogues in the City still functioning, though the oldest is in Beyoğlu, and suffered serious damage as a result of the Al Qaida attack. Balat, cheek by jowl with the Fener – the Phanar – for which we still mourn, has started to look up somewhat since various Istanbul painters, writers, or simply would-be artists have chosen it for permanent residence.

It's a pitiably poor neighbourhood, but it has the fascinating sub-stratum of history. Well and truly drenched with the tears of the Jews who were mercilessly expelled from Spain in the fifteenth century by Ferdinand and Isabella, it retains the feel of a neighbourhood with coherence. Even if it has been taken over by the recent refugees from Anatolia and who knows what other corner of Turkey. Personally, I like it because for a time I used to visit, as is my custom, the two or three lowly hamams. Tourist attractions they are not. Happily. You won't see a tourist in Balat. A rare species.

And later I came to love, when I embarked upon learning Turkish, to sit in the cheap cookshops to eat baked green beans and aubergines with meat in tomato sauce. A lively neighbourhood, as all poor quarters, anyway, are, the barbers' shops packed – and I'll be damned if I can imagine what they're cutting and what they're shaving until midnight; full of coffee-shops with unnaturally large groups of men playing cards or gazing at the light programmes on television with the blond beauties, a model of unnaturalness for these poor things, who look at them stroking their crotch. As a friend of ours said, these men with their feverish eyes and blue lips are accustomed, on returning to the wretchedness of the family home – married as they are for twenty years, and with a flock of children – to clout their wives before lying down with them for a blind undertaking of tenderness.

And as dawn breaks, clouds of smells of fresh-baked bread cover over the atrocities of the night. Everywhere in Turkey, the bread is delicious. And, in smaller quantities, the bread cakes of Ramadan. In the old days, they used to bake them only for the period of Ramadan, as we do with the *lagana* bread for the first day of Lent. Now they make them all the year round. Those who can pay a bit extra get to taste them. The rest are limited to the cheap daily bread. And always from the radios the mournful songs of love, and the more modern ones with androgynous youths, who shock the connoisseurs. The eternal soundtrack of the crowd.

Yiannis Xanthoulis, *The Istanbul of my Disrespectful Fears* (2008)
translated by Geoffrey-Alfred Cox

* * *

Jewish-born Mario Levi (b.1957) often writes about the city's minorities and misfits, but this extract from Istanbul was a Fairy Tale *is above all a love story, featuring one of the many Stamboullus whose livelihood depends on the sea.*

Moses had a friend by the name of Carlo, a pilot who conducted ships into and out of the waters of the Bosphorus; he boasted of speaking thirteen languages in addition to Yiddish. His breath stunk of alcohol throughout the day although no one had seen him tipsy. According to reliable accounts, this 'somewhat different' man, who was convinced that real adventures and loves could only take place at sea, was in love in his youth with a girl by the name of Sylvia, of Russian stock like he himself was ... His affair with 'that girl' had started at a reception during which the subject was the lack of taste in matters of gastronomy and of the Jews of Polish descent as compared to the Jews of Russian descent. It turned out that he and that girl had been of the same opinion. This common trait had drawn them to each other. [...]

It did not take them long to consider marriage. Wedding preparations were made, mutual promises were solemnly exchanged. But, at the least expected moment, Carlo received a letter of adieu from her, a letter written from the bottom of her heart ... one of those letters one hardly expects to receive that opens the door to disappointments that last a lifetime. [...]

In her letter of adieu, Sylvia, for reasons she could not divulge, was leaving, as she had been obliged to go to Argentina. She was the only woman who could extend a helping hand to her father who had lost all his wealth and honour. Life sometimes invited people to take part in hazardous undertakings. This was an ordeal that an individual had to endure, at the end of which, depending on how things turned out, a man may receive an injury he had not deserved, a wound destined to remain unhealed throughout his life. This may have been the reason why what was called regret became the constant companion of his life. [...]

No sooner had Carlo got the letter than he had rushed to her place; it was in vain. She was nowhere to be found. He could learn nothing from her neighbours. He felt that everybody knew something about her after a fashion, but somehow preferred to remain silent. The next day, he went down to the waterfront. He walked along the streets throughout the nights. He visited the places where Sylvia and he had been together. Finally he saw her in the company of her father aboard the ship about to weigh anchor. Both father and daughter were smartly dressed. Carlo and Sylvia waved to each other. 'Don't ever come. You won't be able to find me in big cities. Even if you do find me, I won't be the same,' said Sylvia. While saying these words, she appeared to be concealing a deep sorrow that lay behind them. Her father was holding her by the arm while her head was inclined down to her breast. Carlo said nothing in return. Not a single word did he utter. He was employed at the accounting department of a big maritime transportation company. He loved to watch the big vessels sailing through the waters of the Bosphorus. This interest drew him to those ships. To his boss, Monsieur Lazzaro, who had been a father to him in every respect, he had confided saying that after his separation from Sylvia he could not continue working behind a desk, that the sea called the man inside him and communicated to him his desire to become a pilot. He explained that as he owned a small vessel of his own, he knew the job and that it would not take him long to get accustomed to this new venture. He asked Monsieur Lazzaro who had among his acquaintances persons of some influence, to be instrumental in arranging for him this job. [...] The result of this was Carlo's exercising the functions of a pilot for a good many years to come ... in order to be able to stir in the wind of ships sailing towards his land from the remotest corners of the earth; in order to be the first to hail that ship that would have brought Sylvia back to him ... However, Sylvia never showed up.

Mario Levi, *Istanbul Was a Fairy Tale* (1999)
translated by Ender Gürol

✳ ✳ ✳

Elif Shafak shows there are more ways than one of being an outsider.

As Zeliha rushed by, the street vendors selling umbrellas and raincoats and plastic scarves in glowing colours eyed her in amusement. She managed to ignore their gaze, just as she managed to ignore the gaze of all the men who stared at her body with hunger. The vendors looked disapprovingly at her shiny nose ring too, as if therein lay a clue as to her deviance from modesty, and thereby the sign of her *lustfulness*. She was especially proud of her piercing because she had done it herself. It had hurt but the piercing was here to stay and so was her style. Be it the harassment of men or the reproach of other women, the impossibility of walking on broken cobblestones or hopping into the ferryboats, and even her mother's constant nagging ... there was no power on earth that could prevent Zeliha, who was taller than most women in this city, from donning miniskirts of glaring colours, tight-fitting blouses that displayed her ample breasts, satiny nylon stockings, and yes, those towering high heels.

Now, as she stepped on another loose cobblestone, and watched the puddle of sludge underneath splash dark stains on her lavender skirt, Zelhia unleashed another long chain of curses. She was the only woman in the whole family and one of the few among all Turkish women who used such foul language so unreservedly, vociferously, and knowledgeably; thus, whenever she started swearing, she kept going as if to compensate for all the rest [...]

She was a thread of lavender, a most unbefitting hue fallen into a tapestry of browns, greys, and more browns and greys. Though hers was a discordant colour, the crowd was cavernous enough to swallow her disharmony and bring her back into its cadence. The crowd was not a conglomeration of hundreds of breathing, sweating, and aching bodies, but one single breathing, sweating, and aching body under the rain. Rain or sun made little difference. Walking in Istanbul meant walking in tandem with the crowd.

Elif Shafak, *The Bastard of Istanbul* (2007)

✳ ✳ ✳

Mehmet Zaman Saçlıoğlu creates a delightful Istanbul character in his short story 'The Intersection' – and hints at the city's traffic problems at the same time. Here's an extract.

The dolmuşes that leave from Kadıköy and go to Bostancı veer suddenly away from the shore as they round the point at Moda and turn into one of the district's somewhat older side streets. This street takes you down the hill to Moda, and from there to Yoğurtçu Park.

The street, which used to be very congested at several inter-sections, was not at all liked by dolmuş drivers coming up the hill. There were traffic lights at only two places here, one at the intersection with Moda Caddesi, the other at the intersection with Bahariye Caddesi. At the other intersections, young kids who had just got their driving licenses (and some that had not succeeded) created a hazard, showing off in their fathers' cars.

The experienced old dolmuş drivers, who drove cautiously, slightly hunched over the steering wheels of their aged, rattle-trap cars, collecting fares and dispensing change, approached these hazardous intersections with their left foot on the clutch and their right poised to hit the brake at any moment.

One day a man started directing traffic at the most treach-erous of the intersections. Although people were slightly taken aback at first, they soon grew accustomed to his presence. Clean-shaven, with glasses, a long raincoat and a whistle in his mouth, the man flawlessly executed the hand and arms move-ments of a bona fide traffic director – stopping cars and giving them the right of way, making all the cars wait for an elderly woman and then saluting her politely – and before long he was a fixture at the intersection.

The local shopkeepers, the neighbours who observed the proceedings from their windows and the drivers who regularly used the street, soon realized that the man was a harmless idiot. What else could he have been? What could a traffic director with no monthly salary, no rank, no social security, no weapon, no uniform and no forms for writing up tickets be other than an idiot?

It was, in all probability, the corner grocer who was the first to determine that this man, who stuffed a slice of kashar cheese into a half loaf of bread for lunch and attempted to direct the traffic with one hand while eating his lunch with the other, was a nut job.

The first time he entered the shop, the man wished the grocer a polite good day, put in his order, and made a couple of gestures to the cars from a distance to show that he was on the job even as he stood waiting at the door of the grocery for his sandwich to be made. To the grocer, who asked him who he was and why he was directing traffic here, he replied: 'Can't talk now, I'm on duty.' He paid without taking his eyes off the street and, taking his sandwich, resumed his post in the middle of the intersection.

The grocer watched the man briefly and then got absorbed in his business. Towards evening, while he was waiting on a customer, he heard a horn-honk and looked for the man but was unable to discern anyone at the intersection. It surprised the grocer to see that this intersection, which had looked after itself for years, had abandoned its old habits and quickly adapted to the traffic director, only to revert to chaos again on his departure.

After the first few days, the traffic director's working hours fell into a regular pattern. With his whistle, his hand and arm movements and a smile on his face, the man, who took his place at the intersection at 7:30 in the morning, directed traffic without a break until five in the evening and disappeared at precisely 5pm. On Sundays the intersection was untended.

In the end, everyone came to accept the man, who observed his weekly working hours punctiliously and solved the traffic problem on the street. Now and then at midday while he was eating his lunch the man would utter a few words, but he never took his eyes off the traffic. He never made school children, pregnant women, or old people wait to cross the street but immediately stopped the cars, not giving the go sign until the pedestrians had reached the opposite kerb.

Before long the grocer stopped accepting money for the man's lunches. He felt indebted to this person who toiled with boundless energy and a smile on his face with no expectation of anything in return. In any case all the poor soul ate was half a loaf of bread and a hundred grams of kashar cheese.

'Why won't you take the money?' he asked. 'Am I a beggar?' The grocer was prepared for all possible questions.

'I beg your pardon, brother, but the Department of Traffic told me not to take money from their officer,' he said. 'They are very pleased with your work and they are going to pay for your lunches from now on,' he explained, quashing any further objections.

This reply prompted the man to take his work even more seriously, to the point of extending his workday by another hour. The grocer gave the same reply to questions about the man asked by people he didn't know who entered his shop as first-time customers.

What do you mean an idiot, my good man? He is more intelligent than any of us. Some so-called great men take office saying they are going to administer the state and then make a hash of it. That man has been directing the traffic all this time without a hitch. He doesn't take a penny for it and he doesn't complain either. God knows I can't tell who is crazy and who is sane.

Mehmet Zaman Saçlıoğlu, 'The Intersection' in
The Book of Istanbul (2011), translated by Virginia Taylor-Saçlıoğlu

✻ ✻ ✻

*Arrested for political activism at the time of the
1971 coup, Oya Baydar went into exile for twelve
years following the coup of 1980. In* Its Warm Ashes
Remained, *Baydar explores the effects of the social
and political climate of the second half of the twentieth century and how it is reflected in the lives of the
ordinary people of Istanbul.*

The daily worries of civil servants with small means ... That
very thin line which moves between being thrifty and stingy,
between being poor and middle class ... The constant problems
of rent, telephone bills, transportation, pocket money. With the
unexpected death of the father, the family budget which has
shrunk from the salaries of two teachers to that of only one
... After the mother comes home from work and the little girls
finish their homework, the supplementary sewing work until
midnight for ready-made clothes manufacturers: the duck and
rabbit figures sewn on the chests of children's coats; the interfacing and tabs sewn on the front of coats, under linings or
collars; the scattered flowers embroidered on the skirts ...

She used to take the pieces of clothing from a dingy old work
place in the back streets of Caşaloğlu and bring them to their
home in Levent. She wouldn't take a taxi to save money; she
would drag all the way to the bus the two huge bags that she
had to put down at every corner to catch her breath. Then she
would shrink with her bags in a corner on the back platform
of the Caşaloğlu–Levent bus which left every hour. The bus
would fill up along the way, with passengers hanging out of
the doors. Tired and weary people who could barely stand on
their feet would look at the young girl's bags almost her own
size and grumble, angry because she was taking up room for
three with only one ticket. She would die from embarrassment,
blood would rush to her face, her palms would sweat, and she
would remain silent.

She was eighteen when one evening, a lovely evening at the end of summer, together with the threads and pieces of cloth in her lap, she threw away the interfacing, the duck and rabbit figures, the colourful embroidery threads, children's dresses of all colours, the frightening old rooms in Caşaloğlu, the dark offices of ready-made clothiers who grew fat on cheap labour, the embarrassment suffered in the crowded back platforms of buses.

It was warm. All the windows of the back room and the verandah door of the little bungalow were open. The sultry smell of honeysuckle and lily from outside filled the room along with the mosquitoes flying towards the light and fresh blood. Her mother was working under the standing lamp, her head bent on her work, detached from the world. That night, she noticed for the first time that the woman's hair had started to turn white, her shoulders had drooped and that she was getting old. 'She isn't even forty-five. I haven't paid attention to her for some time, passing her by as if she were just one of the familiar old pieces of furniture in the house.' She felt a knot in her stomach. She thought about the distance and the lack of communication between herself and her mother and sister.

Feeling the gaze on her body without looking, the tired woman raised her face from her work and looked up with almost empty eyes.

'Did you want something?'

She whispered as she cleaned the bits of thread sticking to her skirt:

'It's over, Mother. Let's finish this business. I won't go to fetch work again. I'm not going to touch a needle or a thread, either.'

She quickly went out to the back garden through the open door. There was a full moon. The lilies looked whiter in the moonlight than they did in the sun. She sat on the veranda steps and inhaled the flower-perfumed air. Happy screams of playing children came from the next garden. 'We too used to run around like them three or four years ago.' She could smell the scent of grilled meat, hear the peals of laughter and the conversations coming from the neighbouring houses. They had been living in this neighbourhood, in this small house long enough to identify each of the neighbours by their laughter, their voices, the smell of the food they cooked. She liked it here, she felt safe amongst her equals. 'This place is my childhood, my adolescence, my whole world; my friends, my confidants, my childhood loves, my dreams ... So what is it that is missing? What is this dissatisfaction, this cold void I feel inside?'

She understood that this small silent house, this neighbour-hood where streets smelt of jasmine and linden, was a prison of peace and security, that the shirt of innocence which had been put on her age of eighteen years was now too tight for her yearning body.

Oya Baydar, *Its Warm Ashes Remained* (2000)
translated by Stephanie Ateş

✻ ✻ ✻

English novelist Barbara Nadel (see her introduction to this anthology) loves Istanbul, though she doesn't ignore its darker side in her very successful series of crime novels set in the city, featuring the detective Inspector Çetin İkmen.

Everyone in Istanbul had a fake something or other. Inspector Çetin İkmen himself had been given a counterfeit Rolex watch by his youngest son for his last, his fifty-seventh, birthday. The child, Kemal, had purchased it from one of the many scruffy-looking vendors of such things who plied their trade underneath the Galata Bridge. As was typical of such purchases, the watch had worked for a week, died and then been put into the drawer of İkmen's office desk. There it would probably languish until the policeman either retired or the watch itself met with some sort of accident. At the other end of the scale, his daughters paid not inconsiderable amounts of money for their fake Prada handbags and his son Bülent felt himself very dashing in his almost perfect replica Police sunglasses. Forgeries, not least because the tourists loved them, were a fact of life. Many young men and women from the poorer suburbs of all the major cities, including Istanbul, worked in the 'knock off' trade. They did so of their own volition.

But in recent years things had changed. Not only in Turkey, but across the world, the trade in forged goods had become a multibillion-dollar industry. Controlled largely by criminal gangs known loosely as 'mafias' (some could indeed be traced back to the original Sicilian Cosa Nostra), these counterfeit businesses were known to run sidelines in prostitution, money laundering, drug dealing and contract killing. Many had dispensed with local cheap-ish labour in favour of slaves from poor former Warsaw Pact countries, Southeast Asia or Africa. Illegal immigrants, desperate to escape the poverty of their own countries, would readily agree to work for nothing in return for a route into a country, like Turkey, on the doorstep of the European Union. What these people rarely knew was how long and hard they would be forced to work in order to pay off their 'debt'.

It had been an unseasonably stifling day in April when the Istanbul Police Department, via one of İkmen's colleagues, Inspector Mehmet Süleyman, had been tipped off about a possible slave factory in a rundown district of Tarlabaşı. Just seconds from the bright lights of the fashionable district of Beyoğlu, Tarlabaşı was a rabbit warren of tenements, illegal brothels and small-time drug dealing operations. It was also home to many, many migrants from the country as well as people from places very far from Turkey. Süleyman who, like İkmen, was principally concerned with the crime of murder, had met with his informant, as arranged, aboard one of the commuter ferries that shuttled people back and forth between the European and Asian sides of the city. The informant, a man known only as 'George', told the handsome policeman that the Tarlabaşı factory had been operating for some time. It produced mainly handbags and, although George didn't actually own up to having any sort of personal connection with the place, it was obvious to Süleyman that he had at some time worked there. Why George was talking to the police about the Tarlabaşı factory was because people were, he claimed, dying in there now. Mention was made of a young African girl who had died from exhaustion. Her body had apparently been disposed of in a fire up in the equally dodgy district of Edirnekapı. The bosses, Turkish mafiosi, George reckoned, were bringing people into the country to work for them in record numbers.

'Like tissues, they use them to do one job and then they throw them away,' George said as the ferry passed beneath the pointed roofs and green gardens of the Topkapı Palace. 'I make things, Mr Süleyman. I make things that are not real or honest, but I do not kill people. I won't have anything to do with that. Not now, not ever.'

Süleyman nodded gravely, put his hand inside his elegant jacket pocket, took out his mobile phone and called Police Headquarters. By six o'clock that evening Süleyman, together with İkmen and a team of rather more junior officers, listened intently as their superior, Commissioner Ardiç, outlined how the operation against the illegal factory in Tarlabaşı was going to work.

It was just after dawn the following morning when they went in.

Barbara Nadel, *Death by Design* (2010)

✳ ✳ ✳

We'll lighten the mood with an informative and amusing piece on the Turkish male and his moustache ...

157

The moustache Ruled for centuries over the Turkish upper lip. At first glance it seems still to be going strong, but in reality it is fighting a rearguard action. One of the most powerful moustaches in history sprouted under the nose of Sultan Selim I. This Selim, nicknamed 'the Frightful', grew one of those splendid specimens about which the Turks used to say respectfully that you could 'hang a corpse on each end' with no problem – something the aforementioned Selim was certainly considered capable of doing. Not long ago the moustache was evidence of a political mindset: devout Sunni Moslems could be identified by the brush style, Leftists by down on the upper lip, Alevites by a Friedrich Nietzsche-style bush, and Fascists by the Genghis Khan model. For the generals in the coup of 1980 this meant that every single moustache was thrown out of university, and they were especially suspect in the torture cellars of the Second Political Department in Gayrettepe. Then in the 1990s Tansu Çiller, the first female head of state, dealt a further destructive blow: she ordered all delegates in her party to be clean-shaven. Here and there the moustache put up heroic resistance. Recently the Istanbul bus company Metro Turizm, one of the largest coach services in the country, ordered its employees to shave off their nose-ticklers. 'We are doing this to try to conform with European Union norms,' explained Sinan Solak, the head of Metro. Beardless into Europe? Not Nihat Sungur, fifty years old, a bus driver with Metro. 'I would rather cut off my head than my moustache,' Sungur said to reporters, and gave his notice. It's clear: anybody who wants to be modern no longer wears a moustache in Turkey. One of the last preserves is the cabinet and parliament in Ankara, of all places. Nearly all the brushes thriving here follow the Islamic cut, and with the best will in the world nobody could attach a corpse to the ends.

Kai Strittmatter, *User's Guide to Istanbul* (2010)
translated by Susan Thorne

✻ ✻ ✻

There has long been a close relationship between Turkey and Germany. Turkish 'guest-workers' in Germany sometimes experience prejudice in their host country, but Esmahan Aykol points out that racial preconceptions are not the preserve of Europeans.

I can't let this pass without mentioning some strange prejudices that Turks have about Germans. For instance, Turks are amazed to see a smiling, cheerful German. They love it when I laugh, because they think I've become really integrated into the community. I haven't yet convinced anyone that I used to laugh when I lived in Germany, even if only occasionally, and that it didn't mean I was excommunicated from society. I even know people who think the reason I came to live in Istanbul was that I couldn't remain in Germany because I was too cheerful.

Esmahan Aykol, *Hotel Bosphorus* (2004)
translated by Ruth Whitehouse

✻ ✻ ✻

One of Istanbul's most famous sons is, of course, the Nobel Prize-winning writer Orhan Pamuk. His memoir, Istanbul, *should be read by anyone wanting to get under the skin of the city and of Pamuk's writing. His 2009 novel,* The Museum of Innocence, *has spawned a very physical spin-off in the form of an actual museum based on the characters and events of the story. Shaun Walker interviewed Pamuk for the* Independent *soon after the museum's opening, in 2012, giving an invaluable insight into the writer's life and work.*

The view from the balcony of Orhan Pamuk's apartment in the hilly district of Cihangir is almost absurdly apt. The minarets of the Cihangir mosque are in close enough proximity that the muezzin's amplified call to prayer renders all conversation impossible; across the Golden Horn stands the Topkapı Palace, seat of the Ottoman sultans; further away still are the high-rise towers and business centres that drive the new Turkish economy.

The view pans across the Bosphorus from the European side of Istanbul, with its tourist sights and expat-heavy districts, across to the Asian side, Anatolia. Taken together, it is a neat empirical manifestation of the philosophical, cultural and geopolitical dilemmas that Turkey's best-known writer explores in his novels.

Pamuk, who turned sixty earlier this summer, has been writing books about Istanbul for three decades, and was honoured in 2006 with the Nobel Prize for literature. Istanbul has a competitive claim to be one of the world's greatest cities, and the prominence of Pamuk as its most prescient contemporary chronicler is undisputed.

This status has been further boosted in recent months with the opening of the Museum of Innocence, which is designed as the counterpart to his most recent novel, of the same name, which came out in 2009.

'It was conceived together, I planned it together – I wrote the book thinking of the museum and I made the museum thinking of the novel,' says Pamuk, sitting out on his balcony in the hot sun. Prior to beginning work on the novel, in 1998, he bought a house in the down-at-heel Cukurcuma district, and made it the location where one of the novel's protagonists, Fusun, would live.

The book and museum are a detailed evocation of the 1970s and 1980s in Istanbul, and Pamuk spent years scouring the flea markets of the area looking for objects that would fit into his novel. 'It's not that I wrote the novel and then looked for the objects. First I would find an object which I would think suitable for my characters and stories, then write about it, and in the end I ended up with a house full of thousands of objects,' he says. Simultaneously he worked with architects on a project to turn the building into a museum to house the objects, which opened its doors earlier this year.

The Museum of Innocence charts the obsession of Kemal, a well-to-do young man from the posh suburb of Nişantaşı, with a young cousin, Fusun, from a less wealthy side of the family. His obsessive love, which verges on creepy infatuation, leads to his emotional destruction, and he hoards objects with connections to Fusun with the intention of building her a shrine – the museum.

The most striking exhibit is in the lobby, a collection of 4,213 cigarette stubs allegedly smoked by Fusun and pilfered by the love-struck Kemal between 1976 and 1984. The cigarettes are pinned to the walls in neat rows with an entomologist's precision, each butt bearing a handwritten caption capturing a moment of Fusun's thoughts, or of events in Istanbul at the time.

Pamuk went to painstaking lengths to get the exhibit right. 'If you put real tobacco there, it will spoil in six months, and it would have been completely ruined,' he says. Instead, 4,213 cigarettes were emptied then filled with a chemical compound made specially to look like tobacco. They were then smoked using a vacuum cleaner, stubbed out using various levels of thoroughness and aggression depending on Fusun's supposed mood at the time of smoking, and scarlet lipstick was applied to the ends.

'At the beginning we overdid it a bit so then we had to clean them and do it all again,' says Pamuk. 'Fusun doesn't wear that much lipstick!'

Given the painstaking attention to detail that Pamuk has put into the beautifully curated museum, and the fact that Kemal is a character from a background not unlike his own, there is a natural impulse when reading the novel to wonder how much the author is drawing a self-portrait.

'Everyone asks me, especially women readers, "Oh, Mr Pamuk, are you Kemal?"' he says. 'No, I'm not, I'm not as obsessive as him, and I was never infatuated with love like this, although of course we all do have things similar to this at some time in our lives. But where I identify with him more is not in terms of my infatuations, but because I too fell out of my class. I'm not in touch with the Nişantaşi bourgeois class in which I grew up, just like Kemal at the end of the novel. Him because they made fun of him falling in love, and me because of politics and literature, which those people never cared much for.' [...]

'Between the ages of seven and twenty-two I wanted to be a painter, so part of creating the museum was to answer this calling,' he says. Some pieces were easy to find, such as old bottles or pictures of Istanbul boats of the 1970s, but items like old toothbrushes or salt shakers were hard to come by.

'The museum honours daily life objects we don't notice, their emergence and disappearance,' he says. 'You have an intimate relationship with your salt shaker, you sit and look at it three times a day. And then one day it breaks, or someone buys you a new one, and it's gone. After they disappear, five or ten years later you see them in flea markets, and then they disappear from there too.'

'Globalism washes away memories,' says Esra Aysun, the museum's director. 'Back then we were like Eastern bloc countries – we were living a secret, isolated life. Now, Istanbul is becoming a duplicate city like every other city in the world and some of these objects are very precious for our cultural memories.'

Pamuk is currently in the middle of writing a new novel, which he says will be called *A Strangeness in my Mind*. His writing process involves locking himself away in the Cihangir apartment, where he is surrounded by shelves of books and inspired by the view out to the Bosphorus and the Sea of Marmara. [...]

'The question we writers are asked most often is: why do you write? I write because I have an innate need to. I write because I can't do normal work. I write because I want to read books like the ones I write. I write because I am angry at everyone. I write because I love sitting in a room all day writing. I write because I can partake of real life only by changing it. I write because I want the whole world to know what sort of life we live in Istanbul, in Turkey. I write because I love the smell of paper, pen, and ink. I write because I believe in literature, in the art of the novel, more than I believe in anything. I write because it is a habit, a passion. I write because I am afraid of being forgotten. I write because I like the glory that writing brings. I write to be alone. Perhaps I write because I hope to understand why I am so very, very angry at everyone. I write because I like to be read. I write because once I have begun a novel, I want to finish it. I write because everyone expects me to write. I write because I have a childish belief in the immortality of libraries, and in the way my books sit on the shelf. I write because I have never managed to be happy. I write to be happy.'

Shaun Walker, 'Orhan Pamuk: Turkey's enemy within finds peace'
The Independent, 20 August 2012

✻ ✻ ✻

And finally a piece from Sarcophagus, *by Cem Mumcu regarding the millions of potential Stamboullus who never saw the light of day.*

How effective was it to have separate days or hours for men and women? How many male bodies, slipping into the plash of hot water, clad in *peştamals*[1] and *takunyas*[2], would have entered this reverberant space without the fantasy of a woman in their fancies, on their minds, in the steamy darkness of their

---

1   Loin-cloth of cotton or silk.
2   Special wooden clogs to prevent the wearer slipping on wet floors. They usually have leather straps and are decorated with silver or mother-of-pearl.

souls and on their erections aroused by nakedness? How many thousands, hundreds of thousands, indeed millions of sperm might lie in the nooks and crannies of the marble stones, wriggling their heads and tails, each with the capacity to become a baby? How many millions of children's corpses, that is, how many millions of potential human beings or unbornnesses might be found in the *kurnas*[1], on the floor and on the water-stained stones? How many thousands of women would have bled onto the semen deposits or sated the wetness of their private parts on the warmest section of the *göbektaşı*[2], aroused by their imminent ovulation?

How many millions of children's unborn corpses would the hamam have hidden away between its stones; how many millions of unborn infants' tombstones could it be composed of? Who knows how many potential geniuses, how many retarded, schizophrenic, suicidal children, men and women this paradise of semen and eggs, with its wet, warm and frightening interior, has housed in their death …

Cem Mumcu, *Sarcophagus* (2004)
translated by Buşra Giritioğlu

---

1 Marble wash-basin.
2 Large, heated platform in the hot room, traditionally located in the centre of the room.

"I was fourteen when we boarded the British ship
which was to take our small family
from the Karaköy pier to the New World"

Oya Baydar

Exiles

Istanbul is a city that many people depart from and
very many come to. Here we meet some of the people
who leave, and many who arrive as exiles from their
home territory. First, three young men arriving in
Istanbul from rural Turkey – from an autobiograph-
ical novel by the much-loved writer Orhan Kemal

(1914–1970). Istanbul has a museum dedicated to him, while the Orhan Kemal Novel Prize was established in 1972. Kemal was particularly keen to portray the lives of the city's poorer inhabitants.

'We're there!' exclaimed Hasan.

We rushed up on deck. The ship was anchoring at Galata.

Istanbul was shrouded in a fine mist. We were facing the Galata Bridge. Trams were shuttling to and fro, and people were milling around, looking like a mass of ants from a distance. The dirty waters of the port were crowded with barges and steamers. The hubbub of voices permeated the blanket of smoke and the smell of coal.

'Well I never,' marvelled Gazi. 'Well I never … '

'What's that?'

'Well, I mean, it's Istanbul. Istanbul! Look at how beautiful it is!' […]

There's so much in Istanbul to amaze people like us, fresh from the sticks. It's marvellous! For all its wonders, though, what use is Istanbul to a young man who has just stepped off a boat with all of sixty kuruş to his name?

So the three of us set off for Karaköy, went up Bankalar Road and over to Beyoğlu. Gazi was wide-eyed every step of the way. He was completely lost for words.

After that we toured Istanbul, that wonderful city of legends. We were so mesmerised by it all that we completely forgot about out girlfriends and the Gedikli Academy. We were ready to die for any one of the stunning women we spotted.

Eventually we had our fill of the wonders of Istanbul. This was because we were almost always hungry, and beautiful sights didn't fill our stomachs.

Orhan Kemal, *The Idle Years* (1950)
translated by Cengiz Lugal

✳ ✳ ✳

In a short story by Mehmet Bilâl (b.1962), we witness another young man arriving from the provinces. He is overwhelmed by the sights, sounds and bustle of the great city.

When he first disembarked, the crowd and noise that he found in Sirkeci had sent his head spinning. The tram siren, the honking cars, the people scurrying along the muddy sidewalks, all of it had unnerved him completely, and so he ran, straight to the sea with its billowing waves a few hundred metres in the distance, sprinting, as if toward some kind of miracle. While catching his breath he stood looking out at the ships rocking back and forth in the water, the greedy seagulls squawking in the air, the men fishing from the Galata Bridge, the larger bridge connecting the two sides of Istanbul, and the misty beauty of the opposite shore, which extended before him like a living, breathing post-card. He was hungry, as usual. It was then that he purchased his very first simit in Istanbul and quickly devoured it, right down to the last sesame seed.

Finding the coffeehouse that the imam had told him about proved quite a task. In the narrow streets crammed full of jostling pedestrians, salesmen screaming out their pitches, store on top of store on top of store, heaps of merchandise piled high upon tables, and dark office buildings, he was looking for a coffeehouse with a certain name but an uncertain address. 'Walk straight ahead, turn right, then go uphill ... ' 'You're at the wrong place, brother. You gotta go down this street until you see a kiosk on the corner, then you turn left there, and then ... '

The cigarette smoke stung his eyes and seared his nose the moment he stepped into the coffeehouse. He scanned the room, searching for his stepfather. There were men yelling, playing cards, rolling dice in a game of backgammon, watching television. He looked at each face. When the apprentice carrying tea on a suspended tray asked him who he was looking for, he told him. But why was he looking for him? 'I know him from back home,' the young man said, and gave him the name of the town. That loosened the apprentice's tongue up a bit. He told the young man that the latter's stepfather wasn't there at the moment, and that he only stopped by every once in a while. There was a hotel where he hung out sometimes though. He could tell him the name of the hotel, if the young man wanted to try there.

It was nearby. It wasn't nearly as difficult to find as the coffeehouse had been. He passed through a number of dark, narrow, muddy, potholed, lookalike streets before arriving at the hotel. It had single and double rooms, as well as twelve-person rooms with bunk beds, what the receptionist referred to as 'bachelors' rooms'. He asked about his stepfather. Perhaps he was staying there? 'What do you want with him, huh, boy?' the receptionist snarled in response. He repeated what he had said to the coffeehouse apprentice. He wasn't 'up to no good'; he was just hoping to find his friend from back home. The receptionist told him that his stepfather did stay there, but that he didn't show up every night. Now, did he want a room or not? He whipped out the money for a bed in one of the bachelors' rooms.

> Mehmet Bilâl, 'The Stepson' (2008)
> in *Istanbul Noir*, edited and translated by
> Amy Spangler and Mustafa Ziyalan

✻ ✻ ✻

As much as one might prepare oneself for arriving in the city, the reality doesn't always match the expectation.

When we got off the train, we were greeted by the very humid and heavy air. [...]

We dragged our suitcases and walked towards one of the exits of the Haydarpaşa train station. It was not the exit that one sees in the movies, the one which migrants arriving to the city for the first time would stand in front of and give a long look at the city. It was the one with the steps that led down to the taxi stand, with small shops lining both sides. I stopped after a couple of steps down. I looked up and saw the boat terminal in front of me. The jetty that was in front of the terminal came almost up to the tip of the peninsula we were on. Seagulls were descending over the sea and then going up. But it was not as crowded as I expected it would be.

I had tried to prepare myself well for this first meeting with Istanbul. I knew that the city would assault me from the first day, with its towers, palaces and minarets. It would not relent until it had made an impression on me, until it had managed to turn my seventeen-and-a-half-year life into a cassette inadvertently erased, and converted the city in which I was born and raised into a rural small town.

That is why I was very conscious of the fact that I had to resist Istanbul. With all my might, with all the folds and creases of a brain I did not have, with the skin of my teeth and my nails. I knew very well what would happen to me if I did not do this. I knew this country girl well by now. It had been seventeen and a half years, after all.

'What you are looking at is the Kadıköy boat terminal. Boats go to Karaköy and Beşiktaş from there.'

'Which boat do we take, then?'

'For this time let us allow ourselves to be spendthrifts. We'll take a taxi. Otherwise it's going to be difficult with these suitcases.'

Fırat left his bag at my feet and walked towards the taxis. The driver, reading a newspaper, leaning on the bonnet, immediately noticed him. Fırat made a sign with his arm extended and palm turned left. The driver made furious circles in the air with his hand raised up. While he was opening the trunk, Fırat came near me and grabbed both our suitcases from their handles.

169

I was trying very hard to keep my eyes open in the taxi. The trip had tired me and the tiredness hit me like a ton of bricks. My consciousness was slipping into sleep. A bit later, while passing through a wide avenue, I saw a hand offering me a small bottle of cologne. I found myself staring at his eyes through the rear view mirror.

'Here, little sister, take this. It'll do you good.'

'Has Armaşan' brand cologne had eighty percent alcohol, and with it, I could open my eyes a bit. I massaged my wrists and neck with it. I thanked him and gave the bottle back. Traffic was not too heavy. It was a bit more crowded than on the waterfront. Fırat was looking much fresher more alert than I was. He was making light conversation with the driver, joking around. He was telling the driver that the best thing to do would be to buy a Beetle made in Brazil and have it turned into a convertible in the workshops in Bursa. Listening to them talk, I learned that there had been torrential rains in Istanbul last week. That must have been why it was so humid and heavy.

We turned off the main road that we had been following since Kadıköy. We went into a side street lined with three-to-four storeys high apartment buildings. Trees on both sides of the street gave a sense of coolness, as well as providing shade for the balconies of the apartments. The driver was trying to read the street signs at every intersection.

After having passed a multitude of streets that looked all the same, we stopped in front of the phone booths that we had seen. I looked around me while the taxi driver was returning change. There was a small mini-market in the corner, a candy store next to it, and just in front, two public phones, one of which was obviously out of order. The way the street looked did in no way match the image of Istanbul I had in my mind, but it was a nice place. One could want to live there after a certain age.

'Are we there?'

'Almost there. We have to make a phone call.'

'Do we have much further to go, still?'

'The place is about fifty metres ahead. We stopped here to make the phone call.'

While he was phoning I went to the market. I bought a large bottle of mineral water and a newspaper. Then I saw Fırat looking troubled, gazing towards the direction we were supposed to go. He was playing with the phone tokens, nervously.

'Ertugrul is not home.'

'So, what do we do now?'

'We wait here. Maybe he went to the grocery store.'

I showed him the small market we were standing in front of: 'Here is the grocer's,' I said.

'Perhaps there is another one on the other side of the street. He knew the time we were supposed to arrive. Let us wait.'

We put the bags together and sat on the low wall, on the sidewalk. I offered Fırat the plastic bottle. He took it, and downed almost half of it in two gulps. He then splashed his face and wetted his hair.

It was a very quiet and silent street. There were only the sounds of the commuter train line and the classroom chime from an invisible school that must have been nearby, which played a wailing Beethoven's Ninth chorale.

Tuna Kiremitçi, *Leave Before I Fall In Love With You* (2002)
translated by Jak Korı

✻ ✻ ✻

In recent years Istanbul has seen a daily influx of people from the interior of the country, exiling themselves from their roots in the hope of finding a better life in the city. Their arrival on the overnight buses is described by Jeremy Seal.

There was no sign of Ahmet that January morning, a morning so cold that any sign of him and the warmth of his car would have been welcome. What light there was reflected weakly off grey potholes of crushed ice. Refrigerated wind blew in pulses off the street as if timed to signal the arrival every half-minute or so of another overnight bus from Anatolia. They swung into Istanbul's bus station from Trabzon, Konya, and Amasya, distant cities of the Turkish interior and the Black Sea coasts. Glimpsed faces at the windows stared out at the blear dawn, and what they saw was concrete, skittering litter, and unfamiliarity at the beginning of a new life.

They clambered from the buses, these families, gathered their shapeless coats around them, and started to unload their belongings. There were old cardboard boxes bound by string that once held cartons of soap powder. There were blankets and rolled-up mattresses. There were suitcases straining with necessity. There was an ironing board and a small table and an empty bird cage, and piles of pots with impolite bottoms seared by cooking.

A thousand people were moving to Istanbul today, just as a thousand people had done so every day for the last ten years, turning the city's outlying villages into sprawling suburbs housing hundreds of thousands. Not long before, I guessed, the day had come when these families had finally realized that there was nothing for it but to leave, the cruel, indifferent processes of economics and history turning the screw tight until it could no longer be borne. Such was their situation that the things which mattered, their friends, perhaps a tree, a courtyard, or a scrubby hillside, views from a window that they and their grandparents had known as long as they could remember, had become sentimental luxuries that they could no longer afford. Today, economic necessity had defeated a thousand more Anatolians, and the old life became the past as they shouldered their ironing boards and empty bird cages and took the only chance remaining at the jostling margins of the big city.

Jeremy Seal, *A Fez of the Heart* (1995)

❊ ❊ ❊

Where do these new arrivals live? What kind of life can they expect? What impact do they have upon Istanbul? In this extract from The Other, *Ece Vahapoğlu gives us some pointers.*

New Istanbul suburbs like Ümraniye began as settlements built by conservative migrants from the countryside, and although Ümraniye, on the Anatolian side of the Bosphorus, was the most swiftly urbanizing of these districts and its population was increasing rapidly, it was exemplary in preserving its conservative character. Hikmet Bey had moved there as a youth. It formed a striking mosaic of neighbourhoods rich and poor which reflected the country's most recent era of development with its own up-to-date modern high society as well as secluded networks of families insulated from urban life.

The Akansan family had migrated from the central Anatolian town of Kayseri. Hikmet Bey and Nadide Hanım were both born there. With his native talent for business, Hikmet Akansan was like most Kayserians hard-working, clever, and charitable. The people of Kayseri drive a hard bargain and know the value of money, but do not hesitate to share their wealth when it comes to good works. Hikmet Bey was that sort of person. He loved money but knew how to spend it for the good of his community. In short, he was a typical Kayseri man. Once he'd set himself up in business in Istanbul he returned to Kayseri to find a proper wife.

His relatives had suggested Nadide Hanım. In no time at all they were married and moved to Istanbul immediately. While the children grew up, Nadide Hanım's life was in the home and her neighbours made up her circle of friends.

173

Now, thanks to the success Hikmet Akansan achieved through his enterprise, wit and the network of relationships he established, their home was filled with expensive furnishings. There were two huge plasma television screens in the house, one in the guest salon and the other in the family living room. The floors were covered with thick carpets and fine flat-weave Kayseri kilims bordered with flower and vine motifs. Crystal gewgaws decorated every corner of the house. But Nadide Hanım now wanted to move. She had her eye on the beautiful villas of Çavuşbaşı, also on Istanbul's Asian shore. Her eldest daughter Müberra was living in a large, airy villa in Florya on the European side, and could not praise the peace and quiet there, and her rich neighbours, enough. But once a person gets used to one side of the Bosphorus, it is not easy to move to the other side.

Ece Vahapoğlu, *The Other* (2009)
translated by Victoria Holbrook

✻ ✻ ✻

In contrast to the earlier extract from İnci Aral's
The Colour Saffron, *set in a poor neighbourhood,
the section below from the same novel depicts the
city's wealthy pleasure-seekers. With their 'borrowed'
identities, as Aral calls them, they seem to be exiles
both from themselves and the deeper culture of their
country.*

He looked at the ever-moving, undulating crowd around him. Those standing around with their drinks in their hands, others sitting at tables in the dining section, bursting into loud peals of laughter showing their white teeth, others easy-going, relaxed types who still had on their dark glasses in the dim light ... Naturally people had put on their masks before leaving their homes. All dressed up and ready to look lively, pretty and healthy, to give out positive energy and to play the games which had rigid rules ... Perhaps they sometimes dreamt of changing the games but never the rules. Or was it the other way around?

What ruled at that moment was the contentment of being lucky, beautiful, rich and free from all control and pressure. The weakest and sickest aspects of some of these people would be exposed as night advanced. Full of the pride and confidence of their class, they would surpass their limits of alcohol and drugs and reveal without any scruples the pent-up boredom they felt.

'Where have you been, my love? Have you cast a spell over me? I think about you constantly ...'

He turned around to the slender, soft arms wrapped around his neck from behind, and that familiar, somewhat heavy perfume of wild carnations. Fundi!

She was wearing a cocoa-coloured satin skirt which sat tightly around her lovely buttocks, leaving half of her thighs uncovered. She had combed back her hair to a bun on top of her head. Her over-made-up green eyes filled half of her face. Sometimes the look in those eyes would be shadowed by sadness, but her smile was always irresistible. This tiny jet-set painter was a real wild cat! [...]

Almost all knew each other in this circle and he had met most of the women. Some of them looked interesting and profound at first sight. However as most of them preferred to live with borrowed identities, they became shallow before too long. It wasn't easy to sharpen one's personality or quickly pour it into a personality-cast so as not to be left out. On the other hand, as their appearances had been groomed and polished with almost the same methods, they were astonishingly identical. Their blondeness, their dark tan, their habit of flinging their hair from side to side, their exaggeratedly scanty clothes were so similar that it was almost impossible to differentiate between these women, to find and love one who had different characteristics.

The men were the same. They had lost their right to be themselves. They were now trying to cheer up their loss by their latest fashion clothes, accessories and personal articles such as watches, glasses and mobile telephones. It was obvious at first glance that they spent at least as much time and money as the women did in their efforts to become cool, robot-like types with their well-cut hair carefully styled and soaked in gel, their tattoos and their extra-regular facial features.

The woman passing in front of him was wearing white boots that went up to her thighs. The short legs she was trying to hide in those boots seemed to be even more crooked to Volkan. On the other hand, what was amazing were her large, firm breasts which had been oiled and polished. These artificial breasts which were protruding out of her dress did not at all go well with her short, skinny body. When he looked at the face of the woman sitting in the red armchair by the lamp, he recognized the meaningless, empty visage of a woman with whom he had had a one-night stand in the days when he was still a rookie. Their eyes met for a moment but the woman was looking at him with unseeing eyes. A cold breeze passed through Volkan. He had an uncomfortable feeling of decay and regret. He swayed a little in his seat as if falling back.

İnci Aral, *The Colour Saffron* (2007)
translated by Melahet Behlil

❊ ❊ ❊

Perhaps even greater is the impact made by the city upon an 'exile' arriving from a faraway country. Maureen Freely no doubt uses her own childhood memories of arriving in Istanbul from America in her novel Enlightenment.

There are no words to describe my first impression of the real thing. It hit me like a hand, ripping the pictures out of my head and tearing them to shreds. I can recall a thousand swirling details of that first drive in from the airport, but I have no sense of the whole. There was the yellow haze rising from the Sea of Marmara but not the sea itself; the flock of tankers and fishing boats but not the horizon on which they sat; the red and crumbling fragments of the old city walls but no history to explain them. I could barely breathe from the stench of burning flesh I could not yet trace to the tanning factories, the injured violins that I could not yet accept as music, the belching chaos of jeeps, trucks, horses, carts and Chevrolets. Tiny gypsies wove amongst us with flowers no one wanted, and crooked old men with sofas strapped to their backs. Pressed against the sky was a forest of minarets and domes. The Golden Horn, which wasn't golden. The Bosphorus, so blue it stung my eyes.

The city thinned as we crawled along the European shore, winding our way from bay to promontory, and promontory to bay, through narrow streets that opened without warning into coastal roads, coming so close to Asia at some points that we could see the windows of the houses and at other times veering so far back into Europe that we could see no windows whatsoever, but I had no idea where we were by then, no idea at all. Until that day, I had never seen a landscape that wasn't planned or protected, or a street that wasn't zoned.

After an hour that seemed like a day, our bus turned up a steep and narrow cobblestone lane. We crawled up past a cemetery in which the tombstones wore turbans. Skirting a dark and crenellated tower, we climbed higher still, to pass through a stone gate covered with ivy. Beyond was a cool green hush and a leafy campus that consoled me because it looked so much like the one we'd left behind in Boston. There was a path. I followed it around a corner. I stepped out onto a terrace, and there it was: my golden destination. My picture from the *National Geographic*. The castle on its wooded hillside; the Bosphorus with its endless parade of tankers, ferries and fishing boats. Lining its Asian shore, the villas and palaces that seemed close enough to touch, and behind them, the brown rolling hills that must, I thought, stretch as far as China.

Maureen Freely, *Enlightenment* (2007)

✳ ✳ ✳

Then there are those who have exiled themselves from Istanbul to seek a different life elsewhere. In this extract from Soufflé, *by Aslı Perker (b.1975), we meet a mother whose daughter has gone to live in Paris.*

When the phone rang at ten past four, one hour ahead of Paris time, Ferda looked at the clock on the wall and smiled. She was glad that the steam in the pressure cooker had just come out and she had turned the heat low and set the timer for twenty minutes. This way she could talk to her daughter freely. Her daughter who lived in Paris called her every Friday at the same time, just before she left work. She said talking to her mum at the end of the week helped her start a very happy weekend. She would ask Ferda about everyone, every incident that took place, in detail, and almost request a report of things she was missing by not being there. How was her aunt, was her uncle well, did the cousins who had a fight make up, did her other uncle still live in that house or move to another place; she wanted to know everything. She would sometimes be curious about the price of the honey at the deli across the street, if the branches of the tree in front of their building had been trimmed, and she sometimes asked how Ferda marinated the celery root dish.

Ferda didn't understand why her daughter who had been living in Paris for the last six years was interested in the price of the honey or the branches of the tree, but never asked the reason. She was happy to talk to her as long as she could. Besides, this way she felt as if they lived in the same place, shared the same issues, and this helped her not to go crazy missing her baby girl. Her daughter always said the same thing, 'It's only a three-hour flight, why don't you jump on the plane and come over whenever you want? Plus I come to Istanbul very often. You can come for breakfast and go back for dinner if you like you know.' Ferda couldn't tell her daughter why jumping on a plane didn't work. Being a mother was nothing like that. She wanted her daughter to live downstairs or across the hall. She wanted to go to her place for a cup of Turkish coffee in the morning, or cook for her so that she wouldn't have to do anything after coming home tired from work. How helpful she was to her son and her daughter-in-law. She took care of her grandchildren, cooked for them. They just had to stop by at the end of the day and grab their tupperware filled with food so they never had the problem of low blood sugar. She could never tell these things to her daughter though. If she did, God forbid, her daughter could even move farther away being scared of a lifelong trap.

She actually understood why Ela moved to Europe. When she visited Paris the first time to see her daughter, she silently wished that she had been born there. That was a beautiful city. Every street, every corner was an artwork, all very refined. The transportation was easy, and so was walking. Ela had taken her to a couple of farmers' markets and searched for the approval of how beautiful they looked in her mother's eyes. Ferda thought they were beautiful too. The whole thing looked like a movie set, but it could never replace the farmers' market of Feneryolu for instance. The farmers' markets of Paris were only one-tenth of the Istanbul markets. But she couldn't deny really enjoying the cheese stands there. She confessed that being proud of the Cyprus Cheese, the İzmir tulum, the kasseri or the braid cheese was silly after seeing the variety they had.

While she made her daughter's most favourite dish, stuffed grape leaves, in that tiny Parisian kitchen, Ela showed her a couple of samples from the French cuisine. She thanked God that her daughter was good in the kitchen. They were able to talk in the same language that way. What if she was a kid who didn't know the difference between dill and parsley? She knew a lot of young women like that. So whenever her daughter called her to ask for a recipe she felt proud. She told her friends how Ela loved cooking, how she tried the most difficult recipes. She wanted to say to them, 'She's not going to be one of those new housewives who cannot put food in front of their husbands,' but she didn't since she didn't know if the man her daughter was going to marry was going to care about that at all. Ela didn't care for Turkish men. Ferda knew from the movies that French men had as much appetite as Turkish, but the difference was that they cooked themselves. They didn't think the woman should be the one who is cooking in a household; they had a different culture. Ela's beautiful gift was going to be wasted, but this was the least of her concerns if her daughter married a French man.

Aslı Perker, *Soufflé* (2011)
translated by the author

✳ ✳ ✳

Over the centuries, some Stamboullus have been sent into enforced exile. Here's a rather bizarre example.

The tradition of men in drag emerged when women were banned from dancing in public. In 1805 there were some six hundred dancing boys in the coffee shops and squares of Istanbul. Most of them came from Greek, Armenian and Jewish communities. They were so popular they often caused riots, with members of the audience throwing tea glasses and getting into fights over their different merits. They imitated the hip swaying and shimmying of the women's dance and added variations all their own. One of these involved the dancer painting a comic face on his belly and working his muscles so that the face alternately smiled and frowned. In 1837 these boys were thought to be causing such a disturbance they were outlawed by the sultan and many fled to Cairo.

Wendy Buonaventura, *I Put A Spell On You* (2003)

❋ ❋ ❋

Oya Baydar is possibly using her own experience of exile (see the introductory note to the extract from Its Warm Ashes Remained, *towards the end of the 'Stamboullus' section) in this short but moving extract from her novel* The Gate of the Judas Tree.

I was fourteen when we boarded the British ship which was to take our small family from the Karaköy pier to the New World. It was the end of summer. My mother was wearing a white linen dress, which reflected the dark blue glitter of her black hair and her black eyes. She was waving to Aunt Irene and Uncle Dimitri at the pier while trying to control little Marianne who was trying to climb onto the railing of the deck. Rings of rubies, diamonds, emeralds and jade, which she wore over her white mesh gloves, were sparkling on every finger of her elegant hand. My father wiped his eyes while pretending to clean his glasses with the white silk handkerchief which he always kept in the left pocket of his smart dark coloured linen jacket. Aunt Irene was holding a pink handkerchief which she occasionally brought to her eyes or to her nose. I remember that my stomach churned and my eyes clouded over when the whistle blew twice and the boat started to weigh anchor. What does an adolescent who is barely pushing a moustache leave behind in a city he abandons, what does he carry inside his heart? Which tastes, which perfumes, which colours, which memories?

Istanbul was the smell of wood shavings, resin, polish, aloe, frying fish, seaweed and jasmine. It was the climbing yellow roses, the mimosas and the jasmines of Büyükada, the Judas trees of the Beylerbeyi copse, the aromatic pink strawberries of the Arnavutköy hills. It was the shared taxis that left

Taksim for Nişantaşı, the dim coolness of the Covered Bazaar, the appetizing smoke of the Sultanahmet meatball restaurant, the smell of the Flower Arcade which was a mixture of fried muscles, roasted *kokoreç*, beer and a whiff of the toilet; and it was also the bittersweet memory of undeclared puppy love for a little girl with long blond hair and a bouffant skirt.

Oya Baydar, *The Gate of the Judas Tree* (2004)
translated by Stephanie Ateş

✻ ✻ ✻

And exiles returning to the city may have some surprises in store ...

'How long is it exactly since you last were here?'

'Ten years next June.'

'Then you're in for a shock.'

They swung around the bend, and there it was, the famous view. To the left, the Galata Bridge with its swarming crowds. To the front, the swarm of ferries and fishing boats coming in and out of the Golden Horn. The hills of the European city, the Galata Tower and the church spires mingling with the domes and the minarets and the tenements spilling down the hill to the Bosphorus, the hills of Asia. The Bosphorus was grey and choppy, dissolving into a mist. But then the sky broke through the clouds, and there it was, the great arcs of the new bridge joining Europe to Asia.

Maureen Freely, *Enlightenment* (2007)

✻ ✻ ✻

We finish with one of the city's most famous stories of exile – and return from exile.

For several centuries, packs of wild dogs have quarrelled over, and divided between them, the Muslim districts of Istanbul. Each district, especially in the Turkish sector, had its own pack, fed by its residents. The dogs were masters of the streets. They often forced passers-by to make detours and hated to be disturbed. It was impossible to go about at night without a hefty stick to arm oneself against their attacks. Philip Mansel tells the story of a drunken sailor who fell over in the street in the Galata area and of whom, next morning, only the bones were found. He also tells how, after the inauguration of the first tram route, they had to send employees ahead to clear the dogs that were obstructing the tram-lines.

In the end the power of the dogs came to challenge that of the sultans. Abdülmedjid decided to gather up all the city's dogs and exile them to one of the Princes' Islands. Up until that time only emperors, empresses, religious leaders, princes and princesses had been deported to the Princes' Islands, though only after the men had had their eyes gouged out and women their heads shaved. No-one objected to these banishments; it was in a spirit of mockery that the Red Islands, as the Turks called them (or Priests' Islands, according to the Greeks) were nicknamed Princes' Islands. The deportation of the dogs threw up more problems. When the wind blew from the Sea of Marmara, one could hear them, from the Asian side, baying to the moon. The population declared their attachment to these creatures, and the sultan had to bring the exiles back by boat.

Daniel Rondeau, *Istanbul* (2002)
translated by Erica King

"Hagia Sophia ... huge, fairly unadorned, with shafts of light breaking on matt walls, dark arches all around"

Eduardo Reyes

Built to last

One of the legacies of Istanbul's past is its glorious architecture – probably the chief reasons many people visit the city. The most famous building is Hagia Sophia (originally the Byzantine Christian Church of the Holy Wisdom) which has probably spawned more words than any of the others. First, Edmondo de Amicis waxes lyrical on the subject of its famous dome.

The chief marvel of the mosque is the great dome. Looked at from the centre of the nave below, it seems indeed, as Madame de Staël said of the Dome of St Peter's, like an abyss suspended over one's head. It is immensely high, has an enormous circumference, and its depth is only one-sixth of its diameter which makes it appear still larger. A narrow gallery runs round the base and above this gallery there is a circle of forty arched windows. At the top of the dome is written the sentence pronounced by Mehmet II, as he sat on his horse in front of the high altar on the day Constantinople was captured: 'Allah is the light of heaven and of earth'; and some of the letters, which are white upon a black ground, are nine metres tall. As everyone knows, this aerial miracle could never have been constructed with ordinary materials: its vaults were built of pumice stone that floats on water and with bricks from the island of Rhodes, five of which weigh only slightly more than a single normal one. Each brick was inscribed with David's sentence: '*Deus in medio eius non commovebitur; adiuvabit eam Deus vultu suo.*' At every twelfth course of bricks, the relics of saints were enclosed. While the workmen laboured, the priests chanted, Justinian in a linen tunic watched, and an immense crowd gaped in wonderment. And such a reaction need not astonish us when we think that the construction of this 'second firmament', so marvellous even in our own day, was in the sixth century an undertaking without precedent. The vulgar crowd believed it was suspended in the air by magic, and, for a long time after the Conquest, when the Turks were praying in the mosque, they had to force themselves to keep their faces towards the east and not turn them upwards to 'the stone sky'. The dome, in fact, covers almost half the nave, so that it dominates and lights the whole edifice, and a part of it may be seen from every side; whichever way you turn, you always find yourself beneath it, and your gaze and your thoughts repeatedly return to rise and float within its circle with an intensely pleasurable sensation, like that of flying.

Edmondo de Amicis, *Constantinople* (1877)
translated by Stephen Parkin

✣ ✣ ✣

Journalist and architecture enthusiast Eduardo Reyes recalls the impact Hagia Sophia had upon him as a teenager.

I went to Istanbul in the late 1980s on a school cruise, at an age when the world was unfolding before my inexperienced eyes at a tremendous rate. At fifteen, the urge to describe something, or to win an argument, with reference to a book I had read, was just beginning to be replaced by reference to things I had seen, and Hagia Sophia made a huge impact on my teenage mind.

My experience of 'big' architectures in the UK and US had been very different to this. Till then, I had found, important buildings were cleaned, their sculptures and paintings labelled and floodlit. They were well-kept and nicely curated – the rotunda at the National Trust's Ickworth was balanced by a great gift shop.

But Hagia Sophia – wow. Oddly, from the outside, lit by the mid-morning sun with the 'mighty Bosphorus' behind, I didn't quite get it. Only by stepping into this building – huge, fairly unadorned, with shafts of light breaking on matt walls, dark arches all around, unfamiliar symbols hanging where a contested cross had once been – did I get the proper sense of this incredible structure.

Hagia Sophia makes sense of St Peter's, St Paul's, the Blue Mosque, the East London Mosque and the US Capitol. Once through that first set of arches, I raised an old borrowed camera upwards towards the dome. 'You'll never get a picture in this light,' a teacher advised me (a large disappointed Canon with a flash atop hung around his neck). I lowered my flashless camera, found a setting that allowed an exposure of a full second, and held it as steady as I could – and squeezed the button.

I no longer have that picture, but it was good considering the limitations. There was the inner dome, the light from its surrounding windows, an Islamic pendant and, at the edges of the picture, the unanswerable gloom and shadows that had impressed me the most.

Here one could see – despite the picture being grainy in places – was the kind of space that someone had conquered by owning, rather than destroying. It had been competed over and, to my teenage eyes, it was not clear that the competition was definitely over.

Eduardo Reyes, 'Big Architecture' (2011)

❊ ❊ ❊

William Dalrymple catches a glimpse of the divine.

At the end of the Hippodrome, then as now, rises the great dome of Justinian's Hagia Sophia, the supreme masterpiece of Byzantine architecture, and still, in the eyes of many, the most beautiful church ever built. No other Christian building is so successful in transporting one to the threshold of another world, or so dazzlingly intimates the imminence of the transcendent. In the golden haze of its interior, with its extraordinary play of light and space, precious stone and mosaic, under a dome that blazes like the vault of Heaven, even the solid walls seem to cease being barriers and become like passages into a higher reality. When it was first built in the 530s, Procopius, in one of his finest passages, described the overwhelming effect it has on the visitor. 'So bright is the glow of the interior that you might say that it is not illuminated by the sun from the outside but that the radiance it generated within,' he wrote in *The Buildings*. 'Rising above is an enormous spherical dome which seems not to be founded on solid masonry, but to be suspended from heaven by a Golden Chain. Whenever one goes into this church to pray, one understands immediately that this work has been fashioned not by human power and skill, but by the influence of God. And so the visitor's mind is lifted up to God and floats aloft, thinking that He cannot be far away, but must love to dwell in this place which He himself has chosen.'

The power of the building has not been diminished by fourteen hundred years of earthquakes and rebuildings, the destruction of much of its mosaic, the stripping of its altars, nor even a city fire which caused molten lead from the dome to run down the gutters in a flood of boiling metal. As you stand in the narthex you can see even the gossiping tour groups falling silent as they enter the dome chamber; if anyone talks they do so in a hushed whisper. The sacred breaks in on the mundane; and one immediately understands what a Byzantine monk must have felt when he touched a relic or gazed at a sacred icon: for a moment the gates of perception open and one catches a momentary glimpse of the Divine.

William Dalrymple, *From the Holy Mountain* (1997)

❊ ❊ ❊

But for one visitor, the Hagia Sophia was not the most beautiful of the city's mosques.

Perhaps I am in the wrong, but some Turkish mosques please me better. That of Sultan Suleyman is in an exact square with four fine towers on the angles, in the midst a noble cupola supported with beautiful marble pillars, two lesser at the ends supported in the same manner, the pavement and gallery round the mosque of marble. Under the great cupola is a fountain adorned with such fine coloured pillars I can hardly think them natural marble. On one side is the pulpit of white marble, and on the other the little gallery for the Grand Signor. A fine staircase leads to it and it is built up with gilded lattices. At the upper end is a sort of altar where the name of God is written, and before it stand two candlesticks as high as a man, with wax candles as thick as three flambeaux. The pavement is spread with fine carpets and the mosque illuminated with a vast number of lamps. The court leading to it is very spacious, with galleries of marble with green fountains covered with twenty-eight leaded cupolas on two sides, a fine fountain of three basins in the midst of it. The description may serve for all the mosques in Constantinople; the model is exactly the same, and they only differ in largeness and richness of materials. That of the Validé is the largest of all, built entirely of marble, the most prodigious and, I think, the most beautiful structure I ever saw, be it spoke to the honour of our sex, for it was founded by the mother of Mohammed IV. Between friends, St Paul's Church would make a pitiful figure near it, as any of our squares would do near the Atmeydan, or Place of Horses, 'at' signifying horse in Turkish.

Lady Mary Wortley Montagu, *Turkish Embassy Letters* (1716)

✳ ✳ ✳

Equally important to the flourishing of the great city were the 'hans', providing shelter and storage for the many traders bringing their goods to Constantinople.

Yet cheek by jowl with the grand mosques are dozens of little-known *hans* that served a large and flourishing community of foreign traders by offering both lodging and warehousing – and were amply provided with stout doors and massive stone walls for the purpose. Some *hans* provided for the spiritual well-being of the merchants as well, by including a small mosque. Istanbul benefited from being both at the doorstep of Europe and at the western terminus of the silk routes: it was at the *hans* that the caravans from Asia, laden with spices, silks and porcelains, were put up.

At one time there were scores of *hans*. Evliya Chelebi, the most peripatetic of seventeenth-century Turkish chroniclers and a man who wrote extensively about Istanbul, describes two dozen of the largest *hans*. Most were known primarily by the goods traded within: woollens, cloth, slaves, honey, furs. Still others were known chiefly by the peoples living there: Bulgarians, Egyptians and Persians.

The neat distinctions of commodity and nationality no longer apply, and those *hans* that survive are given over to many small and frequently unrelated industries. They are often in sad disrepair and somewhat ill used by the tinkers and merchants who tenant them. But the *hans* are loud with echoes of the past and, to any tourist determined enough to seek them out, convey a deep and indelible impression of the daily life of Istanbul as it was four centuries ago.

John K. McDonald, 'Istanbul's Caravan Stops' (1983)
The New York Times April 17, 1983

❋ ❋ ❋

The Harem (or Seraglio) – the women's quarters of the Topkapı Palace – have always been popular with tourists, even in the eighteenth century ...

I have taken care to see as much of the seraglio as is to be seen. It is on a point of land running into the sea; a palace of prodigious extent, but very irregular, the gardens a large compass of ground full of high cypress trees, which is all I know of them, the buildings all of white stone, leaded on top, with gilded turrets and spires, which look very magnificent, and indeed I believe there is no Christian king's palace half so large. There are six large courts in it all built round and set with trees, having galleries of stone; one of these for the guard, another for the slaves, another for the officers of the kitchen, another for the stables, the fifth for the divan, the sixth for the apartment

190

destined for audiences. On the ladies' side there are at least as many more, with distinct courts belonging to their eunuchs and attendants, their kitchens, etc.

Lady Mary Wortley Montagu, *Turkish Embassy Letters* (1716)

✳ ✳ ✳

Gül İrepoğlu conjures the wonderful library built within the grounds of the palace early in the eighteenth century.

Erecting a new build in the middle of the inner palace called Enderun, in this Third Courtyard of the imperial palace that only admitted the emperor's closest, was no mean feat. Erecting a new building with an entirely new purpose just behind the majestic Audience Chamber – as if in competition with it – and on the foundations of the Pool Pavilion that one had demolished especially for this purpose, this most certainly was no mean feat. The library was but one of the innovations of 1719, that most dynamic year.

No one had considered dedicating an entire building to books to date; true, books had always been precious and the most priceless of all belonged to the sovereign himself, but those books had always been safeguarded in the treasury. And here was Ahmed Han, venturing to spend a fortune on a building specifically for books alone, that Enderun officials may read. It was rumoured that Nedim the Poet would be entrusted with the curatorship, the poet who praised the innovations of the emperor so, and whose verses rejoiced in the finer things in life. The cupboards were filled with theological books, and literary also; there were books on sciences, medicine and history. Enderun ağas were known to be partial to books on dream interpretations.

The chief imperial architect had raised the building over a semi-basement, that those priceless treasures within, those manuscripts, plain and illuminated, would be properly safeguarded from humidity. This building combined the unassuming splendour of antiquity with the cheerful insouciance of its own time.

The drinking fountain in front, set between the twin staircases, was as unthreatening and inviting as the library itself: a heart-shaped gilt handle on the tap and carved tulips bending elegantly on either side. The staircases led to a porch, slender columns supporting arches, a veritable portal for the supplicant to enter a hallowed chamber. The emperor had been pleased, and the chief architect's reward reflected the favour.

Levnî savoured the bright warmth that enveloped him as he entered the library, having climbed the stairs and passed under the porch. His emperor had asked for an honest appraisal of this new work, so the companion had come unaccompanied, to get a full impression.

The gilded and painted dome was like a reflection of the rich world that was contained within the library. The colourful flowers in the rows of vases looked eternally fresh, especially the tulips. Daylight, soft, not dazzling, streamed down onto the readers from the clerestory windows of the bays on three sides of the central chamber.

A deliberate quiet spread from the golden hexagonal flagstones on the floor to the veins of the porphyry columns, and from the tranquil repetition of the blue-and-white tile patterns on the walls to the subtle sheen of the silver screens and the mother-of-pearl of the built-in cupboards. These fabulous tiles produced two hundred years ago, when the Ottomans enjoyed the peak of their power, had already graced the walls of other emperors' pavilions: as those other pavilions succumbed to the effects of time, so were these priceless tiles carefully prised off, that they may be reused: and here they were, displaying the pride of yet another emperor.

Gül İrepoğlu, *Unto the Tulip Gardens: My Shadow* (2004)
translated by Feyza Howell

✳ ✳ ✳

*Another of the architectural wonders of the city
are the Cisterns – an amazing feat of engineering
built at the same time as the Hagia Sophia. Until
1987, when they were restored, one could only row
through them (as James Bond did in* From Russia
With Love*). Now there are walkways, atmos-
pherically subdued lighting, a café, and sometimes
musical performances. A good place to visit on a hot
day and no longer the fearsome experience suggested
by Edmondo de Amicis.*

I entered the courtyard of a Muslim house, went down a damp
and gloomy staircase by the light of a torch to find myself
under the vault of Yerebatan Sarayı, the great Cistern Basilica
of Constantine, the extent of which, or so the common people
of the city believe, has never been ascertained. The greenish
water is lost to sight under the black arches, illuminated here
and there by a ray of pale light which only accentuates the
horror of the surrounding shadows. The torch threw a fiery
gleam upon the arches near the door and revealed dripping
walls and endless rows of columns wherever one looked, like
tree trunks in a dense flooded forest. With a pleasurable sensation of terror the imagination wanders off down those long
sepulchral porticoes, hovers above the gloomy waters and
loses itself in giddying circles among the innumerable columns,
while the dragoman, in a low voice, tells fearsome tales of those
brave enough to explore those subterranean solitudes in a boat,
hoping to discover how far they extend, only to return after
many hours of frantic rowing, with their hair standing on end
and their faces transfixed with horror, while the distant vaults
echo with loud laughter and shrill whistling; and as for others
who never came back, who knows what became of them?
Perhaps they were driven mad with terror, or died of starva-
tion, or were carried away by some mysterious current far from

Stamboul. This lugubrious vision vanished immediately in the broad daylight of the Atmeydanı square. A few minutes later I was again underground among the two hundred pillars of the dry cistern called Binbirdirek, where, lit by some feeble rays that filter down through the arches, a hundred Greek workmen were weaving silk and chanting some warlike song in high-pitched voices. I could hear the confused noise of a caravan passing overhead. Then once more the sunshine and the open columns, in a tomb-like silence broken only by a fair sound of distant voices – and so on until evening, a mysterious, thought-provoking pilgrimage, after which I was haunted for a long time by the image of an underground lake, into which the metropolis of the Byzantine Empire had sunk and vanished, and where the gay and heedless city of Stamboul would one day disappear in her turn.

Edmondo de Amicis, *Constantinople* (1877)
translated by Stephen Parkin

✻ ✻ ✻

You can't possibly visit Istanbul without savouring the Grand Bazaar. We've already been there, in passing, in other extracts, but here Philip Mansel gives us some of its history.

All the merchants of the city, whether Muslim, Greek, Jewish or Armenian, met in the bazaar on the brow of the hill between the Golden Horn and the Sea of Marmara. The streets of Constantinople were unusually quiet. The bazaar, however, greeted visitors with a rush of heat, colour, perfumes and noise: 'Buy my fine cloth, one thousand kurush! Buy my fine cloth, two thousand kurush!'

The bazaar is an immense stone edifice, so large that it was said that no native of Constantinople ever saw it all. Surrounded by high grey walls and surmounted by a roof of cupolas perforated with holes to let in light, it contains a labyrinth of arcaded alleys, crowned by plaster vaults stencilled in elaborate Ottoman blue and red arabesques. Each alley was lined on both sides by stalls, known as *dolaps*, about seven or eight feet wide and three to four feet deep, decorated with flowers and pious messages from the Koran. There were some four thousand stalls, about a tenth of all those in the city as a whole. Each *dolap* had a bench in front where the vendor displayed his wares. Most stall-keepers were Muslims and built a small recess for ritual ablutions, where they retired before performing their prayers on the bench. The bazaar was a miniature city with its own mosques, courtyards and fountains: one was erected by an imperial princess 'in honour of a shoemaker who sent home his work punctually'.

The bazaar was opened every morning at about half past eight with prayers for the Sultan and his soldiers and the souls of all past members of the bazaar, and an injunction: 'There will be no cheating! There will be no hoarding! There will be no sale of goods without security!' The tradesmen then filed in. The stalls closed at about six in the evening.

The nucleus of the bazaar was the Bedesten, or covered market, now called the Old Bazaar, built by Mehmed II in 1456–61. By 1473 there were a hundred and twenty-four shops inside and seventy-two outside the Bedesten. Over two thirds were Muslim-owned. The Bedesten was surrounded by four gates, of the skullcap-sellers, the cloth-sellers, the jewellers and the second-hand booksellers. The latter's reputation for meanness was such that the phrase 'worse than a second-hand bookseller' entered bazaar lore. Outside the Bedesten every product had its particular street. In the street of the arms dealers, the sixteenth-century French traveller Philippe du Fresne Canaye was entranced by 'harnesses in silver gilt with very fine carving, a lot of golden vases, very rare plumes with rubies and turquoises in such quantity that it is impossible to regard them fixedly … In short one sees so many beautiful things there that it is very difficult to leave without putting one's hand in one's purse.' The rents from the Bedesten went to the *vakif* or endowment which supported Aya Sofya.[1]

The bazaar also contained state-designated safes built behind the stalls, where individuals deposited jewels and money. It was probably more free of crime than markets in the West. Merchants could leave stalls unattended; pastry-sellers trusted members of the public to pay for the wares they left on a small round tray. In 1591 a robbery of safes in the Grand Bazaar was an unprecedented horror. The culprit was a young man who worked for an Armenian jeweller – he hid the goods under the straw matting on the shop floor. He was hanged in the Sultan's presence. It was not until the nineteenth century and the advent of modern tourism that the bazaar acquired a reputation as a nest of vultures.

The bazaar combined the roles of shopping centre, stock exchange and bank. It was also a club where merchants met to plan transactions and voyages. Dudley North missed the bazaar more than anywhere else in Constantinople, for he had found there 'almost any kind of thing that any man desires or uses'. Above all it was a meeting-place. In London, despite the coffee-houses and the Exchange, 'those that wanted him, could not find him, any more than he them'.

The bazaar was surrounded by twenty-one hans, like the Buyuk Valide Han, built to foster trade. Consisting of two or three arcaded storeys around a tree-filled courtyard, the hans accommodated goods and animals on the ground floor, and craftsmen and merchants on the first and second floors. Unlike most houses in the city, hans were made of stone.

Philip Mansel, *Constantinople:*
City of the World's Desire, 1453–1924 (1995)

❊ ❊ ❊

---

1 Another spelling of Hagia Sophia (Ed.)

*William Dalrymple takes us to the Hippodrome where
chariot races used to take place. Now a pleasant green
place, the road around it is said to follow the original
race-track.*

In the cool of the evening I walked over to the Hippodrome.
In what was once the stalls, where the violent Byzantine circus
factions once knifed it out, large Turkish ladies in headscarves
now sit quietly gossiping on park benches. Their husbands
squat nearby, under the chestnuts, cracking pistachio nuts. The
occasional salesman with a glass cupboard on wheels wanders
past, hawking paper cones full of chickpeas. Gulls hover silently
overhead. It is strange to think that the hippodrome once held
120,000 people – double the present-day capacity of Wembley
Stadium.

The obelisk of the Emperor Theodosius still stands in the
centre of the old racetrack, rising from the plinth where it was
placed in the 430s. A carving on the side shows the cat's-cradle
of ropes and pulleys which was used to raise it. On another face
is carved a picture of the Emperor in the imperial baldachin
overlooking the races; these are illustrated at the base with a
series of small relief carvings of what look like horse-drawn
bathtubs.

Between the Emperor and the charioteers stand his body-
guard, a remarkably effeminate gaggle of fops with long sloppy
fringes, every bit as willowy as St John Damascene's blood-
and-fire sermons might have led one to expect. Certainly these
gentle cosmopolitans not only look remarkably unthreatening,
they appear to be much more interested in the races than in
guarding the Emperor. Here could lie part of the explanation
for the large number of successful assassination attempts in
Byzantine history.

William Dalrymple, *From the Holy Mountain* (1997)

✳ ✳ ✳

> *Another famous architectural feature of the city, the* yalıs *are waterside mansions traditionally made of wood and ideal as a cool, summer retreat.*

Air, light, summer, *yalı*. Happy, breezy palaces of the aristocratic and the rich. Ottoman princes, Greek bankers: two centuries ago they were already escaping the oppressive summer heat in their *yalıs*, their villas on the shore. Courtiers waited all year for a signal from the sultan, then loaded their splendid *Kayık*, slender boats, and transformed the move into a festival. Each house had a boat dock and a magnificent garden up the hill. The wood structure gave protection from the sun yet admitted the cool breeze which the *Poyraz* brought from the northeast. Even the windows were different from those in city houses, allowing the play of light: fully adjustable shutters, brightly painted on the interior side, captured light reflected from the surface of the water and conveyed it into the interior. In many places the boat docks have been sacrificed to a street along the shore. The gardens are still there: peonies, oleander, hydrangeas, bougainvillea, roses, lavender, persimmons, and mulberries. Not easy to pick, the mulberries: one person shakes the tree, the others hold an outspread sheet underneath. Early in the year there is an intoxicating scent and an intoxicating view when the explosion of Judas Tree blossoms on the slopes lines the Bosphorus with pink to the left and right. *Yalı* comes from the Greek *gialos*, or 'bank.' Where the coast road runs behind the *yalı*, they still sit directly on the water today: the Bosphorus knows no high or low tides. You don't need to worry about floods here, though the wash from powerful tankers is another matter. Many an idler has been roused from his dreams by their wake.

Kai Strittmatter, *User's Guide to Istanbul* (2010)
translated by Susan Thorne

*American Chris Hellier gives a detailed description of
the* yalı's *construction and history.*

[A] glimpse of a perfect ceiling is to be caught by any one who
rows up the Asiatic shore [of the Bosphorus] from Anadolu
Hisar ... this ceiling, and the whole room to which it belongs, is
the most precious thing of its kind in all Constantinople, if not
in all the world.

That was how American writer H. G. Dwight in 1907
described what is today the oldest surviving *yalı* (*yah*-lih), the
home of Köprülü Amcazâde Hüseyin Pasha, who served as
grand vizier under the Ottoman sultan Mustafa II in the last
decade of the seventeenth century. Though its terra-cotta-rose
paint has long since faded and its timbers have grown weary,
the grand house still stands on the Bosphorus shore, one of the
several dozen remaining *yalıs* of the former Ottoman elite.

It was in the latter half of the seventeenth century, when the
Empire stretched from Mecca to Budapest and from Tunis to
Tabriz, that it became fashionable for Ottoman viziers, admi-
rals, and civil and miltiary pashas to build prestigious summer
homes along the Bosphorus, the strait that separates Europe
and Asia. These homes were called *yalıs*, a word deriving from
the Greek *yialos*, or seashore.

Like the Newport 'cottages' of the American elite in the late
nineteenth century, *yalıs* in their time functioned as extravagant
retreats where the owners and their families escaped the
sweltering bustle of the city. Today, however, Istanbul's
remaining *yalıs* are glimpses into Ottoman high culture across
more than two centuries, and the social standing of their
owners gave these homes important roles in society, politics,
and architecture.

Only a handful of the earliest *yalıs* still stand. These were
invariably built of timber and roofed with red tiles. The exterior
walls were stained a deep earth-toned red, known as 'Ottoman

rose,' which made the façades stand out against the forested slopes with their pink cherry blossoms, green-leafed chestnuts, and slim, dark cypresses. During the eighteenth and nineteenth centuries, the increasing popularity of European tastes led to the supplanting of the traditional red façade by pastel shades.

The arrangement of rooms within each *yalı* harks back to the earliest Turkish houses that, like the Turks themselves, can be traced to Central Asia. From the *sofa*, or central salon, where a freestanding fountain cooled the summer heat, internal doors typically led into four corner rooms.

The cruciform central hall often included one or more recessed sitting areas that overhung the Bosphorus waters, thus affording unobstructed views. Here, members of the household received their guests.

Like all larger Ottoman houses, *yalıs* were divided into a *selamlık* for the men and a *haremlık* for the women – though the women's side was sometimes a separate building. Each *yalı* also had its *hamam*, or bath, often made of marble, which was divided into steam and cool rooms. Men and women used the *hamam* at different, designated times of the week.

Upper-class ladies often spent summer days on excursions in the gardens and the extensive grounds that surrounded nearly all *yalıs* on the landward side. Enclosed footbridges, known as 'privacy bridges,' often spanned the narrow access road behind each house and connected the enclosed gardens with the forested grounds, allowing the women of the household private passage to the grounds. Over the last century, road-widening projects have torn down all but one of these.

Towards the end of the nineteenth century, when the number of *yalıs* had reached its peak, a highlight of the summer social season was the *mehtâb*, one of the most extraordinary spectacles of an affluent and aesthetically refined era. On summer evenings when the moon was bright and the Bosphorus calm, rich and poor alike would throng the shore to watch and listen as a flotilla of private boats – sometimes numbering in the hundreds – would weave its way north in a snakelike procession, often calling at prominent *yalıs* on both shores along the way. In the lead was a special concert boat fitted with a raised platform on which an orchestra performed, or vocalists accompanied by the flutelike *ney*, the stringed dulcimer, and the *saz*.

With such prominent owners, *yalıs* invariably also played host to history. In the central *sofas*, viziers received visiting ministers and heads of state, treating them first to banquets and later to negotiations that, in several instances, altered the shape of the empire. The far-reaching Karlowitz Treaty – which ceded to Austria territories in the Balkans, including Hungary and Transylvania – was ratified in the Köprülü Yalı in 1699. The Küçük Kaynarca Treaty recognising Crimean independence was also signed there in 1774. Early in this century, negotiations with German officials in the Sait Halim Pasha Yalı led to Turkish involvement in World War I.

Architecturally, *yalıs* were bellwethers of style. From the earliest, entirely Ottoman *yalı*, they gradually adopted features that reflected Istanbul's rising fascination with European designs. From the 1730s to the early 1800s, a style now called 'Turkish baroque' brought elaborate decorative schemes to the Bosphorus and encouraged the replacement of traditional built-in cupboards and divans with European-style, freestanding furniture.

In the latter half of the nineteenth century, this gave way to a neo-Western classicism, the 'empire' style – a term the Ottomans borrowed from the French – that produced several of the largest *yalıs*. Toward the close of the nineteenth century, this was overshadowed by an eclectic 'cosmopolitan' style wherein several *yalıs* became ensembles of European towers and Ottoman onion domes, each ornamented with Islamic motifs. Finally, during the decade prior to World War I, a Turkish expression of Art Nouveau influenced some of the last of the Ottoman *yalıs* to be built.

Yalıs were rarely built for longevity. In Ottoman Turkey there was no hereditary aristocracy that bequeathed property from one generation to another, as was the custom in Europe. A pasha's position depended on his relations with the sultan. Should the pasha fall from grace or the sultan fall from power, the family's fortunes fell as well, and the *yalı* often became impossible to maintain.

Indeed, temporality is intrinsic to timber buildings. Winter rains and the moist sea air both encouraged rot. On an unseasonably chilly July day in 1910, the romantic French novelist Pierre Loti, staying at the *yalı* of his friend Count Ostrorog, noted that 'a balmy dampness fills my bedroom overlooking the sea, like an old ship whose hull is no longer watertight.'

Simple forms of heating, such as the common open brazier, or *mangal*, caused several devastating fires. Later, in the 1940s and 1950s, rising land prices took a further toll. Thus only a handful of eighteenth-century *yalıs* have survived, and a number more from the nineteenth century. During the 1980s, some of these received new leases on life as a new class of moneyed Turkish entrepreneurs revived the prestige of a historic Bosphorus summer home.

Today, the remaining *yalıs* are protected buildings, divided into several categories according to their architectural importance. One, the eighteenth-century Bostancibaşi Abdullah Ağa Yalı at Çengelköy, has been acquired by the Ministry of Tourism, and it is being remodeled to accommodate a restaurant and a souvenir shop.

The future of the best eighteenth-century *yalıs* now seems brighter than at any time this century.[1] Several have actually remained in the same family for generations, and their current owners are committed to their upkeep. The Çürüksulu Yalı at Salacak, for instance, is maintained largely as it was originally conceived by one of Turkey's leading industrialists.

---

1   Note that the article was written in 1996, so this refers to the twentieth century. (Ed.)

Istanbul Socialite Ayşegül Nadir is restoring the Sa'dullah Pasha Yalı. Restoration of this oldest of the *yalıs* was first planned in 1915, but was derailed when, following World War I, the Ottoman era ended with the establishment of the modern Republic of Turkey.

Chris Hellier, 'Mansions on the Water' (1996)
in *Saudi Aramco World*, April/May 1996

✳ ✳ ✳

Some of the yalıs *of the early eighteenth century were particularly sumptuous and the site of dazzling social occasions.*

Üsküdar's Salacak quarter had a particularly jolly time of it in 1718. The grand vizier's splendid new yalı dazzled all. The grounds backed onto a wide swathe of cypress woods, and bijou gazebos, spray fountains and flowerbeds in a rainbow of colours graced the gardens; verily, this was a palace on a small scale. The water distribution point built at the site they call Doğancılar supplied the mansion and its vast gardens as well as Üsküdar itself.

No more *plus ça change* for the new Grand Vizier İbrahim Pasha; a new and brilliant lifestyle, that was his pleasure. All the finest things in the world would enfold him, refinement elevating his lifestyle, all the challenges of the new and untested making it all so very worthwhile …

The mansion named Şerefabad had been constructed with the singular aim of pleasing Sultan Ahmed, playing host being İbrahim Pasha's foremost consideration. The verses inviting the emperor had to come from the celebrated poet Nedim; beholden upon the statesman was rewarding the man of letters handsomely:

Every breath, its water and air add life to life
Your arrival imbues the universe with teasing and restraint

Which day will my sovereign honour us, all a-flutter,
Come, just see Şerefabad once, my majestic sovereign ...

Master of racing words as his pen flourished elaborately,
Nedim had delivered once more: Ahmed Han did honour the
mansion his son-in-law had built with such attention to detail.
The imperial caïque delivered the emperor up to the landing
stage. The emperor first rested a while in the main room of the
over-adorned mansion, and then moved to the wooden garden
gazebo by the waterfront. He praised his son-in-law's fine taste
in selecting this site, tasting the delicacies placed before him,
whilst enjoying the view: Leander's Tower that looked close
enough to touch, his own home at Sarayburnu, the port and
Galata on the other side of the city.

This was the first of so many more: waterfront villas called
yalıs would line the banks of the Bosphorus, all competing with
one another. Each more flamboyant than the rest, each bearing a
more pretentious name that the rest, each staging more dazzling
shows and each receiving ever more exaggerated praise.

Gül İrepoğlu, *Unto the Tulip Gardens: My Shadow* (2004)
translated by Feyza Howell

✳ ✳ ✳

Another reminder of the city's architecturally gracious
past is the Sultan Ahmet Fountain.

It is one of the richest and most original monuments of Turkish
art. But, more than a monument, it is a marble jewel which a
gallant sultan placed on the forehead of his beloved Stamboul.
I believe that only a woman could describe it well. My pen
is not fine enough to trace its image. At first sight it does not
look like a fountain. It is in the form of a small square temple,
with a Chinese-style roof with undulating slopes which project
a long way, giving it a somewhat pagoda-like appearance. At
each of the four corners there is a small round tower, with little

204

grated windows, or rather four charming little kiosks, which are matched above the roof with four slender little cupolas, each one surmounted by a graceful pinnacle, and all encircling a larger cupola in the middle. On each of the four sides there are two elegant niches flanking a pointed arch, and under each arch a jet of water falls into a small basin. An inscription runs all round the edifice which says: 'This fountain speaks to you in the verses of Sultan Ahmet; turn the key of this pure and tranquil spring and invoke the name of God; drink of this inexhaustible and limpid water and pray for the Sultan.' The little edifice is all of white marble, which is scarcely visible under all the decorative ornament which covers the wall surfaces; there are little arches and niches and columns, rosettes and polygons, ribbons and lace carved in marble, gilding on blue ground, fringes around the cupolas, inlays under the roof, many-coloured mosaics and arabesques of many forms, which draw the eye in and almost irritate one's sense of wonder. There is hardly an inch of surface which is not carved and gilded and fretted. It is a miracle of grace, richness and patient craft, which should be kept under glass; it's as if it's not made only for the eyes but must have a flavour – one would like to suck a piece of it; or it's a jewel case that one would like to open, and find inside a goddess in the form of a doll, or a gigantic pearl, or a magic ring. Time has in part dimmed the gilding, blurred the colours, and blackened the marble. What must this enormous jewel have been like when it was first unveiled, glittering and new, a hundred and sixty years ago? But old and blackened as it is, it is still supreme among all the smaller marvels of Constantinople; and it is besides so utterly Turkish that it takes its place among the small number of images which spring immediately to mind whenever the name Stamboul is heard, and form the background to our enduring memories of the Orient.

Edmondo de Amicis, *Constantinople* (1877)
translated by Stephen Parkin

* * *

Ottoman structures are not the only interesting archi-
tectural feature of the city. Turkey-based travel writer
Pat Yale enlightens us about its more recent heritage.

As with most cities with long histories tailing them, Istanbul
is a palimpsest on which every generation has left its mark.
There's something here from every era for those with the time
and inclination to hunt it out.

Take Art Nouveau, for example. This is a wonderful, flamboyant style of turn-of-the-twentieth-century architecture most
strongly associated in its different forms with France, Germany,
Austria, the Czech Republic, and Italy. But Istanbul too has
its Art Nouveau legacy, much of it concentrated in Beyoğlu,
Sirkeci, Bebek, Arnavutköy, and Büyükada, but with the odd
stray in Çamlıca, Tarabya, Yeniköy, and Çubuklu too.

The best place to set out on an exploration of Art Nouveau
in Istanbul is the Galata/Tünel end of İstiklal Caddesi in what
is now Beyoğlu but was once Pera, the part of town where the
ambassadors and foreign merchants lived until the founding
of the Turkish Republic. Like most of Istanbul, Pera was originally furnished with wooden houses, but a sequence of fires,
most disastrously in 1870, led to a decision that all new buildings should be in stone. It was this more than anything else
that threw open the doors for the modish European style to
infiltrate the area.

Architect Raimondo d'Aronco was first off the drawing
board. Born in Italy in 1857, d'Aronco had arrived in Istanbul
in 1893 to work on designs for a planned Istanbul Exhibition
of Agriculture and Industry that never materialized after a
terrible earthquake struck the city in 1894. Fortunately by then
he'd caught the eye of Sultan Abdülhamid II who employed
him to restore some of the damaged buildings. Between 1900
and 1901 he built a house for the sultan's tailor, Jean Botter,

that was the city's first Art Nouveau structure. Today it still stands beside the Swedish Consulate, a soot-blackened, crumbling shell of a building festooned with gorgeous stone roses, giant sphinx-like heads and wonderful wrought ironwork that includes dramatic protruding flowers. Inside, even the windows contain stained-glass roses [...].

Once you know what you're looking for it's not hard to spot the classic features of Nouveau Istanbul-style in the clusters of stylized flowers carved on facades, and the swirling, circular designs on wrought-iron balconies, window grilles and metal doors. To modern visitors these look very attractive. However, at the time they were a novelty that didn't find approval with everyone. There were probably as many complaints at the turn of the twentieth century about the new high-rise apartment blocks and their tiny interior spaces as there are today about the even higher-rise concrete apartment blocks; and it turns out that then, as now, many of the new stone buildings were thrown up as investment properties by speculators who wanted to spend as little as possible on them, hence the fact that the Art Nouveau trimmings tend to be strictly façade-deep only. [...]

Art Nouveau is usually thought of as a style of architecture appropriate to stone buildings, but Turkey, with its long tradition of wooden houses, soon found a way to adapt it to local needs. Some of the finest of all Istanbul's Art Nouveau buildings are those that line the waterfront at Arnavutköy. Ironically these lovely houses that now look so individual appear to have been built using ready-made window and doorframes that could be fitted by local builders without the need for expensive architects.

Pat Yale, 'Istanbul's Forgotten Art Nouveau Heritage'
in *Sunday's Zaman* 3 January 2010

✳ ✳ ✳

Flip over a twenty lira banknote and on the reverse you'll see a man in his prime with a big, bristling moustache. This is Kemalettin Bey, an architect whose time seems to have come at last after years in which his work went virtually ignored. But Kemalettin Bey was, with Vedat Tek, one of the prime movers behind a turn-of-the-twentieth-century style of architecture that, unlike the Art Nouveau that started to adorn Istanbul at the same time, drew its inspiration from indigenous styles, particularly those of the Selçuk and Ottoman periods.

Originally called the Neoclassical Turkish style or even the National Renaissance style, this type of architecture is better known nowadays as First National Architecture (Birinci Ulusal Mimarlık). Unlike the spectacular mosques and palaces of the Ottoman period such as the Sultanahmet Cami (Blue Mosque) or Topkapı Sarayı (Palace) to which tourists flock in their thousands, the buildings of the First National style were designed to serve more mundane purposes. Many of them housed – and still do house – workaday government departments. Consequently, they're buildings that people tend to walk past every day without necessarily even noticing them.

First National Architecture had its heyday in the first three decades of the twentieth century when the collapse of the Ottoman Empire and birth of the Turkish Republic led to a growth of interest in Turkish nationalism. Although both Kemalettin Bey (1870–1927) and Vedat Tek (1873–1942) had studied overseas – Kemalettin Bey in Germany, Vedat Tek in France – and although both worked in a multicultural milieu when they returned to Istanbul, they are thought to have been influenced by the ideas of the Turkish nationalist Ziya Gökalp, and to have sought to develop an architectural style that would reflect his ideology. Both men produced works that either aped traditional designs – viz Kemalettin Bey's mosque on the Bebek waterfront and Vedat Tek's mosque behind the Büyük Postane (Main Post Office) in Sirkeci – or mixed in elements of Art

Nouveau, as in the enormous wooden mansion Kemalettin Bey designed for Ahmet Ratip Pasha in Çamlıca. Kemalettin Bey even joined forces with his old tutor August Jasmund to work on Sirkeci train station, a fine example of Oriental Gothic. But both men's most interesting works are those that showed off the characteristics of First National Architecture.

The trademark features of this style are: the decoration of the façades of buildings with panels of Kütahya tiling; thick, pointed windows; overhanging gables; protruding stone roundels; and marble maqarna (stalactite) corbels. Every tourist who stays in Cankurtaran and walks up to Sultanahmet Square will have seen a building that displays all these features without necessarily recognizing what it was. In 1996 the dustcovers finally came off the magnificent building that had been designed in 1919 to serve as Sultanahmet Prison but which had been restored to serve as the luxury Four Seasons Hotel. Although its façade bears all the hallmarks of Vedat Tek's work there is no certainty that he was in fact its architect. Much less mystery surrounds the names of those unfortunates who passed spells inside its walls while it was still a prison, amongst them Billy Hayes, the infamous anti-hero of the dreadful *Midnight Express*, and the far more illustrious writers Nazım Hikmet and Yashar Kemal.

The Four Seasons kickstarted a trend which has been gaining pace in recent years; namely the restoration of the First National buildings and their conversion for new uses. So not long after the Four Seasons opened, the Fourth Vakıf Han, a monumental pile in Sirkeci designed as a business centre by Kemalettin Bey, was converted into what is now the Legacy Ottoman Hotel. Perhaps the most extraordinary makeover was the one given to what started life as a vast abattoir in Sütlüce and is now the Haliç Kongre Merkezi (Golden Horn Conference Centre). Covering 20,000 square metres of land, this was originally the city's largest slaughterhouse, and was only retired from service in the 1980s. Now it can be admired in all its revived splendour as you stroll across the Old Galata Bridge, relocated upstream to provide a pedestrian walkway over the Golden Horn from Eyüp to Sütlüce.

Pat Yale, from 'Nationalism in Stone: Istanbul's Forgotten Treasures' in *Sunday's Zaman* 17 January 2010

"What must it be like to lose power, a city, an empire?"
César Antonio Molina

From *hüzün* to *huzur*:
the city in all its moods

*Hüzün is a little more complicated than 'sadness'
– it involves a kind of nostalgia or regret for what
was glorious but is now past, but also a strange kind
of pleasure in that emotion – and huzur isn't quite
defined as 'joy' or 'happiness'. But precise definitions
aside, this section tries to capture some of the varied
moods the city can evoke in its residents and visitors.
Ayfer Tunç (b.1964) suggests that melancholy loneliness can be transformed into huzur simply by gazing
out over the Bosphorus.*

The house was freezing cold. It felt like the wind was blowing through it. The lazy custodian of our palatial turn-of-the-century apartment building hadn't got up yet to turn on the central heating. I threw one of Osman's sweatshirts over my thin silk nightgown. It was a polar fleece and it warmed me up. I went into the living room. The big window in the high-ceilinged living room was like a television screen marred by static snow showing a flat, grey Istanbul from the top of our hill. Istanbul was sleeping soundly under an ashen mist. […] I stood in front of the window watching the greyish screen slowly come alive in waves. Small motorboats and big city ferryboats appeared on the Bosphorus. A tanker passed through the screen like a creature swimming through the morning mist. The fog was rising and one by one the lights that had pierced the darkness went out. An extreme and violent exuberance surged inside me.

Ayfer Tunç, *The Night of Green Fairy* (2010)
translated by Alexander Dawe

✻ ✻ ✻

Another instance of the views offered by the city having the power to lift one's mood – from Behçet Çelik (b.1968).

While passing through the marketplace, he had no thoughts of going down to the park on the shore. He intended to pick up something to eat and head straight home after taking a short walk. He enjoyed walking, the cool winter sun, and the deserted avenues. It was something he hadn't done in years, wandering idly about at this time of day – on a weekday. So there were times when this place was quiet, deserted like this. Perhaps he hadn't even wandered around here at this time of day back in his schooldays. Leaving the shops, the stores, and the office towers behind, he walked through narrow streets, between low-rise apartment buildings, until he emerged onto a wide, open space that looked down onto the sea, and he suddenly felt happy.

Clusters of clouds veiled the sun, but they were unable to stop a silvery stirring on the sea out beyond from swaying merrily, flickering and fluttering, almost as if winking. So this was how the sun struck the sea at this time of day – yesterday around this hour it was lunchtime at the office. For a while he gazed in awe at the twinkling light. It wasn't just the angle of the sun, the view, and the light that struck him, but the stirring within him – was it silvery too? – also seemed strange and unfamiliar.

Behçet Çelik, *The Drone of the World* (2008)
translated by Amy Spangler

✳ ✳ ✳

Both sadness and pleasure mingle in this piece by Spanish writer and diplomat César Antonio Molina. He visits the Edirnekapı (Edirne gate) and recalls the fall of the Byzantine city in 1453 – one of the most significant dates in Turkish history. Could the sorrow of the then emperor, imagined here, be compared with the sense of loss when the Ottoman empire finally fell at the end of the First World War? ... a loss which, according to some, lies behind the feelings encapsulated in the very word hüzün.

'As he stood there erect before the gate and impregnable in his sorrow,' is the opening line of Odysseas Elytis' poem about Constantinus Paleologus, the emperor who lost Constantinople and Byzantium. Impregnable in his sorrow. What must it feel like to lose power, a city, an empire? What must it be like to be everything, and then, in an instant, nothing? Wherefore Constantine, Theodosius, Justinian? The impregnable sorrow that prevented him from delivering himself to death makes him immortal in his pain, nobody could hurt him now, he has become a soul on perpetual pilgrimage. [...]

I am standing before the Edirnekapı, the gate through which most of the army entered early in the morning of the 29th May

1453. Like the Yedikule and Adrian gates, the dimensions of the opening are not very generous. They look more like the gates to a palace than a city. The construction and doorway are beautiful. When Jesus said that it would be harder for a rich man to get into the kingdom of heaven than for a camel to pass through the eye of a needle, he was referring to a small secondary gate that actually existed in the walls of Jericho or Jerusalem. These gates within gates were known as the eye of the needle. The Edirnekapı inserts a semi-Gothic brick arch into the imposing wall, which then disappears a little way underneath the two sturdy capitals supporting either side of the semicircle. Two people, one on top of the other, would be unable to get through if the one on top didn't bend over. No more than four people standing side by side would fit lengthways. You can see the jambs which framed the door that was dismantled, broken up, burned and then replaced by the conquerors. Today the gateway is diaphanous, open, beseeching. No-one goes through here, it doesn't mean anything any more, not even to tourists. A plaque, in Turkish, makes it even more mysterious. We understand only the dates: the Muslim 857 and the Christian 1453. We have to guess at the rest of the text. I am underneath the arch of the Edirnekapı. It is currently protecting me from a large January snow storm. I didn't know that it snowed so often and so copiously in Istanbul. [...]

When I got out of the car, on the inner side of the wall and, of course, the gate, I saw the great white carpet stretching out further on, up to the long, wide avenue. Now it is full of my footprints. They are just the same as those of other travellers walking in no particular direction. When Sultan Mehmet came through the Edirnekapı it was the end of May and the drifts had long since melted. 'It's difficult to believe that a living city lies within these dead walls! No other place in the world presents such a melancholy panorama as this path flanked on both sides by ruins and cemeteries,' wrote Gautier. Captivated by the snowflakes, I lean against the wall. I feel the fatigue of being oneself. I feel the fatigue of the many others who will come after me. I am a waiting being and end up discovering the disappointment of not knowing what I am waiting for. [...]

When the weather clears I come out from beneath the lintel and, going back over my tracks, look at the construction of which this gap is an insignificant part. 'Landscape, when seen properly, influences the life of the observer,' said Thoreau. Here, before this gate where so much blood was shed, I feel free. Joyful to have found it without having to defend or conquer it. Whilst it allows our thoughts to pass through, it will remain. I take refuge in neither the past nor the future, but on the border that the gate forms between one and the other.

César Antonio Molina, 'Impregnable in His Sorrows' (2010)
translated by Kit Maude

✻ ✻ ✻

A Kurdish author (though writing in Turkish), Suzan Samancı (b.1962) does not always write about the political issues of the Kurdish situation. In the extract below, however, the narrator has been in prison for political activities. The stress of trying to cope with the unfamiliar mood of the noisy, energetic city does not, however, dim the joy of freedom.

Not a soul came to meet me when I was released. My legs were rusty scissors, my arms walking canes. I was taking refuge in the salvation of my backpack, getting lost in the crowd and trying to follow people I thought might be the right ones. I was taking a breather at bus stops, reading signs, and when I asked after an address or the time, the words would get knotted up in my throat. The eyes of the man sitting on the bench twitched. 'It's obvious you're not from around here!' he said.

What torture not to inform me of my release date! When I heard the sound of the sloppy mouthed warden, my wish to have committed a crime worthy of a life sentence was more than a mere passing thought. 'There's a big ol' roaring world out there!' the other inmates laughed. The headcount that struck you like the vilest swear word, the door of rusty iron, the drippy faucet ...

I don't recall how long I sat at the stop. I kept getting lost in thought, staring at the skyscrapers, the huge billboards, from the other side of that foreign wind. I was watching the hurried steps of all those people with their telephones to their ears, and their synchronized arms, and I felt I might suffocate. That's how they release you, just toss you out, just like that. If they'd let me know the day beforehand, my sister would've come ... When I got on the bus, I took the twenty lira bill from my pocket and held it out, asking 'How much?' The driver's bulging eyes became crossed and he shook his head, saying, 'Good heavens, have you been living under a rock! You need a ticket, a ticket!' A red-headed woman sitting in the front row spoke up, 'I've got an extra.' I sat down next to her. She looked at me from over the rims of her glasses and smiled, 'Hmm ... You're from the countryside I imagine!' [...]

When I got off at Taksim, I didn't know which way to go; as I looked around blankly, children selling handkerchiefs and gum stuck to me like ticks. I asked them what their names were. 'Rojda, Mizgin, Welat, Şilan ... '[1] One of them laughed as she yelled out, 'Sister, this one's name is Ajda, Ajda!'

The evening rush, Istanbul with its huge, droning belly! A shiver went down my spine. In a state of mind like those who long for freedom yet recoil from it, I headed for the phone booth. When I had trouble using the card I had bought, I asked the people in line for help. 'You're putting it in backwards,' one of the men grumbled. My breathing grew quick. 'Hello,' my sister said. When I told her I was in Taksim, my voice cracked; I swallowed. I sat down on the bench next to the flower-sellers.

---

1 These are all Kurdish names.

The boisterous Romany women with their giant breasts and wiggly hips were raising a ruckus, smoking cigarettes, their eyes narrowed like foxes observing their prey. I smiled at their brazenness, as they swore like sailors. Words that I was hearing for the first time fluttered in the darkness.

The last time we'd seen each other, my sister had been in poor spirits. I didn't ask her what was wrong. I knew. It was Sinan, the conflict between them, their inability to get along. Yet how sincere and protective she had been when we had first set out to overturn the system. [...]

My eyes are dazzled by this atmosphere, which flickers, full of laser lights. As I pondered the overwhelming distance created by luxury, my sister cried out, 'Ayten!' I froze. She embraced me, sobbing. I buried my face in her neck; it was the scent of my mother. I looked at my sister out of the corner of my eye. Is this my sister? I asked myself. She'd gained weight, her hair had thinned, her face had grown wrinkled before its time. As if reading my thoughts, she told me, 'I'm useless.' As we walked down İstiklal, I kept tripping; I didn't know what to say. The lights, the crowd, they were frightening. Young people were joking around, taking rhythmic strides to the music playing in their ears. My sister told me that Sinan had a successful textile business, that he'd expanded and gotten into export. And then she sighed, 'Money changes people, it changes them a lot.'

Suzan Samancı, *In the Melancholy of Wisteria* (2008)
translated by Amy Spangler

✽ ✽ ✽

In this beautiful piece by Oya Baydar, both the sorrow and the joy, the squalor and the beauty of the city are described.

Each city has its own unique colour; its own scent, sound and sorrow. The seasons look different on each of them. Each carry autumn leaves, flowers of the spring, the sun, snow, rain, joy and sorrow differently. Cities often change habits. They are different in the moment, different in memories, in victory and in defeat, at every age and every love.

New York is baby blue, Moscow khaki green, Athens sand colour, Prague pale violet red, Madrid crimson, Parma yellow, Amsterdam silver, Ankara snow white, Paris French rose, Oslo grey, Berlin beaver brown. As for Istanbul, stretching all the way back to the times of the Byzantine era, Istanbul has always been the colour of redbuds.

Some smell of newly-mown grass, some of seaweed, some fish, some rotten leaves, jasmine, linden trees, lilacs, some sewage, some soot, rain, snow, some of blood, carnations, tangerine blossoms, burnt oil, olive pulp, dry weed, incense, mould, herrings, wall-flowers; yet each smells of memories.

At twilight one night, as she watched the city of Istanbul, she noticed that cities also bore daggers that pierced through the human heart. The sky and sea had orange and purple ripples shining across their navy blue surfaces. Towers, domes and minarets had been lit up, and the lights had begun winking in the twilight.

When she spoke the words, 'This city hurts me inside. It pierces my heart like a pointed dagger,' she wasn't after a fancy stanza, or a pompous line. There, at a spot on the bridge with the best view of the Bosphorus, where on one side stood Saray-burnu, Galata, Üsküdar, the Maiden's Tower, the Islands and on the other, the meandering coast leading to the Black Sea, these words had rather escaped her mouth as a cry. At that moment, the city really had pierced her heart like a dagger. She felt excruciating pain.

For years now the city had been a symbol of the hope to return, a refuge for both memories and fugitives, the last stop for trains awaited at foreign stations which were never to arrive. Istanbul with its side streets, cobblestone slopes, its piers beaten by the lodos wind, its redbuds ready to bloom, its street cats, its mosque courtyards overrun with pigeons, its hungry seagulls, its noisy markets, its full moon that lit up beautiful babes, the fishermen under bridges, wooden mansions whose shadowy courtyards smelled of magnolia and pink roses with petals fit to make jam, the lively factories, the muddy shanty neighbourhoods, the main streets bursting with wealth and goods, the outskirts, its city squares that carried the blood stains of the dead.

'This city hurts me inside. All the cities I love hurt me inside. But this one most of all.'

In front of the window which opened out onto Istanbul, she sat in her usual place, watching the city. The city was there, right in front of her, all around her, in the sea, everywhere; it rose in the twilight with its own inner light, shining with its inner radiance. Wearing the armour of the night it hid its purulent sores under its satin redbud robe, concealing all.

Oya Baydar, Returning Nowhere (1998)
translated by İdil Aydoğan

❊ ❊ ❊

The sights, sounds and smells of Istanbul work like magic ...

I was bewitched, I'm sure, by the slow unfurling splendour of the evening, as the harsh heat of the afternoon dissolved into a golden light, and the sea turned from turquoise to azure to pink and silver. The ferries hissed as they slipped past the pier, the glass windows vibrated with every passing tanker, and the speedboat rocked back and forth, back and forth in the waves every ship and boat, large and small, left in its wake. A breeze started up, bringing with it the smell of fish and roasting corn and chestnuts. The windows of the houses on the Asian shore turned gold with the setting sun. [...]

A great black hulk of a tanker was just coming out from behind the southernmost tower of Rumeli Hisar as they sat down in front of Nafi Baba's tomb. For a few moments the whole hill trembled. They watched it threading its way up the Bosphorus, turning from black to grey. As it crossed paths with another tanker coming down from the Black Sea, a horn sounded. As the sharp, violent blast faded into its mournful echo, they heard the backfiring of a car. Then this, too, faded away. A bird that might have been a nightingale began to sing in the tree above. Could it be a nightingale, if it wasn't night yet? Could anything be more beautiful than the Bosphorus when the Judas trees were in bloom?

Maureen Freely, *Enlightenment* (2007)

✳ ✳ ✳

Another nightingale, another visitor moved by the exquisite experience of the city.

A nightingale sings in the cedars and the evening's mist rises from the strait. Waves of cool air flow around us heavy with the scent of honeysuckle and Judas blossoms. Green leaves rustle behind a wooden railing. A sleek, stray cat slips behind the pots and across the top of a wall. In the old Greek house, Kalkan's mother serves us yoghurt soup with mint. Afterwards, we return to the garden for tea and more conversation by the pale light of stars. [...]

I walk down the uneven streets. A line of late-night washing drifts in a roofless ruin. I cross the Golden Horn at Galata Bridge, still bristling with fishing-rods despite the hour, and climb into a hilly neighbourhood of stepped streets and Maritime pines cradled in the Bosphorus's arms. As I walk, I think of the Grand Tourists and the first Intrepids, about the sixties impulse to reinvent the world and today's anxious acceptance of one's place in it. Law students play backgammon under the vines. A yawning, veiled woman pushes a wakeful child on a swing. A sleepless mussel-seller mops his neck with a cloth.

Istanbul touches me in the fluid Arabic script of its İznik tiles, in its expressways built over Roman roads, in a lamb feeding on the grass precincts of a mosque.

Rory Maclean, Magic Bus (2007)

✳ ✳ ✳

The unique moods of Istanbul may arise, in part, from its fabled position of uniting two continents. In this extract from Emine Sevgi Özdamar's My Istanbul, *a potentially tragic incident on a Bosphorus ferry is given a strangely magical twist by the moon, shining down on both continents alike.*

One summer night when I still lived in Istanbul, twenty five years ago, I was sitting on a ship ferrying me from the European side to the Asiatic side. The tea-sellers brought tea to the passengers, loose change clinked in their pockets. The moon was so big, as if the sky above Istanbul was the only place he lived, as if Istanbul was the only place he loved, and he polished himself every day just for this city. Wherever the moon looked, all the doors would open immediately to let him spill inside. Whatever you touched, you would touch the moon too. Everyone held a bit of the moon in their hands. Now the moon lit up two faces next to me on the ship. A boy and a girl. He said, 'So you gave Mustafa your key too. I'm off. Goodbye'. He leapt from the deck of the ship into the sea and plunged into the moonlight. The ship was exactly halfway between Europe and Asia. Without saying a word, the girl remained in her seat in the moonlight. All the other people rushed to the railing, the ship listed under the crowd, even the tea glasses on their saucers slid in the direction of the railing. The tea-seller yelled, 'Tea money. Tea money.' I asked the girl, 'Is he a good swimmer?' She nodded. The ship's crew threw two lifebelts after the boy, but he didn't want a lifebelt. The ship turned around and steered towards the boy, a lifeboat pulled him out of the sea.

The moon followed everything that happened, and when the boy was taken to the captain with wet clothes and wet hair, the moon lit him up like a circus clown in a ring of light. The ship turned around again in the direction of the Asiatic half, the tea sellers found their clients and collected their money. The moon shone down on the empty tea glasses, but suddenly the ship turned around again in the direction of the European side, because it had left the lifebelts in the sea. And the moon was there the whole time, above Europe and Asia.

Emine Sevgi Özdamar, *My Istanbul* (2001)
translated by Lyn Marven

✻ ✻ ✻

To end the section, Istanbul in full celebratory mode.

Life explodes everywhere. The city's energy breaks loose in a general atmosphere of drunkenness and oblivion. The sounds of celebration rise from both shores. Each bend of the Bosphorus sends out its gusts of techno or Turkish music and fresh bursts of noise. All the sound systems are turned up to maximum. In the open-air nightclubs, right by the landing-stages, the closely-packed movements of the dancers create shifting shapes in aquariums of light. Everywhere thighs, breasts and haunches are gyrating, arms raised, while fireworks spangle the sky with continual fountains of light. On both shores, and on the boats as well – pitching and rolling as if their hulls are dancing to the same crazy rhythm, shaking both water and people – everyone seems impatient to throw themselves greedily towards infinite dreams and desires.

Daniel Rondeau, *Istanbul* (2002)
translated by Erica King

"Today, this is where the modern world's fault lines meet: between rich and poor, democracy and the authoritarian, Islam and the West"

Rory Maclean

Here and now

It may have its roots in ancient times, but today's Istanbul is an exciting, thriving, twenty-first-century city.

Istanbul is among the oldest inhabited cities, a metropolis founded on the advice of Apollo's oracle, the western gateway of the Silk Road since the sixth century. Its pivotal location, astride the Bosphorus, flanking the scimitar-shaped Golden Horn, was the most strategic in the ancient world. In its time, 'the City' was occupied by Persia, Alexander and Rome, rising to Christian glory after Constantine, defying Muslim invaders for almost a thousand years. Under the Ottomans it held sway over territories stretching from Hungary to the Persian Gulf, from North Africa to the Caucasus. Today, this is where the modern world's fault lines meet: between rich and poor, democracy and the authoritarian, Islam and the West.

Rory Maclean, *Magic Bus* (2007)

❈ ❈ ❈

Maureen Freely describes the city on the eve of the new millenium – on 2nd November 1999, to be precise.

If I stand on the balcony, looking out over the Asian shore, and the Old City with its domes, its palaces, its mosques, and the great and teeming waterways between them, I can still see the city I remember.

If I'm going somewhere and veer into the back streets, I can smell that damp. The ferries are the same, though they seem less numerous. There are still nut vendors everywhere, and corn vendors, and cheap watch vendors and kiosks selling newspapers, cigarettes, bubblegum and grilled cheese sandwiches. Most shop signs in most back streets are still crooked, most pavements still have potholes, and the vogue for neon has not yet passed.

There are vast new neighbourhoods stretching endlessly in all directions. In poor neighbourhoods we always find a minimarket, a pharmacy, a kebab restaurant and at least three banks. A sweet shop, a damp arcade where they sell flowers, newspapers, meat, fish, and pink quilts, a generic police station and a generic mosque. Men in skullcaps and men in caps and brown suits and men in Tommy Hilfiger; women in Tommy Hilfiger and women in long Islamic coats and tightly knotted scarves.

In the rich neighbourhoods it's endless rows of skyscrapers, malls, glittering showrooms displaying all the world's most expensive cars, designer clothes and designer ice cream, bathrooms, furniture, computer software. The dark, damp sinister streets of Tepebaşı are changed beyond recognition, lined with bright and beautiful restaurants, cafés, clubs, and salsa bars; the stretch along the Bosphorus between Ortaköy and Kuruçeşme, where there were once only coal depots, is a glittering strip with vast open air clubs and there are, I'm told, so many bouncers and valets and famous football players with famous model girlfriends that in the early hours of a summer morning it can take up to an hour to creep half a kilometre.

Those old Ottoman villas that were falling into their foundations – these days, no rich man can be without one. There aren't many left but those that are left have been restored and are so sumptuous they hurt your eyes.

Maureen Freely, *Enlightenment* (2007)

❊ ❊ ❊

Food writer Anya von Bremzen loves the modern city, but like many residents and visitors, is aware of the way in which a vanished past sometimes seeps into the trendy present.

Gritty and glamorous, secular and devout, antique and up to the minute, Istanbul is flooded with pleasure seekers these days, and no wonder. A former capital of Christian and Ottoman empires, this sprawling metropolis has it all: history to give Rome a run for its churches and statues, water panoramas to rival Hong Kong's, and a many splendoured cuisine all its own. At times, I'm swept along with everyone else into the jet-setting restaurants and boutiques of some newly gentrified enclave. But I also have my own, private Istanbul. Having fallen in love with the city over years of visits, I recently bought an apartment overlooking the Bosphorus, the strait that separates Europe from Asia. I do much of my hanging out now in my leafy neighbourhood of Cihangir, famous for its sidewalk cafés and fin-de-siècle apartment buildings. And off the tourist trail, I delight in watching the city's new gloss dissolve into a black-and-white cityscape veiled in *hüzün*, a feeling defined by the novelist Orhan Pamuk as a kind of collective nostalgia for the vanishing, crumbling past.

Anya von Bremzen, 'The Soul of a City' in *Saveur* (April 2009)

✳ ✳ ✳

Michael Booth on a modern shopping experience in the old Grand Bazaar as he retraces the steps of Hans Christian Andersen.

The Grand Bazaar's 5,480 retailers put any modern shopping mall to shame. If you have a pressing need for painted ostrich egg lamps, Iranian caviar, Viagra, clockwork dervishes, fabulous carpets, gold, counterfeit Louis Vuitton, mother-of-pearl chess sets, jewelled daggers, clothing with tempting labels such as 'Fashion', 'Design', and 'Trend' and pointy-toed slippers, this is your one-stop shop. There is no Swarovski, no Benetton, and no monster dildos; it is, however, the only place in the world where you can still buy those patchwork leather pouffe covers that your hippie aunt had in the 1970s.

The bazaar remains one of the world's great crossroads. I sat for a while in a corner café, watching faces from virtually every ethnic background pass by – from Georgian to Somali to Californian. And if you close your eyes it really does sound like a beehive, with the buzz of a hundred deals being done; the air being sucked through a hundred teeth.

Andersen bought a fez, and so did I.

In the bazaar, he who hesitates is fleeced. You soon learn not to make eye contact with any of the traders; their powers of persuasion are relentless, they will leave no ploy unturned in order to get your attention, hold it and then sell you something against your will. One man selling Turkish Delight and candy noticed that I was writing something down, and cornered me: 'Hey! You write my name? My name Eddie Murphy! You see my face? Ha, ha!' I looked at him. The resemblance was uncanny. I don't know who his resemblance was uncanny to, but with six billion to choose from I am sure there must be someone – though it wasn't Eddie Murphy.

Stallholders kept approaching me in French for some reason, and I began to sympathise with Andersen's frustration at constantly being mistaken for an American. That said Americans can actually be useful in the Bazaar. I soon learned that if you can get in the slipstream of a group of them, their outgoing, guilelessness acts as a kind of minesweeper through the crowds of touts. By such means I was eventually able to find my way out of the labyrinth, although the American family I had attached myself to began to cotton on towards the end – I think they thought I was stalking their daughter. Leaving the frenzied commotion of the Bazaar, with its cacophony of 'Yes, my friend, you say hello? You buy? You buy carpet? Why not?' I felt like a pearl diver surfacing for air.

I spent the rest of the day touristing around the sights of Sultanahmet beneath a watery spring sun. I visited the Topkapı Palace, the museums and the Hippodrome, with its ragbag collection of ancient obelisks, pyramids and columns. The female slave market that Andersen described with hushed horror – 'A young mother gives the breast to her child, and they will separate these two' – is no longer there (I mean the building that housed it, obviously I was hardly expecting to find women on sale), but the palace, the Blue Mosque and the Hagia Sophia remain the city's great tourist attractions.

Michael Booth, *Just As Well I'm Leaving* (2005)

The present-day Bazaar isn't just for tourists ...

Despite her hurry, as she wound her way through the Grand Bazaar, Zeliha slowed down. She had no time for shopping but would go inside for just a quick glance, she assured herself, as she surveyed the storefronts. She lit a cigarette and as the smoke curled from her mouth, she felt better, almost relaxed. A woman who smoked on the streets was not highly regarded in Istanbul, but who cared? Zeliha shrugged. Hadn't she already waged a war against the entire society? With that she moved toward the older section of the bazaar.

There were vendors here who knew her on a first-name basis, especially the jewellers. Zeliha had a soft spot for glittery accessories of all sorts. Crystal hairpins, rhinestone brooches, lustrous earrings, pearly boutonnières, zebra-stripe scarves, satin satchels, chiffon shawls, silk pom-poms, and shoes, always with high heels. Never a day had she passed by this bazaar without ducking into at least several stores, bargaining with the vendors, and ending up paying far less than the amount proposed for things she had not planned to purchase in the first place.

Elif Shafak, *The Bastard of Istanbul* (2007)

✳ ✳ ✳

Geert Mak takes his leave of the city which, despite its shining modernity, is for him about the lives of the ordinary people he encountered during his stay.

It was a late Sunday afternoon, darkness was drawing in. The Black Wind had picked up again, the thermometer made it only a few notches past zero. The newspapers told of heavy snow clouds on their way from Germany and the Balkans. The cold wind blew along the gutters of the old Greek neighbourhood, up and down the hillsides, around the ruins of the elegant mansions, past the sagging bay windows, the flapping curtains, the lone bakery, the crying babies, the dimly lit cake and soap shops on the street corners. Little girls were out skipping, or doing something complicated with a long piece of elastic. The boys played football, or clattered along after me on their roller skates across the paving stones: 'Hello! Hello!'

I had said my goodbyes. The lottery girl had given me a free ticket, the insole vendor and the bookseller had given me a hug. No one was out on the bridge any more, even the insole vendor had stayed at home, the only fishing pole in use was that of the man from the bank, but for him being cold was part of the sport. The rest of them were watching television, they were sitting in the coffeehouse, they were lying in bed and dreaming their dreams: the head nurse of a visa to see her grandchild; the bookseller of a good marriage for his daughter; the waiter of his son becoming a professional footballer; the perfume seller of the grass around the village of his youth; the blind flautist of murdering his first wife; the tea vendor of two thousand dollars to buy a truck and set up a transport-cum-smuggling business in his village; the umbrella salesman of taking the whole of England to court; the insole vendor of a cheerful meal with all his children; the oldest sister of a divorce; the policeman whose beat the bridge was of a TV course, a diploma, a better pay grade and then retirement; the lottery girl of her sister performing as a backing singer on a television programme – and the man with the drum was still far away.

It grew colder. The coloured laundry flapped on lines across the narrow streets. Smoke crawled low through the neighbourhood, people everywhere were busy scavenging for wood, the men sawed and chopped, splinters flew, in the darkness of the basement homes the fires in the plate-metal stoves were glowing red.

At dusk the rain slowly turned to wet snow and then the flakes began to fall, white and regal; above the Blue Mosque even the flying souls were gone from sight.

Geert Mak, *The Bridge: A Journey Between Orient and Occident* (2007), translated by Sam Garrett

✻ ✻ ✻

A slightly more 'hard-nosed' aspect of contemporary Istanbul ...

I drove along the coastal road from the airport to the hotel, with the Bosphorus opening out into the Marmara Sea on one side and a mixture of lower- and middle-class neighbourhoods with their tall ugly buildings on the other. The traffic wasn't too bad for a Friday and I was even able to drive at full throttle. It was perhaps the first time since coming to Istanbul that its frenzied beauty, which had survived both indifference and efforts to destroy it, did not play on my mind.

Esmahan Aykol, *Hotel Bosphorus* (2004)
translated by Ruth Whitehouse

✻ ✻ ✻

A humorous word of advice about taking an Istanbul taxi – from a recent German visitor.

The concept: *Map*.
Definition: *Pretty wall decoration.*

That's what it says in the Sauren Dictionary, the popular Turkish Internet encyclopedia. And that's what an Istanbuler's genes say, too. 'Where maps of cities and countries are concerned, the Turk has a genetic defect,' says our friend Serdar, himself a Turk. 'He CANNOT read anything like that.'

It's not as if there were no maps of the city. In fact there are very beautiful and very thick ones. Maps in ring binders. Hardcover maps. Folding maps. But not a single taxi driver has ever been seen with such a map. Sometimes a stained copy is stashed in the rear seat pocket of a taxi. This is for giving away, for the tourists in the back seat. If somebody takes it out, looks for a street on it, and holds it under the taxi driver's nose, he'll wrinkle his forehead, rotate the map 180 degrees, scratch his neck for a while, and finally ask: 'Is that over by Topkapı Palace?' First of all you're lucky that the taxi driver is familiar with the Topkapı, and secondly you've learned something: orientation here works by means of reference points. And inquiries. There is an old proverb: *Sora sora Bağdat bulunur*, 'You get to Baghdad by asking.' After all, that's how the Turks managed to progress from central Asia to the Bosphorus: 'Brother, how do you get to Constantinople from here?'

The best approach for the district of Beyoğlu, for example, is to locate everything in relation to the Marmara Hotel on Taksim Square. It is risky to just give the name of a street and then make yourself comfortable in the back seat. The taxi driver will always drive off. He just won't arrive. He will set off in roughly the right direction and hope for an encouraging word from the passenger after that. If none is forthcoming, he will nervously snap at the customer: 'So? Now?' one or two kilometres before the destination.

Kai Strittmatter, *User's Guide to Istanbul* (2010)
translated by Susan Thorne

❊ ❊ ❊

*A quick visit to one of Istanbul's exclusive clubs –
though, as usual, it's the view that steals the show.*

Volkan walked in step to the music along the corridor before entering the dim, humming depths of the club. As he passed, the light which filtered through the stained glass panels on both sides sprinkled him with lace-like spots resembling coloured flowers.

The place had been prepared for unexpected cold weather, early rains and strong winds. Portable panels and windows which were removed during summer, opening the entire space towards the seashore, had been put back.

That night, the weather was lukewarm and pleasant as if autumn would never end. The large windows were wide open to the smells of rotting leaves and the sea. The dense odours of alcohol, food and perfume were mingling with a pure breeze from the fresh air.

He walked behind the waiter along the side of the dance floor and sat at a table with a view and at equal distance to the bar and the dance floor. Although it was a weekday, most of the tables were occupied. In this club of the elite, management, service and food were exactly suited to the quality, the tastes and expectations of the patrons. From the glasses to the armchairs, from the lamps to the mirrors, everything had been cleverly designed to emphasise expensive privilege. This was a small island hidden from the shame and sin-filled world of crude people and the obtrusive eyes of the paparazzi. It was a kind of refuge, a place to meet, to see and remember each other, to effervesce and let go. Everything seemed to breathe a slight dissatisfaction under the well-arranged lights.

He leaned back. The night outside the windows was enchanting. The copper moon rising from behind the skyscrapers on the hill and the fidgetty colourful reflections of the opposite shore falling into the calm, dark blue glitter of the sea sparked off a pure feeling of eternity and insignificance. Man was transient, a moment's entity for nature, and the earth was a great sage who accepted the variability of life as a valid contrast, a temporary obligation, while poor mankind pointlessly continued to struggle with it.

İnci Aral, *The Colour Saffron* (2007)
translated by Melahet Behlil

* * *

A crime novel with a psychological dimension, Blame the Apple, *by Cem Selcen (b.1962), provides some interesting snapshots of modern Istanbul, given depth through historical details about the city.*

The environs of the bank were looking, as always, like the Perşembe Pazarı. On Banka Street, where there was no room to walk because of the cars that had double parked on the right hand side, the tea-man was giving out tea to people who had stopped by to catch a breath, and who were perched on little chairs squeezed onto the side walk, and a little further ahead, the iron, sheet metal and aspirator sellers were loading goods in front of their doors or telling each other off. As the name of the street changed from Banka Street to Zincirli Han Street, the traffic of people seeking, asking for, buying and selling those strange goods which filled the store windows and the streets also increased. At the end of the street, one would get greeted by the exploding daylight and the dark howl of the traffic. As for that street to the left of the bank block, Bereketzede Medrese Street, which seemed less busy, there, one of those mosque medreses was silently waiting for its time in the midst of all that noise.[1] At the end of the street, again beyond the same howling view of that avenue, a sliver of the Golden Horn with its sparkling grey waters and those slightly crooked seeming minarets of Eminönü Mosque could be seen.

And then, that famous Sabahattin Evren Avenue, which was also renowned as the Perşembe Pazarı Street ... The one place in Istanbul where one can find any sort of technical tool. Colourful hoses, sizes of ball-valves, cage wires, various wheels, strange loops with no apparent use, cogs, vices, aspirators, fans, bands, tractor parts, pickaxes, plastic fences, steel rods, white basins, tiles, water filters, sets of shiny faucets, door handles and much more ... they all await their customers, spilling out onto the street. Among all this hubbub of materials stand a few sycamore saplings on the sidewalk whose leaves you can't tell the colour of. They live on, supported by those little rods surrounding them.

---

1 Medrese is the Ottoman term for an education institution of any kind or level.

I stopped between the two streets, that is on Kardeşim Street at the entrance to the Hardware Bazaar, which was right behind the Central Bank, and looked at its back façade which was getting uglier with fire escapes and slum-style additions. After all these years around this structure, I was taking in the stunning fact that its back façade was completely different from the front.

Cem Selcen, *Blame the Apple* (2007)
translated by Çiğdem Aksoy

❉ ❉ ❉

Many of Istanbul's residents enjoy the thriving modern city, but some find it hard to forget those for whom life there is a contstant struggle – as in this extract from 'Big City Hunter', by Çiler İlhan.

Everything moves faster in this new city. And is (more) planned. My planner's soul that divides the day into sixty-minute segments of fifteen degree latitudes now divides the sixty-minute chunks into sub-minutes – that is the only way we all can fit into twenty-four hours these days: a tiny infant, a big job, other two- and four-legged members of the family (I've not even begun to speak of family, friends, exhibitions, or dance) and deep within, the baleful guilt of every line I've yet to write. How it all pounces upon me from the corners at the most unexpected moments. Donning colours and taking shape. When I blow the single candle (that has been the standard for some time now) topping my birthday cake, bananas within, chocolate icing without; when I struggle to find, in the boutique in the corner, a few rags to flatter my body, still one size too large (for me); when I'm in the swimming pool with the ceiling handpainted in blue (the palest blue, to simulate the sea), the pool that hosts my resolute backstrokes and in whose too-narrow car park I consistently scratch the side of my car, for instance. It is at these moments, tiny or huge, of satisfaction or happiness filled with joy, that the disappointments of a dark, handsome youth, who lives in Sultanbeyli, who's 'never come down to Istanbul', whose life is limited to commuting between the single-room house he shares with his mother recovering from a stroke, his father who has no social security insurance, siblings all snatching at some job or another, and the factory that extracts fourteen hours of work a day come and latch themselves upon me. [...]

The first time I met Istanbul, a long coach trip spent entirely on my grandmother's lap was beginning to break into sunrise. I was too big to sit on my grandmother's lap (but she was tight, and had likely saved my fare 'for a rainy day'), but too young to understand why countless people were on the roads before morning had yet broken. 'Why,' I had asked my beautiful, tight grandmother with the green eyes and the retroussé nose, 'Why do they get up so early?' 'Their homes are quite far from their places of work, they get up this early to get to work on time, and take the bus, and the buses are so crowded, and the distances so long ... ' That's how Istanbul settled into my heart: admiration, amazement, and a concealed (and lasting) concern for those countless people whom I didn't know, but who got out of bed well before they'd done with the night, traipsing the bridges in order to earn some money.

Would he disappear if I closed my eyes? The young boy who pops up before me on the verdant road flanked with well tended trees that takes me from home to work, whose skinny arms strain as he pushes the paper bale on wheels to move it out of the way, terrorised by a cacophony of impatient car horns were it to block the road for the briefest of moments, his trainers ripped at the sole and uppers, and yet his face clean, despite probably lacking access to water for regular washing. I do, he doesn't.

Çiler İlhan, 'Big City Hunter' (2010)
translated by Feyza Howell

* * *

Although mainly known as a fantasy writer (of the 'Perg legends' series), Barış Müstecaplıoğlu has also written in other genres. The extract below, from the crime novel The Brother's Blood, *reflects a very real Istanbul of today.*

Taksim Square was magnificent as usual; as well as bringing together many eras of history in architecture, it also embraced countless numbers of people who were unlikely to be seen together standing side by side anywhere else. Although there was yet no sign of the usual evening crowds, there were people about even that early in the morning; a famous model in a smart outfit and high heeled shoes was walking along quickly while a gypsy boy in rags was passing by her. A little further ahead, two prominent leaders of an Islamic community were in a heated discussion. Across the street from them, a tall and broad-shouldered transsexual was watching her reflection in the shop window with admiration.

Imposing consulate buildings and sleazy bars, very expensive clothes shops and restaurants catering for the local traders had cluttered both sides of the road; an office building that was clad in shining glass was rising opposite a century-old building with ornate carvings and prayers were being said in a little mosque near the cinema where porn films were being shown.

If Istanbul was a huge mosaic, Taksim would have had to be the most colourful tile of it.

A dairy company had set up a promotion stand under the giant screen opposite the entrance of the underground station. Pretty girls in miniskirts were trying to hand out miniature milk cartons to the passersby. The smile on their faces looked as though it had been stuck with glue.

Yasemin looked at the church spire at the entrance of Istiklal Road as if it were an old friend whom she hadn't seen for a long time. A huge seagull had settled on the cross at the top and was looking quite content. The nostalgic tram, the

Square and the towering Hotel Marmara were exactly as she remembered.

Barış Müstecaplıoğlu, *The Brother's Blood* (2007)
translated by Stephanie Ateş

* * *

As he is about to leave Istanbul, Jeremy Seal has an insight into how the old city is transforming itself into a great, twenty-first-century metropolis.

I walked through the litter of brittle leaves towards the Golden Horn. Thin strips of sunlight were falling over Istanbul but did not pierce the low cloud above Eyüp's mosques and cemeteries just as the city itself, engulfing outlying villages on all sides, had advanced to Eyüp's periphery, and abruptly stopped. It was as if the predatory maw of development, of shops, tower blocks, and advertising hoardings had picked at Eyüp and turned away from a taste too rich even for its indiscriminate palate.

I was leaving Eyüp's graveyards and dusty cypresses when a rusty street sign surprised me. It read *Feshane Caddesi*; I was on Fez Factory Street. 'Oh, it still stands,' a tailor told me from the gloom of his shop, what light there was catching on the array of pins stacked alarmingly between his teeth. 'But they no longer make fezzes there, you know. Fezzes are banned these days.'

His directions led me to a large square building, squatting low roofed on its haunches and staring out across the murk of the Golden Horn. On the waterfront decrepit fishing smacks were beached. A pair of earthmovers stood in the mud. The roof of the building gleamed with fresh green paint.

I walked the building's considerable perimeter until I surprised a man standing in a back doorway, smoking.

'Hello, tourist,' he addressed me in English. 'You want to see inside?'

When I replied that I spoke Turkish, he looked relieved and impressed, and by way of welcome took me firmly but mutely by the forearms. His introduction was typical. Many Turks possess a single line of English which is invariably buffed by constant use to such a shine that visitors to Turkey merely assume from the subsequent smiles, nods, and conspicuous lack of English that their new, evidently fluent friend is only touchingly shy.

He was called Osman, and was the site foreman, keeping an eye on the project until work resumed in the spring.

'So they used to make fezzes here?' I asked him.

His dismissive expression, a glance over his shoulder, graphically painted a past safely out of reach. 'But now,' he said with enthusiasm, 'it is a modern art museum,' and he offered to show me round.

The interior was largely finished and comprised white expanses of space where paintings would soon hang. 'Gallery,' intoned Osman respectfully, 'conference centre,' or 'store room,' as we wandered among the old cast-iron pillars made in Belgium early in the last century, passing random bags of cement looking like suitably experimental artistic statements, thoughtfully positioned in emptiness.

Our footsteps fell heavy in the silence. All that remained was the shell of a building, a lifeless blank prepared for the display of modern art from which the slightest echo of Mahmud II's imperial fez factory had been erased. The absent builders had repaired the roof and the windows, repointed the walls and relaid the floors, rewired and repainted until the building was cleansed of its history.

Jeremy Seal, *A Fez of the Heart* (1995)

❊ ❊ ❊

No self-respecting modern city can do without its football teams. Daniel Rondeau found himself on an Istanbul ferry on match day.

A particular kind of restlessness held sway at the landing stage. The faces of the people hurrying towards the quayside were lit up with excitement; they were calling out to each other, greeting each other with slaps on the back, congratulating each other, while one of the ferry sailors, positioned on the boat's bridge, shouted into a loud-hailer: 'We're going to the match, tonight it's the match, hurry up, departure in three minutes, we're going to the match.'

And the passengers jumping onto the gangway responded excitedly with, 'To the match! We're off to the match!'

Trabzon's football team was going to meet Istanbul Spor in the Super League championship. The kick-off was in less than two hours, in the Beşiktaş stadium.

'To the match! To the match!' all those arriving continued to shout.

On the quayside, on the adjacent ferries, in the tobacconists – everywhere the same jubilation reigned. An explosion of joy greeted the departure of the boat. An unbelievable number of passengers took their mobile phones out of their pockets and called Trabzon. They all wanted to give a live commentary of that crossing of the Bosphorus which would bring them closer to the stadium where their team was going to do well. Others had taken out of their bags tape-players already loaded with cassettes on which they had recorded the official anthem of the Trabzon supporters. From one end of the boat to the other, it created a cacaphony dominated by the voices of those who united to take up a chorus when, by chance, two machines sent out, simultaneously, recordings that were almost synchronised. The young men, wearing maroon and blue hats and football shirts, began to dance among themselves, while the girls clapped their hands with a restraint that wouldn't last. A young man with a crew cut had the idea of asking the captain to broadcast a cassette over the boat's radio system.

'If he's from Trabzon, he'll do it!' called out a thin old man whose build was still athletic.

'He's a Laz[1] from Trabzon. He's going to do it ...' exclaimed the young man, giving a 'V' for victory sign a few moments later, as he came back down from the upper deck. He wasn't able to finish his sentence as his voice was drowned out by the sound system at full volume. The passengers were finally able to dance and sing in unison.

Daniel Rondeau, *Istanbul* (2002)
translated by Erica King

❊ ❊ ❊

Writer and story-teller Sally Pomme Clayton gives a fascinating insight into an unusual side of contemporary music-making in the city.

Music lessons are a popular form of tourism in Istanbul. There are so many incredible musicians living in the city, that students come from all over the world to take lessons with a chosen master. F took lessons at the Beşiktaş Music School, and I was the lucky beneficiary, as we stayed in an old apartment in Beyoğlu. I dreamt over the city, while F walked along the Bosphorus to study clarinet. His teacher, E, is educated in both Eastern and Western musical traditions. Their lessons flow between classical pieces and folk tunes, Western scales and makams – the Turkish modal system created from half and quarter-tones.

E is a singer and researcher with the Mehter Band, who play the historical music of the Ottoman military bands. We are invited to Topkapı Palace to watch them perform. From 1299 until 1826 every Sultan had their own Mehter Band. The band had barracks at the Palace, and played for the Sultan every day.

---

1 The Laz people come from a coastal district of the Black Sea. 'Lazistan' is divided between Turkey and Adjarie, in the south west of Georgia. (Ed.)

The giant kös drums (kettledrums), davul (bass drums,) ringing hand-drums, crashing cymbals, staffs covered with bells, trumpets, horns, and powerful zurnas (shrill reed instruments), led the army to battle, filling the soldiers with courage. There are descriptions of Mehter Bands consisting of four hundred drummers terrifying their enemies with a sound like thunder.

The band appear, marching and shouting warrior commands. There are over fifty musicians wearing traditional costumes. The clothes have been meticulously researched and re-created from drawings and manuscripts – striped red and gold robes hang over loose red trousers, bright cumberbunds wrap round the waist, some musicians have daggers tucked inside belts. Each section of the band wears specific head-gear, tall felt hats, turbans, colourful caps. They all wear large fake moustaches. The historical setting of Topkapı is the true home of the band. They bring to life the authentic sounds that would have accompanied the Ottoman army as they marched through the Balkans, Greece, and Middle East.

The following week E invites us to a performance at The Military Museum. It is very hot, F wears shorts and I put on a sleeveless dress, stuffing a shawl into my bag just in case. We go through airport-like security, our bags are scanned, and we try and find a patch of shade. We watch the same vibrant performance but, surrounded by disused tanks and guns, the military function of the music is very present.

The Mehter Band was abolished in 1826. In an attempt to Westernise Turkey, including the music, Italian musicians were hired to retrain the band and teach them to play western style music on western instruments. The Ottoman music was re-scored, delicate half-tones and wavering quarter-tones removed, replaced by whole tones and four square rhythms. The results did not last. Under Kemal Ataturk the band was allowed to perform secular aspects of their repertoire. Then during the 1950s the government used the Mehter Band as a symbol to represent original

Turkish culture and identity. In 1952 the Mehter Band was reformed and attached to the Istanbul Military Museum.

After the performance E takes us to where the band rehearse. We follow him round the back of the museum, and find ourselves in a real army barracks with soldiers in uniform, jeeps, and lorries. E shows us sleek, sound-proofed practise rooms, and a large rehearsal space with perfect acoustics, shelves of instruments, and rows of music stands. E has been researching the Mehter repertoire, searching for old songs. I ask if he has ever found a lost musical score. He nods, 'Yes. We have patched songs together from fragments of music, re-made songs from notes made by travellers and scientists, archaeology can help us, and paintings. But now we are looking at Western music for signs of Ottoman music. Bach, Mozart, Haydn, Beethoven all composed music inspired by the Mehter Band. They heard Turkish tunes and wrote them down. This notation remains.' It is remarkable that the army is funding such valuable research. 'Now,' said E, 'come and meet my General!' F looks nervously at me. He tries to shake off the invitation, but we are whisked upstairs and down corridors. E knocks on a door. I quickly put the scarf round my shoulders. F can't do anything about his shorts.

A tiny room is filled with a desk and the General sits squashed behind it. Tea immediately appears. We speak a mixture of Turkish, English and German. F explains his passion for Turkish music and language. I am shown books of photos of the Mehter Band performing all over the world. Suddenly the General produces a kanun – a large plucked zither of honey-coloured wood. The instrument has at least seventy strings, and they ring and glitter under the General's hands. The sound is intricate, refined. The melody gradually rises upwards, curling and climbing, then sinks back down, only to climb again, this time reaching one step higher. The particular flavour of the makam is revealed in this ornate ascending and descending progression.

As the makam rises, we are lifted up with it, lifted beyond words and histories, and the tiny room is filled with radiance.

Afterwards, when we are released through security, F and I stare at each other amazed.

'Do you think the General realized you were Greek?' I ask. 'I'm not sure. Probably. The whole thing was so strange. I was embarrassed by my shorts, and didn't want to insult anyone. All I could see were those pictures behind the General. The photo of Atatürk seemed alive, his blue eyes staring down at me. And beneath it, the painting of the Ottoman army on horse-back – trampling over Greeks lying dead on the ground in their embroidered waistcoats. Then the General played a makam for us!'

We sit in Taksim Park and eat ices in crystal glasses with tiny silver spoons. How easy it would be to dismiss the Mehter Band as a nationalistic form of music. But this music has been played for over a thousand years. It has crossed backwards and forwards between East and West, and is still doing so. It has been twisted one way and re-shaped another, to convey different sets of ideals. Yet it has survived, kept alive by passionate musicians.

How easy it would be to feel insulted by shorts, shoulders, photos, or paintings. Music had taken us all beyond that.

Sally Pomme Clayton, 'With music in Istanbul' (2011)

* * *

In this final piece, by travel writer Rory Maclean, we are reminded of the complexity of the modern city where an irresistible kaleidoscope made of past and present seduces visitors from all over the world.

Modern Istanbul's complex geography renders it all but unmappable: three dozen districts swelling over seven hills, no single centre, fingered by water, jumbled in time. Age dilutes its fluidity. I can't keep a grip on its currents of slippery politics, of chaotic transport, of residents drawn together to argue, talk and trade. Its light is maritime, a sea lies over each shoulder, yet the city is two thousand miles from any ocean. A ten-minute stroll takes me from a sleepy Greek fishing village to a Hapsburg cul-de-sac reminiscent of a Klimt painting. Across the horizon surge waves of new world tower blocks. In the expanding spiral of my wandering, I find its anarchic streets, its shifting colours, its millions of voices, its dreams of a legendary past at once foreign and familiar.

Rory Maclean, *Magic Bus* (2007)

Selective Index

*after name indicates a writer whose work is extracted in this anthology.

A

Abdülhamid II, Sultan (1842–1918) 266
Adrian Gate 214
Ahmed Han 61, 191, 204
Aksu, Sezen (b. 1954, singer/songwriter) 86
Altunizade (district) 131
Anatolia/Anatolian 2, 94, 106, 112, 145, 160, 172, 173
Andersen, Hans Christian* 39–41, 48, 49, 226
Ankara 158, 218
Aral, İnci* 11–12, 127–9, 174–6, 231–2
architecture 24, 60, 184–210
Armenian(s) 2, 29–30, 41–2, 60, 69, 95, 125, 143, 180, 194, 196
Arnavutköy (district) 181, 206–7
Art Nouveau 201, 206–7
Atatürk Bridge 50
Atatürk, Mustafa Kemal (1881–1938) 1, 49, 100, 143–5, 241–3
Atmeydanı Square/Atmeydan ('Place of Horses') 194
Aykol, Esmahan* 79–80, 121–2, 159, 230

B

bachelor rooms 96, 109
Bağdat Caddesi (Baghdad Avenue, notable high street on Anatolian side) 95
Bahariye Caddesi (most famous street in Kadıköy district) 150
Balat (old Jewish quarter in Fatih district) 145
Bankalar Caddesi/Road (Banks Street, Ottoman financial centre, Beyoğlu district) 166
Baydar, Oya* 79
Bebek (historic neighbourhood in Beşiktaş district) 114–15, 119, 206, 208
Bedesten/Old Bazaar/Covered Bazaar/covered market 74, 195–6
Beşiktaş (district) 61, 169
Beşiktaş Music School 240
Beşiktaş stadium 239
Bey, Kemalettin (1870–1927, architect) 208–9

Beyazıt (district) 65
Beylerbeyi (neighbourhood in Üsküdar district) 79, 114, 181
Beyoğlu (district) 49, 95, 115, 145, 156, 166, 206, 231, 240
Bilâl, Mehmet* 167–8
Binbirdirek (dry cistern) 194
bird(s) 26, 30, 76–7, 84, 96, 220
Black Sea 10, 11, 12, 17, 18, 25–6, 84, 85, 93, 94, 103, 120, 142, 172, 218, 220, 240
Blue Mosque 26, 47–8, 94, 143, 186, 208, 227, 229
Booth, Michael* 8, 48, 49–51, 109–10, 226–7
Boralıoğlu, Gaye* 90–1, 134–9
Bosphorus 3, 11, 12, 13, 15, 17, 18, 20, 21, 22, 24, 25, 34, 43, 50, 57, 70, 80, 85, 93, 94, 106, 107, 111, 113, 114, 115, 121, 140, 147, 148, 160, 162, 174, 177, 182, 186, 198, 199–202, 212, 218, 220, 222, 223, 225, 230, 239, 240
Bosphorus Bridge 131
Bostancı (neighbourhood in Kadıköy district) 150
Bostancibaşı Abdullah Ağa Yalı 202
Buonaventura, Wendy* 180–1
Büyükada (largest island in the Sea of Marmara) 181, 206
Büyük Valide Han 196
Byrne, David* 7, 57–9
Byzantine 1, 3, 8, 12, 71, 90, 123, 143, 187, 194, 213, 218
Byzantium 1, 3, 33, 76, 115, 213

C

Caferağa Sports Arena 52
Caşaloğlu (district) 153–4
Çamlıca (hill on Asian side) 126, 206, 209,
Camuroğlu, Reha* 65–7
Cankurtaran (neighbourhood in Eminönü district) 209
Çavuşbaşı (neighbourhood in Bykoz district) 174
Çelık, Behçet* 212–13
Çengelköy (neighbourhood in Üsküdar district) 202
Christians 38, 63, 70, 72, 74, 76, 187, 190, 223, 225

Christie, Agatha   48
Cihangir (neighbourhood in Beyoğlu
   district)   99–100, 159, 162, 226
cistern(s)/underground reservoirs   4,
   193–4
Clayton, Sally Pomme*   240–3
coffeehouse(s)   24, 47, 167–8, 229
Constantinople   1, 9, 29, 34, 35, 36,
   39, 49, 60–75, 108, 123–4, 185, 189,
   194, 199, 205, 213, 231
Constantinus Paleologus (last Byzantine
   emperor, 1404–1453)   213
Covered Bazaar/covered market/
   Bedesten/Old Bazaar   74, 195–6

D

da Vinci, Leonardo   26, 124
Dalrymple, William*   12, 22–3, 75–6,
   187–8, 197
d'Aronco, Raimondo (1857–1932
   architect)   206
de Amicis, Edmondo*   8, 9, 10–11,
   29–30, 31, 33–5, 185–6, 193–4, 204–5
de Beauvoir, Simone*   45–7
de Nerval, Gérard*   9
Dervish(es)   24, 30, 40, 226
devşirme (re. Ottoman
   administration)   72–4
dog(s)   13–15, 72, 90, 119, 130, 133,
   182–3
Dolapdere (neighbourhood in Beyoğlu
   district)   122–3
Dolmabahçe Palace   81
dolmuş (shared taxi)   11, 127, 150

E

Edirnekapı/Edirne Gate   157, 213–4
Edmunds, Marian*   53–4
Eminönü Bridge   46
Eminönü Mosque   233
Etiler (neighbourhood of Beşiktaş
   district)   134–5
Evliya Chelebi (han)   190
Eyüp (district)   210, 237
Eyüp Mosque   77

F

Farhi, Moris*   143–5
Fenerbahçe (football team)   115
ferry/ferries   9, 17, 18, 19, 20–1, 22–3,
   24–5, 27, 48, 51, 81–2, 83–4, 106,
   107, 112, 113, 140, 149, 156–7, 177,
   182, 212, 219, 221, 224, 238–40
fez/fezzes   28, 40, 41, 45, 66, 226,
   237–8
First National Architecture (National
   Renaissance style)   208–9

First World War   49, 144, 213
Flaubert, Gustave*   43
Florya Plain   76–7
Flower Arcade   182
flower(s)   14, 41, 52, 62, 63–4, 79, 80,
   95, 96, 133, 134–9, 177, 192, 195,
   216, 217, 224
flower-seller(s)   134–9, 216
food and drink
   ayran (yogurt drink)   101
   baklava   104
   börek   9, 99
   boza (drink)   15
   çay bahçesi (tea garden)   99
   ciğer şiş   101
   coffee   46, 101, 104–5, 107–9, 179
   fish   17, 32, 51, 89, 98–9, 110, 115
   halva   99, 111
   'Imam Fainted, The'   98
   kabak graten   100
   kahve   104
   kebab(s)   9, 51, 98, 99, 101, 224
   köfte   99, 101, 104
   kokoreç   67, 105–7, 182
   künefe   101
   mantı (dumplings)   100
   mezze   98
   meyhanes (taverns)   99, 144
   mirra (bitter, thick coffee)   101
   muhallebi (milk pudding)   102–3
   pilav(s)   99
   quince   94, 101, 112, 116
   raki (drink)   17, 58, 106, 120, 144
   salep (drink)   112–3
   simit   4, 81, 118, 121, 167
   sutlaç   105
   tea   4, 9, 17, 50, 55, 79–80, 99–100,
      107, 108–9, 113, 114, 121,
      129–30, 143, 221–2, 233
   tulum cheese   101, 179
   Urfa kebab   101
   yahni   101
football   115, 229, 238–40
fountain(s)   24, 40, 71, 80, 188, 189,
   192, 195, 200, 203, 204–5
Four Seasons Hotel   209
Freely, John*   12–13, 16–17
Freely, Maureen*   19–20, 83–4, 107,
   176–8, 182, 219–20, 224–5
Füruzan*   81–3

G

Galata (old name for Karaköy,
   neighbourhood in Beyoğlu
   district)   10, 33, 39–40, 49–50, 166,
   204, 218

Galata Bridge   8, 13, 16–17, 26–7, 29–30, 65, 142, 155, 166, 182, 210, 220
Galata Tower   43, 182
Galatasaray (sports club and football team)   91, 115
garden(s)   10, 11, 25, 44, 61–4, 71, 79–80, 126, 132, 154, 190, 198, 200, 203
Gate of Salutation   71
Gautier, Théophile (French writer 1811–1872)   214
German/Germany/Germans   121, 159, 201, 208
Gökalp, Ziya (1876–1924, Turkish Nationalist)   208
Golden Horn   10, 12, 17, 22, 28, 29, 34, 43, 44, 46, 50, 70, 86, 96, 177, 182, 194, 220, 223, 233, 237
Golden Horn Bridge   26–7, 124
Golden Horn Conference Centre   209
Grand Bazaar   4, 8, 194–6, 226–7, 228
Grand Vizier   61, 63, 68–9, 73, 199, 203
Greek(s)   1–2, 22, 28, 30, 41, 43, 69, 95, 100, 123–4, 125, 132, 180, 194, 198, 220, 228
Gülsoy, Murat*   93
gypsy/gypsies   3, 30, 58, 96, 122–3, 130–2, 177, 236

H
Hagia Sophia (also known as Aya Sofya, Hagia Sofia, Santa Sofia, St Sophia)   1, 8, 10, 57, 94, 121, 123, 184–196, 227
hamam/Turkish bath   53–4, 55–7, 145, 200
Hamidiye Mosque   65–6
han(s)   189–90
Harem/Serail/Seraglio   30, 71, 75, 190–1, 200
Haugaard, Mikka (novelist)   39–41
Haydarpaşa train station   168
Hellespont   12
Hellier, Chris*   199–203
Hikmet, Nazim (1902–1963, writer)   185–6
Hippodrome   104, 115, 187, 197, 227
hippy/hippies   2, 3, 47–8, 104–5, 226
Hotel Marmara   231, 237
Hükümenoğlu, Hikmet*   119–20
hüzün   211–22, 226
huzur   211–22

I
İlhan, Çiler*   113–15, 234–5

imam(s)   4, 98, 118, 144, 167
Imperial gate   70
İrepoğlü, Gül*   61–3, 72–4, 75, 191–2, 203–4,
island/islands   15, 22, 34, 183, 218, 232
İstikal Caddesi/Istikal Road   206
Iznik tiles   221

J
James Bond   193
Janissaries   72–3
Jasmund, August (German architect, 19th/20th century)   209
Jew(s)/Jewish   2, 28, 30, 50, 69–70, 72, 75, 76, 95, 125, 144, 145, 147, 180, 194
Judas tree(s)   15, 79, 181, 198, 220

K
Kadıköy (district)   12, 52, 150, 169–70
kaftan(s)   30, 62, 67–9
Kalıca (a 'village' on the Asian side)   18
Karaköy (modern name for Galata, a neighbourhood in the Beyoğlu district)   65, 166, 169, 181
Kardeşim Street   234
Kaygusuz, Sema*   80–1
Kemal, Orhan*   165–6
Kemal, Yashar*   76–7, 121–3
Kinglake, A. W.*   21–2
Kiremitçi, Tuna*   32, 51–2, 92, 168–71
Kıvılcım, Gönül*   132–3
Kuruçeşme (neighbourhood in Beşiktaş district)   225

L
Legacy Ottoman Hotel   209
Levent (a business and shopping district)   87–8, 153
Levi, Mario*   146–8
lodos (wind)   85–9, 90, 94–5, 218
Loti, Pierre (1850–1923, writer   44–5, 202

M
Maclean, Rory*   17, 47–8, 103–5, 220–1, 223–4, 243–4
Mahmud II, Sultan (1808–1836)   45, 125, 238
Maiden's Tower   124, 218
Mak, Geert*   25–7, 31, 48–9, 84–5, 142–3, 228–9
Mamboury, Ernest (1878–1953, scholar)   93

247

market(s) 46, 74, 77, 112, 115, 130–1, 160, 162, 171, 179, 195–6, 219
Marmara, Sea of 11, 12, 17, 34, 56, 57, 70, 83, 95, 162, 177, 183, 194, 230,
Mehmed/Mehmet II – the Conqueror (c.1432–1481) 26, 70–1, 99, 103, 185, 195, 214
Mehter Band 240–3
Meryem, Hatice* 139–42
Michelangelo 18, 26, 124
Military Museum 241–2
Ministry of Tourism 202
Moda (neighbourhood in Kadıköy district) 150
Moda Caddesi (street) 150
Molina, César Antonio* 213–5
Montague, Lady Mary Wortley* 35–9, 74, 78, 188–9, 190–1
months
    January 78, 95, 112, 172, 214
    February 95–7, 106
    April 61, 79, 156
    May 79, 106, 214
    August 81–2
    December 95
Mosque of Mehmet II 10
mosque(s) 1, 5, 9, 10, 11, 12, 15, 21, 43, 52, 63, 68, 70, 71, 76, 99, 118, 185, 188–9, 208, 224
muhallebi 102
Mumcu, Cem* 163–4
Museum of Innocence 159
music/musicians 58–9, 63, 87, 104, 217, 222, 240–3
Müstecaplıoğlu, Barış* 131–2, 236–7

N

Nadel, Barbara* 1–5, 155–7
nargile 107
nationalism 76, 208–10
Nedim, Ahmed (1681–1730, poet) 191, 203–4
Neruda, Jan* 27–9, 41–2, 107–8
nightclub(s) 50, 222

O

Old Bazaar (built 1456–61)/ Covered Bazaar/covered market/ Bedesten 74, 195–6
Orient Express 48–9
Oriental Gothic (architectural style) 209
Ortaköy (neighbourhood in Beşiktaş district) 121, 225
Ottoman 1, 4, 10, 12, 19, 34, 44–5, 60–76, 99, 145, 192, 199–203, 225

Ottoman Empire 1, 45, 49, 60–76

P

Pamuk, Orhan* v, 2, 159–63
Pera (modern Beyoğlu district) 10, 14, 30, 39–40, 50, 206
Pera Palace Hotel 48–9
Perker, Aslı* 178–80
Perşembe Pazarı Street 233
Philippe du Fresne Canaye (French traveller 16th century) 195
Pointe du Serail (Seraglio Point/ Sarayburnu, where Topkapı Palace is situated) 57
Princes' Islands 183
Procopius (of Caesarea, c.500–565, Byzantine scholar) 187
Pudding Shop, The (specific) 3, 103–5
pudding shops (general) 101–2

R

Republic, Turkish 1–2, 45–7, 100, 203, 206, 208
Reyes, Eduardo* 186–7
Rondeau, Daniel* 20–1, 57, 93, 115–16, 182–3, 222, 238–9

S

Sabahattin Evren Avenue 233
Saçlıoğlu, Mehmet Zaman* 14–15, 17–18, 93–7, 108–9, 111–13, 130–1, 150–2
Sait Faik (1906–1954, writer) 119
Salacak (neighbourhood of Üsküdar district) 202, 203
Sarayburnu (Seraglio Point, where Topkapı Palace situated) 94, 204, 218
Scutari 11, 29, 33
Seal, Jeremy* 44–5, 171–3, 237–8
seasons
    spring 1, 79–80, 84, 111, 227
    summer 4, 25, 64, 80–3, 198, 200
    autumn 92–5, 231
    winter 4–5, 45, 84, 92–7, 108–9, 111–13, 130–1
    New Year 87–8, 95
Selcen, Cem* 232–4
Selçuk/Seljuk (historical period, 1071–1243AD) 208
Selim I, Sultan (1470–1520) 158
Seraglio/Serail/Harem 30, 71, 75, 190–1, 200
Seraskerat (tower) 10, 33
Shafak, Elif* 91–2, 111, 117–19, 149–50, 228
simit-seller(s) 81, 118

Sinan, Mimar (c.1490–1588, architect) 15, 57
Sirkeci (district) 167, 206, 208,
Sirkeci train station 209
Şişhane (district) 91,
St Irene, church of 71
Stamboul 10, 21–2, 34–5, 41, 46, 194, 204–5,
Strittmatter, Kai* 18–19, 85–6, 105–7, 157–8, 198, 230–1,
Suleyman the Magnificent/Great, Sultan (1494–1566) 68, 73
Suleymaniye Mosque 10, 52, 91, 188
Sultan(s) 22, 45, 66–76, 103, 160, 183, 195, 198, 202, 240,
Sultan Ahmet fountain 80, 204–5
Square 143
Sultana Valide Mosque 10
Sultanahmet (district) 2, 47, 227
Sultanahmet Square/Sultan Ahmet Square 209
Sultanbeyli (district) 235
Sulukule (old neighbourhood of Fatih district) 3, 58
Sütlüce (neighbourhood of Beyoğlu district) 209–10

T
Taksim Park 243
Taksim Square 76, 91, 231, 236
Tanpınar, Ahmet Hamdi* 23–5, 91, 125–7
Tarabya (neighbourhood of Sanyer district) 19, 114, 206
Tarlabaşı (neighbourhood of Beyoğlu district) 114, 156–7
taxi(s) (see also *dolmuş* – shared taxi) 32, 47, 153, 169–70, 230–1
tea garden 99–100, 121
Tek, Vedat (1873–1942, architect) 208–9
Tepebaşı (neighbourhood of Beyoğlu district) 91, 225
Theodosius, Emperor (347–395AD) obelisk of 197
Tilmaç, Feryal* 86–9
tolerance 75–6
Topkapı (Palace) 52, 68, 70–1, 73, 94, 99, 121, 157, 160, 190–1, 208, 227, 240–1
Torolsan, Berrin* 101–3

traffic 46, 100, 128, 134–7, 150–2
tulip(s) 44, 62–4, 68, 84
Tunç, Ayfer* 211–12
Tünel (neighbourhood of Beyoğlu district) 206
Turkish bath/*hamam* 53–4, 55–7, 145, 200

U
Ümraniye (district) 173
underground reservoirs/cisterns 4, 193–4
Üsküdar (district) 12, 100, 106, 124, 131, 203, 218

V
Vahapoğlu, Ece* 173–4
von Bremzen, Anya* 8–9, 98–101, 225–6

W
Walker, Shaun* 159–63
water-seller(s) 81–3
weather
  cemres 97
  fog 84, 93, 212
  lodos (wind) 85–9, 90, 94–5, 218
  rain 4, 83–4, 91–2, 137, 141, 231
  snow 5, 44, 84, 93–7, 212, 214
  sun 14, 26, 78, 91, 160, 194
  storm(s) 84, 93–5,
  wind(s) 44, 66, 69, 85–9, 90, 94–5, 218
Woolf, Virginia* 13–14

X
Xanthoulis, Yiannis* 55–7, 145–6

Y
Yale, Pat* 206–10
yalı(s) 198–203
Yedikule Gate 214
Yeniköy (neighbourhood of Sanyer district) 18, 32, 114, 206
Yerebatan Sarayı (Basilica Cistern) 193
Yıldız Square 65
Yoğurtçu Park (in Kadıköy district) 150

Z
Zincirli Han Street 233
Zoutendijk, Eveline* 8

Acknowledgements

Oxygen Books would like to thank the many people who have supported *city-pick ISTANBUL* with their enthusiasm, professional help, ideas for texts to include, and generosity. Among them we would like to mention the permissions personnel in the many publishers and agencies we have dealt with. A particular thank you to Nermin Moliağlu of the Kalem Agency whose time and support have been so generously given throughout our project. But great thanks also to Amy Spangler and İdil Aydoğan of the Anatolialit agency, along with Feyza Howell, Jonathan Lee, Rebecca Hart, Eduardo Reyes, Amanda Hopkinson, Wendy Sanford, Michael Munday, and Andrew Furlow. And we would once again like to thank the committee of TEDA for awarding a grant towards production costs.

Amicis, Edmondo de, *Constantinople* (1977), © Alma Classics Ltd, 2010, translation © Stephen Parkin, 2005, 2010. Reprinted by permission of Alma Classics.

Aral, İnci *The Colour Saffron* (2007), translated by Melahat Behlil. Reprinted by permission of the Kalem Agency.

Aykol, Esmahan *Hotel Bosphorus* (2003), translated by Ruth Whitehouse, 2011, Bitter Lemon Press. © Diogenes Verlag AG, Zurich, 2003. Reprinted by permission of Bitter Lemon Press.

Baydar, Oya *The Gate of the Judas Tree* (2004), translated by Stephanie Ateş. Reprinted by permission of the Kalem Agency.

Baydar, Oya *Its Warm Ashes Remain* (2000), translated by Stephanie Ateş. Reprinted by permission of the Kalem Agency.

Baydar, Oya *Returning Nowhere* (1998) translated by İdil Aydoğan. Reprinted by permission of the Kalem Agency.

Beauvoir, Simone de *Force of Circumstance* (1963), translated by Richard Howard, reprinted by permission of the Estate of Simone de Beauvoir and Editions Gallimard, Paris c/o Rosica Colin Ltd, London.

Bilâl, Mehmet 'The Stepson', in *Istanbul Noir* (2008), Akashic Books, New York, translated by Amy Spangler and Mustafa Ziyalan, reprinted by permission of the Anatolialit Agency.

Booth, Michael *Just As Well I'm Leaving* (2005), published by Jonathan Cape. Reprinted by permission of the Random House Group Ltd.

Boralıoğlu, Gaye *Syncopated Rhythm* (2009), translated by Amy Spangler, reprinted by permission of the Anatolialit Agency.

Buonaventura, Wendy *I Put A Spell On You* (2003), reprinted by kind permission of Saqi Books.

Byrne, David *Bicycle Diaries* (2009) Ó Todo Mundo Ltd, 2009. Reprinted by permission of Faber and Faber Ltd.

Çamuroğlu, Reha *A Momentary Delay* (2005), translated by Çiğdem Aksoy, reprinted by permission of the Kalem Agency.

Çelik, Behçet *The Drone of the World* (2008), translated by Amy Spangler, reprinted by permission of the Anatolialit Agency.

Clayton, Sally Pomme 'With music in Istanbul' (2011), © Sally Pomme Clayton. Commissioned for *city-pick ISTANBUL*.

Dalrymple, William *From the Holy Mountain* (1998), © William Dalrymple, reprinted by permission of HarperCollins Publishers Ltd.

Edmunds, Marian 'Don't forget your toothbrush' (2011), © Marian Edmunds. Commissioned for *city-pick ISTANBUL*.

Farhi, Moris *Young Turk* (2004), reprinted by kind permission of Saqi Books.

Freely, John and Sumner-Boyd, Hilary *Strolling Through Istanbul* (revised edition, 2010; first published 1972), reprinted by kind permission of I. B. Tauris & Co Ltd.

Freely, Maureen *Enlightenment* (2007), published by Marion Boyars, © Maureen Freely, 2007. Reprinted by permission of United Agents.

Füruzan, 'In The Park By The Pier' in *Parasız Yatılı* (1972), translated by Nilüfer Mizanoğlu Reddy. Reprinted by permission of Yapı Kredi Publications.

Gülsoy, Murat 'Marked in Writing', from *The Book of Istanbul*, (2010, Comma Press) translated by Amy Spangler, reprinted by permission of the Anatolialit Agency.

Hellier, Chris 'Mansions on the water', originally published in *Saudi Aramco World,* April/May 1996. Copyright © Aramco Services Company.

Hükümenoğlu, Hikmet 'The smell of fish' in *Istanbul Noir* (2008), Akashic Books, New York, translated by Amy Spangler and Mustafa Ziyalan, reprinted by permission of the Anatolialit Agency.

İlhan, Çiler, 'Big City Hunter' (2010), translated by Feyza Howell, reprinted by permission of the Kalem Agency.

İlhan, Çiler, 'Groundnut Sky Cake' (2011), translated by Feyza Howell, reprinted by permission of the Kalem Agency.

İrepoğlü, Gül *Unto the Tulip Garden* (2003), translated by Feyza Howell, reprinted by permission of the Kalem Agency.

Kaygusuz, Sema 'A Couple of People', from *The Book of Istanbul,* (2010, Comma Press) translated by Amy Spangler, reprinted by permission of the Anatolialit Agency.

Kemal, Orhan *The Idle Years* (2008 edition; first published 1950). Reprinted by permission of Peter Owen.

Kemal, Yashar *The Birds Have Also Gone* (1978), copyright © Yashar Kemal 1978, copyright in the English translation © Thilda Kemal 1987. Reprinted by kind permission of the author and Ayşe Semiha Baban.

Kiremitçi, Tuna *Leave Before I Fall In Love With You* (2002), translated by Jak Kori, reprinted by permission of the Kalem Agency.

Kiremitçi, Tuna *The Way of Loneliness* (2003), translated by Jak Kori, reprinted by permission of the Kalem Agency.

Kıvılcım, Gönül *Razor Boy* (2002), translated by Çiğdem Aksoy, reprinted by permission of the Kalem Agency.

Levi, Mario *Istanbul was a Fairy Tale* (1999), translated by Ender Gürol. Reprinted by kind permission of Dalkey Archive Press.

Maclean, Rory *Magic Bus* (2006), reprinted by permission of Penguin Books Ltd.

Mak, Geert *In Europe: Travels Through the Twentieth Century* (2004), translation © Sam Garrett, 2007. Published by Harvill Secker. Reprinted by permission of The Random House Group Ltd.

Mak, Geert, *The Bridge: A Journey Between Orient and Occident* (2007), translation © Sam Garrett, 2008. Published by Harvill Secker. Reprinted by permission of The Random House Group Ltd.

Mansel, Philip *Constantinople: City of the World's Desire, 1453–1924* (1995), © Philip Mansel, 1995, reprinted by permission of John Murray (Publishers) Ltd and the author.

McDonald, John K., 'Istanbul's Caravan Stops' (1983), New York Times April 17, 1983.

Meryem, Hatice *It Takes All Kinds* (2008) translated by Amy Spangler, reprinted by permission of the Anatolialit Agency.

Molina, César Antonio 'Impregnable in his Sorrows' (2010), © Ediciones Destino, S. A. , 2010. Translation © Kit Maude, 2011.

Mumcu, Cem *Sarcophagus* (2004), translated by Buşra Giritlioğlu, reprinted by permission of the Kalem Agency.

Müstecaplıoğlu, Bariş *The Brother's Blood* (2007), translated by Stephanie Ateş, reprinted by permission of the Kalem Agency.

Nadel, Barbara *Death by Design* (2010) Copyright © 2010 Barbara Nadel. Reproduced by permission of Headline Publishing Group Limited.

Emine Sevgi Özdamar, *My Berlin* ('Der Hof im Spiegel') © 2001 Verlag Kiepenheuer & Witsch GmbH & Co. KG, Köln. Translation © Lyn Marven 2012.

Perker, Aslı *Soufflé* (2011), translated by the author, reprinted by permission of the Kalem Agency.

Reyes, Eduardo 'Big Architecture' (2011), © Eduardo Reyes. Commissioned for *city-pick ISTANBUL*.

Rondeau, Daniel *Istanbul* (2002), translation © Erica King. By permission of Gallimard.

Saçlıoğlu, Mehmet Zaman 'The Intersection', in *The Book of Istanbul* (2011) Copyright © 1994 (2010) Mehmet Zaman Saçlıoğlu. The said work is protected by the International Copyright convention. Extract published with the arrangement of ONK Agency Ltd.

Saçlıoğlu, Mehmet Zaman 'Winter' in *Four Seasons Istanbul from 1000 Feet* (2010) translated by Hatice Ahmet Salih and Joan Eroncel. Copyright © 1994 (2010) Mehmet Zaman Saçlıoğlu. The said work is protected by the International Copyright convention. Extract published with the arrangement of ONK Agency Ltd.

Seal, Jeremy *A Fez of the Heart* (1995), reprinted by permission of Pan Macmillan and the author.

Selcen, Cem *Blame the Apple* (2007), translated by Çiğdem Aksoy, reprinted by permission of the Kalem Agency.

Shafak, Elif *The Bastard of Istanbul* (2007), reprinted by permission of Penguin Books Ltd.

Strittmatter, Kai *User's Guide to Istanbul* (2010) published by Piper Verlag, Munich (as *Gebrauchsanweisung für Istanbul*). Translation © Susan Thorne, 2011. Published by permission of Piper Verlag.

Tanpınar, Ahmet Hamdi *A Mind at Peace* (1949), translation © Erdağ Göknar, 2008. Reprinted by permission of Archipelago Books.

Tilmaç, Feryal 'Hitching in the *Lodos*' (2008) translated by Amy Spangler and Mustafa Ziyalan, reprinted by permission of the Anatolialit Agency.

Torolsan, Berrin 'The Milky Way' (2002). Extract from an article originally published in Issue 26 of *Cornucopia:The Magazine for Connoisseurs of Turkey*, Spring 2002. Copyright © 2002 by Berrin Torolsan. Reprinted by kind permission of *Cornucopia* magazine and the author.

Tunç, Ayfer *The Night of the Green Fairy* (2010), translated by Alexander Dawe, reprinted by permission of the Kalem Agency.

Vahapoğlu, Ece *The Other* (2009), translated by Victoria Holbrook, reprinted by permission of the Kalem Agency.

von Bremzen, Anya 'Eating in Istanbul' (2007). Originally published in *Departures*, November/December 2007. Copyright © 2007 by Anya von Bremzen. Reprinted by permission of the author.

Xanthoulis, Yiannis *Istanbul: City of my Disrespectful Fears* (2008), translated by Geoffrey-Alfred Cox. First published by Metaixmio. Reprinted by kind permission of the author.

Yale, Pat 'Istanbul's forgotten Art Nouveau heritage' in *Sunday's Zaman* 3 January 2010. Reprinted by permission of the author.

Yale Pat from 'Nationalism in Stone: Istanbul's Forgotten Treasures', in *Sunday's Zaman* 17 January 2010. Reprinted by permission of the author.

Zoutendijk, Eveline 'Interview' in *Istanbul: The Collected Traveler – An Inspired Companion Guide* © Barrie Kerper (ed.) 2009, published by Vintage (Random House, Inc.). Reprinted by kind permission of Barrie Kerper, and of the author, Eveline Zoutendijk, www.cookingalaturka.com.

city-lit PARIS

'It's terrific ... all the best writing on this complex city in one place'
Professor Andrew Hussey, author of *Paris: The Secret History*

'A great and eclectic set of writings ... an original book on Paris.'
Sylvia Whitman, Shakespeare & Co, Paris

'It's like having your own iPad loaded with different tomes, except that this slim anthology contains only the best passages, bite-sized chunks just perfect to dip into as you sip that pastis in a pavement café.'
The Times

'Whether you're a newcomer to Paris or a die-hard aficionado, this gem of a book will make you think of the city in a completely new way.'
Living France

'The ideal book for people who don't want to leave their minds at the airport.'
Celia Brayfield, author of *Deep France*

£9.99   ISBN 978-0-9559700-0-9

city-lit LONDON

'I can't imagine a more perfect travelling companion than this wonderful anthology'
Clare Clark, author of *The Great Stink*

'The latest offering in this impressive little series concentrates on the spirit of London as seen through the eyes of an eclectic selection of writers ... an exciting selection, with unexpected gems.'
Clover Stroud, *The Sunday Telegraph*

'For those visitors to London who seek to do more than bag Big Ben and Buckingham Palace, this is the ideal guide, a collection of writings that expose not only the city's secret places but its very soul ... I can't imagine a more perfect travelling companion than this wonderful anthology.'
Clare Clark, author of *The Great Stink*

'Brings London to life past and present in a way no conventional guide book could ever achieve.'
Tarquin Hall, author of *Salaam Brick Lane*

' ... a frenzied orgy of London writing. You'll love it.'   *Londonist*

£8.99   ISBN: 978-0-9559700-5-4

city-lit BERLIN

'A gem ... an elegant, enjoyable and essential book'

Rosie Goldsmith, BBC Radio 4

'This wonderful anthology explores what it is really like to be a Berliner by bringing together extracts about the city from a range of genres, including some specially translated. This was the city of Einstein, Brecht, George Grosz, and Marlene Dietrich. It was 'the New York of the old world', a melting pot of new ideas and lifestyles ... This collection is timely: on 9 November 20 years ago, Berliners tore down the hated wall'

The Guardian

'*city-Lit Berlin* gathers more than a hundred extracts from writers on aspects of Berlin's conflicted heritage ... the editors have trawled widely to try to capture the modern city's rule-bound yet permissive tone, as well as its persistent state of cultural and architectural renewal. The result is an eclectic pillow-book ... a stimulating intellectual tour of the idea of the city that would complement any guidebook's more practical orientation'

Financial Times

'This is a sublime introduction to the city'   *The Sydney Morning Herald*

'A welcome contrast to the many formulaic travel guides in print and online, *city-Lit Berlin* reveals the city as seen through the eyes of 60 writers of all description – ... a volume that has greatly enriched the field of travel books.'

Ralph Fields, *Nash Magazine*

£8.99   ISBN 978-0-9559700-4-7

city-pick DUBLIN

'An elegant, incisive and always entertaining guide to the city's multitude of literary lives.'

Lonely Planet Magazine

'*city-pick Dublin* is the latest triumph of distillation. There's everything here from David Norris' defence of the significance of Joyce's *Ulysses* to Iris Murdoch's fictional treatment of The Easter Rising. You'll read about walking and drinking, being poor and being poetic, new wealth and newcomers, old timers and returning natives.'

Garan Holcombe, Book of the Month, The Good Web Guide

'From Sean O'Casey to Anne Enright – the best ever writing on Dublin has been specially published in a new book entitled *city-pick Dublin*'

RTE

'Bite-sized beauties ... You won't find pub recommendations or directions to art galleries in this little guide, but you will get a taste of Dublin's most important natural resource: stories.'

The Dubliner

£8.99   ISBN 978-0-9559700-1-6

city-pick AMSTERDAM

'This latest addition to the excellent 'city-pick' series of urban anthologies weaves together fiction and non-fiction, including more than 30 specially translated extracts, to give an intimate portrait of one of Europe's most distinctive cities.'   ***The Guardian***

'Charles de Montesquieu, David Sedaris and Cees Nooteboom walk into a bruin café. It's not the start of a bad bibliophile joke, but the portrait painted by a new breed of city guide ... It's a simple idea, presenting a metropolis in all its multifaceted glory through the words of great writers; and it's one so good it's astonishing it hasn't been done before. Split into loosely thematic sections, one of the nicest features of this collection are the 70-plus contributors – novelists, journalists, travel writers – span the centuries. There's a thoughtful selection of Dutch writers including not only literary heavyweights like Mak, who are widely known in translation, but also lesser-known authors – Meijsing, Stefan Hertmans, Jan Donkers – some of whom are translated into English for the first time. It makes for some delightful discoveries – even for those of us who think we know this city well'   ***Time Out Amsterdam***

'The latest installment in this much-lauded series, city-pick: Amsterdam showcases all the qualities that have established city-pick as an innovative literary alternative to your average visitor's potted history or guidebook. Eclectic, challenging and deeply involved in its subject, it takes you to deeper, more diverse places than you could ever hope to go elsewhere.'   ***Translated Fiction***

£8.99 ISBN 978-0-9559700-2-3

city-pick VENICE

'The latest addition to this admirable series ... makes any visit to La Serenissima more flavoursome'   ***The Bookseller, Editor's Pick***

' ... the latest literary treat from the city-pick series ... as a guide to the atmosphere and spirit of the city, it's unmissable.'   ***Lonely Planet Magazine***

'For those who love Venice, this book is genuinely unmissable ... short extracts are seamlessly blended into a compelling narrative.'   ***The Sydney Morning Herald***

'Composed of over 50 of the very best writers on Venice, this book is so much more than your average pocket guide ... the perfect companion.'
                                                                          Real Travel Magazine

'This welcome addition to the city-pick series ... with more than 100 extracts, this is a delightful literary guide to La Serenissima.'   ***The Guardian***

£8.99   ISBN 978-0-9559700-8-5

city-pick NEW YORK

'This sublime and 'literary' travel book operates on so many levels. For those who have never been in New York, here are some of the greatest writers painting the city in magical word pictures. For those who know and love the city, here are images so evocative you will feel as though you are there. And for those planning to visit, this is a compendium of everything that is special about the city.'

Bruce Elder, *The Sydney Morning Herald*

'Reyes succeeds in capturing the authentic flavour of the Big Apple … this excellent addition to the city-pick series of urban anthologies.'

The Guardian

'A wealth of atmospheric literary snippets that evoke the 'crush and heave' of New York City – this gazette dips into a host of writers whose themes range through the city's history, jazz and architecture … a prismatic, engrossing and skimmable work, the book suggests further intriguing tangents for further exploration – both on foot and on the page.'

Financial Times

'The hubbub of clamouring voices covers the history of the city, the difference between the five boroughs, the architecture, the famous inhabitants, the experience of living in NYC and more … the multitude of subjects and viewpoints gives a good impression of the heterogeneity and bustle of the great metropolis, and succeeds in painting it as a unique and thrilling place'

The Irish Times

'Regroups the very best of literature written about the greatest cities on the planet from some of its finest authors. The New York edition is divided into 12 sections, including, 'On the Waterfront', 'Big Yellow Taxis etc' and 'Celebrity City', and offers insights into various aspects of The Big Apple as seen through those who have written about it'

Easy Voyager

'Perfect for carry-on, the New York edition is a fast-paced powerwalk through different "themes" or moods of the city … city-pick NEW YORK works both as an excellent, and imaginative, alternative travel guide, and as an easy way for wannabe Manhattanites to pop in and out of the city that never sleeps.'

Katie Allen, *We Love This Book*

£9.99   ISBN 978-0-9567876-1-3